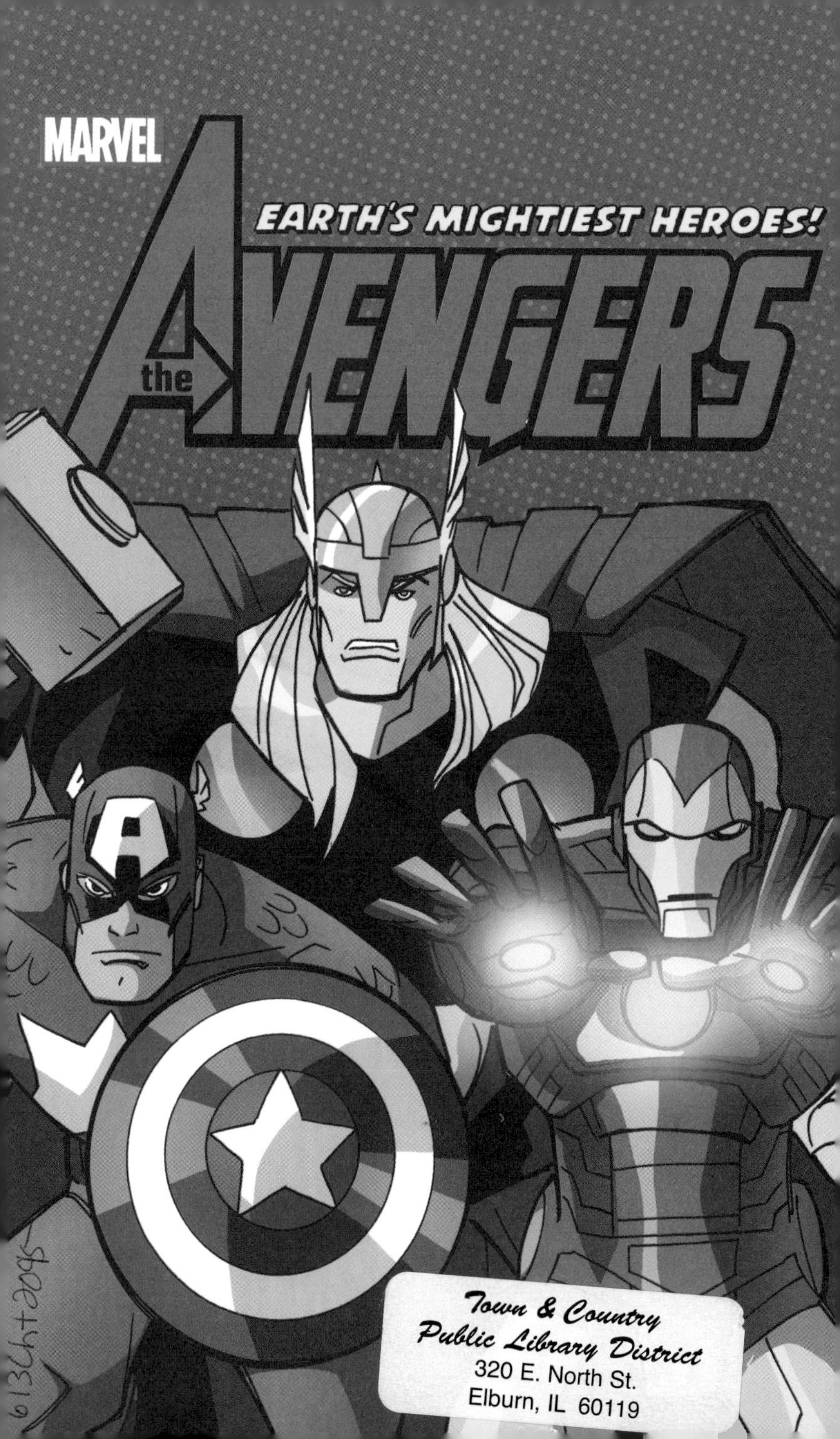
MARVEL
EARTH'S MIGHTIEST HEROES!
the AVENGERS

MARVEL
EARTH'S MIGHTIEST HEROES!
the AVENGERS

Writers
**CHRISTOPHER YOST,
HOWARD CHAYKIN, ROB WILLIAMS,
ELLIOTT KALAN & KARL KESEL**

Pencils
**RAMON BACHS, TODD NAUCK,
TIM LEVINS, CRAIG ROUSSEAU,
CHRISTOPHER JONES & ADAM DEKRAKER**

Inks
**RAUL FONTS, TODD NAUCK, KARL KESEL,
CRAIG ROUSSEAU, VICTOR OLAZABA & POND SCUM**

Colors
SOTOCOLOR & PETE PANTAZIS

Letters
VC'S CLAYTON COWLES

Cover Artists
**KHOI PHAM, CHRIS SOTOMAYOR
& EDGAR DELGADO**

Assistant Editors
ELLIE PYLE & RACHEL PINNELAS

Editor
TOM BRENNAN

Associate Editor
SANA AMANAT

Senior Editor
STEPHEN WACKER

Collection Editor
CORY LEVINE
Assistant Editors
ALEX STARBUCK & NELSON RIBEIRO
Editors, Special Projects
JENNIFER GRÜNWALD & MARK D. BEAZLEY
Senior Editor, Special Projects
JEFF YOUNGQUIST
Senior Vice President of Sales
DAVID GABRIEL
SVP of Brand Planning
& Communications
# MICHAEL PASCIULLO
Editor In Chief
AXEL ALONSO
Chief Creative Officer
JOE QUESADA
Publisher
DAN BUCKLEY
Executive Producer
ALAN FINE

MARVEL UNIVERSE AVENGERS EARTH'S MIGHTIEST HEROES VOL. 2. Contains material originally published in magazine form as MARVEL UNIVERSE AVENGERS EARTH'S MIGHTIEST HEROES #5-8. First printing 2013. ISBN# 978-0-7851-6445-6. Published by MARVEL WORLDWIDE, INC., a subsidiary of MARVEL ENTERTAINMENT, LLC. OFFICE OF PUBLICATION: 135 West 50th Street, New York, NY 10020. Copyright © 2012 and 2013 Marvel Characters, Inc. All rights reserved. All characters featured in this issue and the distinctive names and likenesses thereof, and all related indicia are trademarks of Marvel Characters, Inc. No similarity between any of the names, characters, persons, and/or institutions in this magazine with those of any living or dead person or institution is intended, and any such similarity which may exist is purely coincidental. **Printed in the U.S.A.** ALAN FINE, EVP - Office of the President, Marvel Worldwide, Inc. and EVP & CMO Marvel Characters B.V.; DAN BUCKLEY, Publisher & President - Print, Animation & Digital Divisions; JOE QUESADA, Chief Creative Officer; TOM BREVOORT, SVP of Publishing; DAVID BOGART, SVP of Operations & Procurement, Publishing; RUWAN JAYATILLEKE, SVP & Associate Publisher, Publishing; C.B. CEBULSKI, SVP of Creator & Content Development; DAVID GABRIEL, SVP of Publishing Sales & Circulation; MICHAEL PASCIULLO, SVP of Brand Planning & Communications; JIM O'KEEFE, VP of Operations & Logistics; DAN CARR, Executive Director of Publishing Technology; SUSAN CRESPI, Editorial Operations Manager; ALEX MORALES, Publishing Operations Manager; STAN LEE, Chairman Emeritus. For information regarding advertising in Marvel Comics or on Marvel.com, please contact Niza Disla, Director of Marvel Partnerships, at ndisla@marvel.com. For Marvel subscription inquiries, please call 800-217-9158. **Manufactured between 11/12/2012 and 12/24/2012 by SHERIDAN BOOKS, INC., CHELSEA, MI, USA.**

10 9 8 7 6 5 4 3 2 1

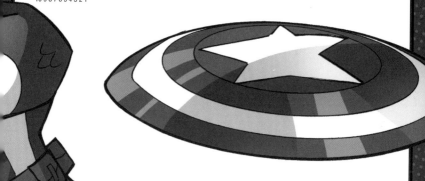

ND THERE CAME A DAY... A DAY UNLIKE ANY OTHER,
HEN EARTH'S MIGHTIEST HEROES FOUND THEMSELVES
NITED AGAINST A COMMON THREAT... TO FIGHT THE
DES NO SINGLE SUPER HERO COULD WITHSTAND...
N THAT DAY WERE BORN...

EARTH'S MIGHTIEST HEROES

THE AVENGERS

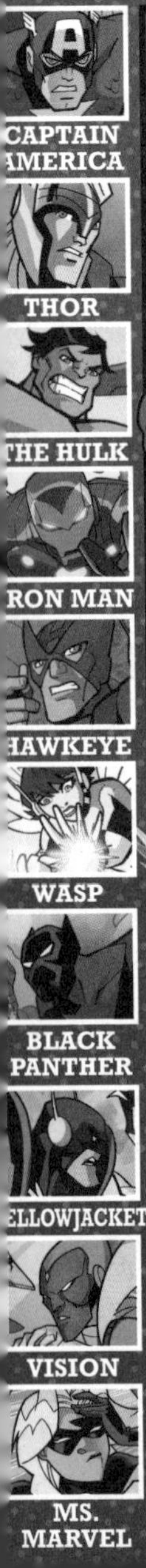

CAPTAIN AMERICA
THOR
THE HULK
RON MAN
HAWKEYE
WASP
BLACK PANTHER
ELLOWJACKET
VISION
MS. MARVEL

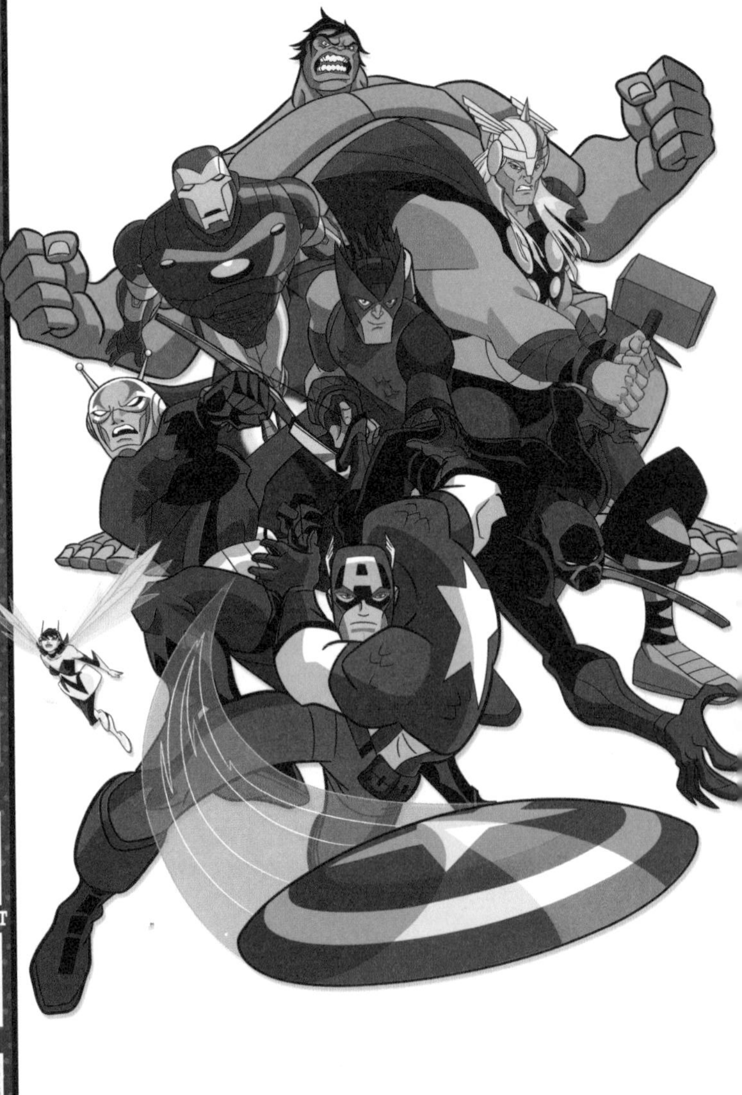

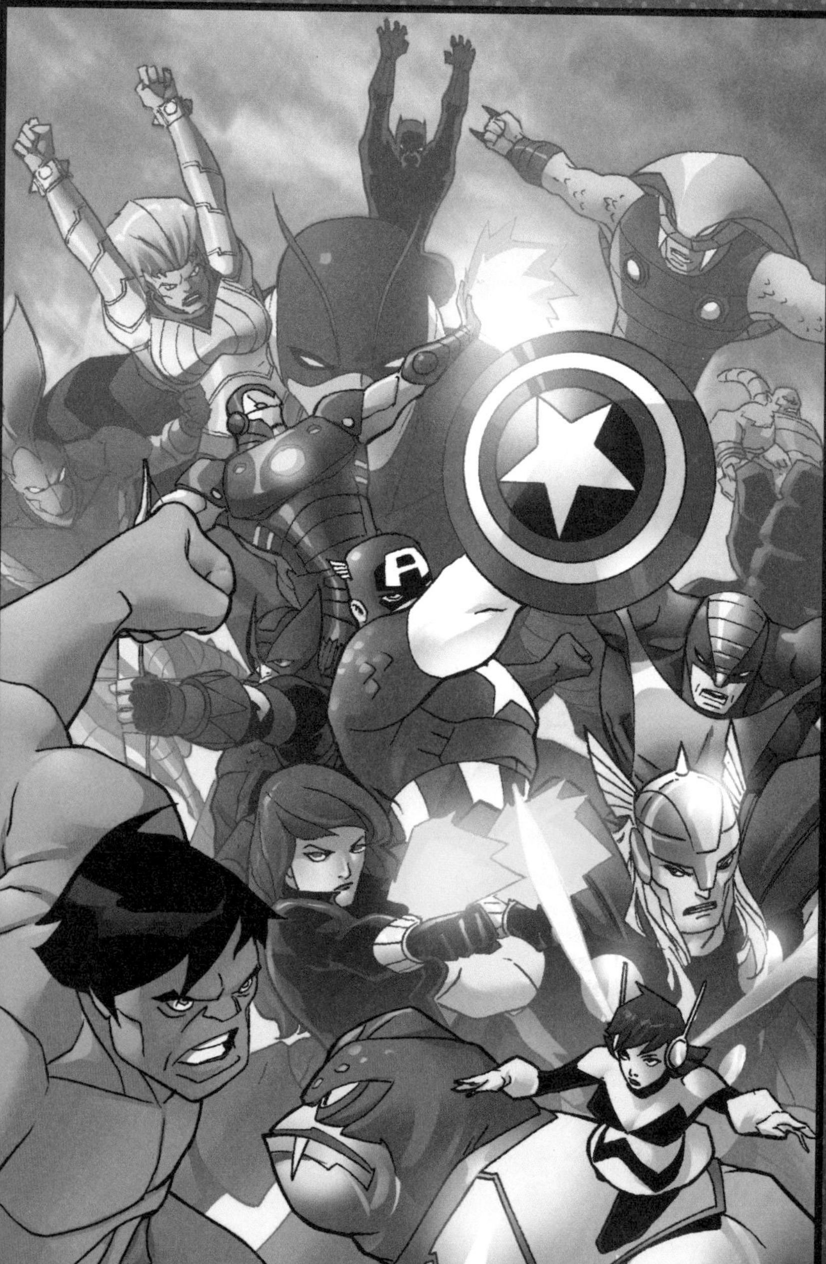

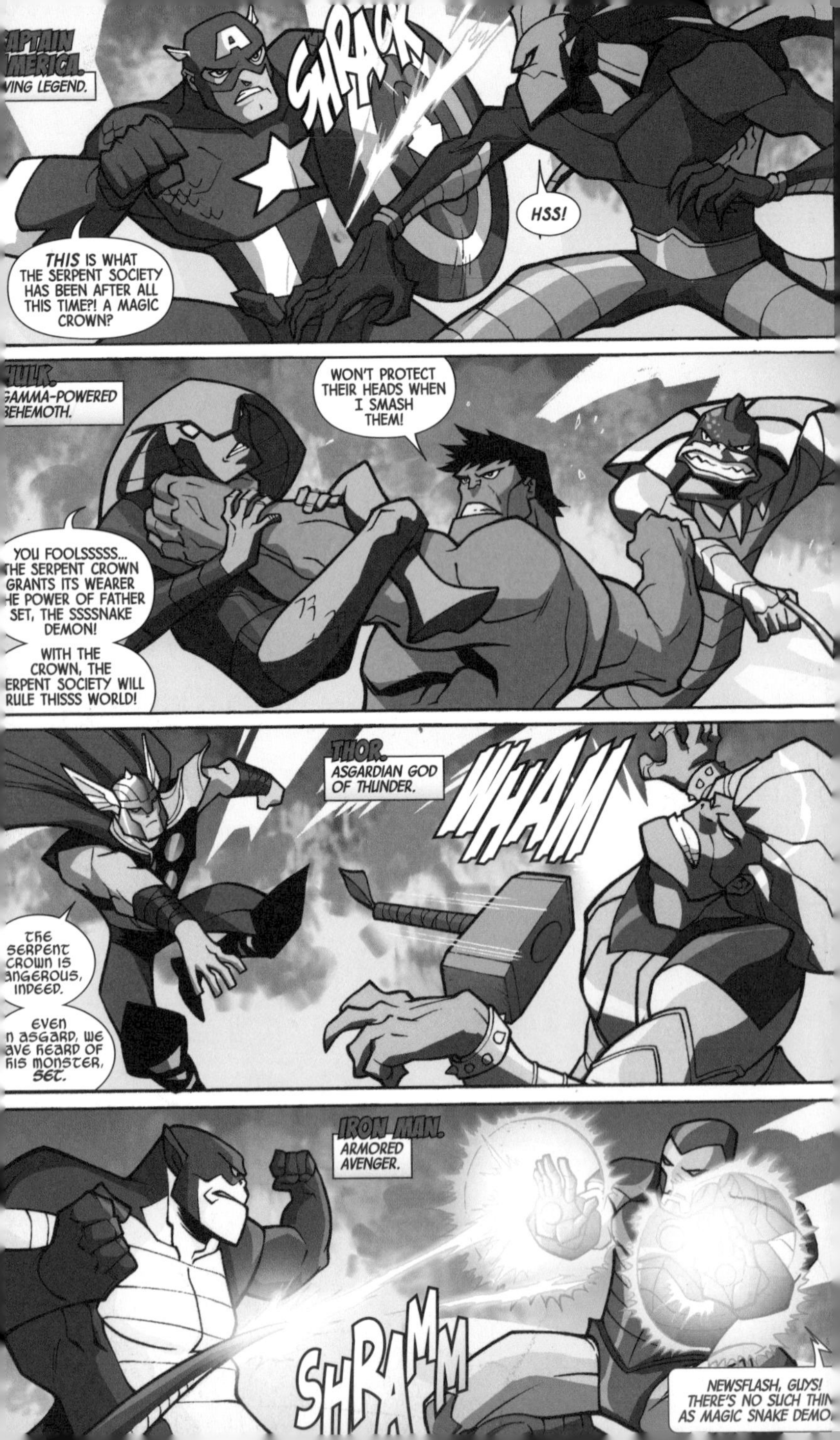

CAPTAIN AMERICA. VING LEGEND.
SHRACK
HSS!
THIS IS WHAT THE SERPENT SOCIETY HAS BEEN AFTER ALL THIS TIME?! A MAGIC CROWN?
HULK. GAMMA-POWERED BEHEMOTH.
WON'T PROTECT THEIR HEADS WHEN I SMASH THEM!
YOU FOOLSSSSS... THE SERPENT CROWN GRANTS ITS WEARER HE POWER OF FATHER SET, THE SSSSNAKE DEMON!
WITH THE CROWN, THE ERPENT SOCIETY WILL RULE THISSS WORLD!
THOR. ASGARDIAN GOD OF THUNDER.
WHAM
THE SERPENT CROWN IS ANGEROUS, INDEED.
EVEN N ASGARD, WE AVE HEARD OF HIS MONSTER, SET.
IRON MAN. ARMORED AVENGER.
SHRAMM
NEWSFLASH, GUYS! THERE'S NO SUCH THIN AS MAGIC SNAKE DEMO

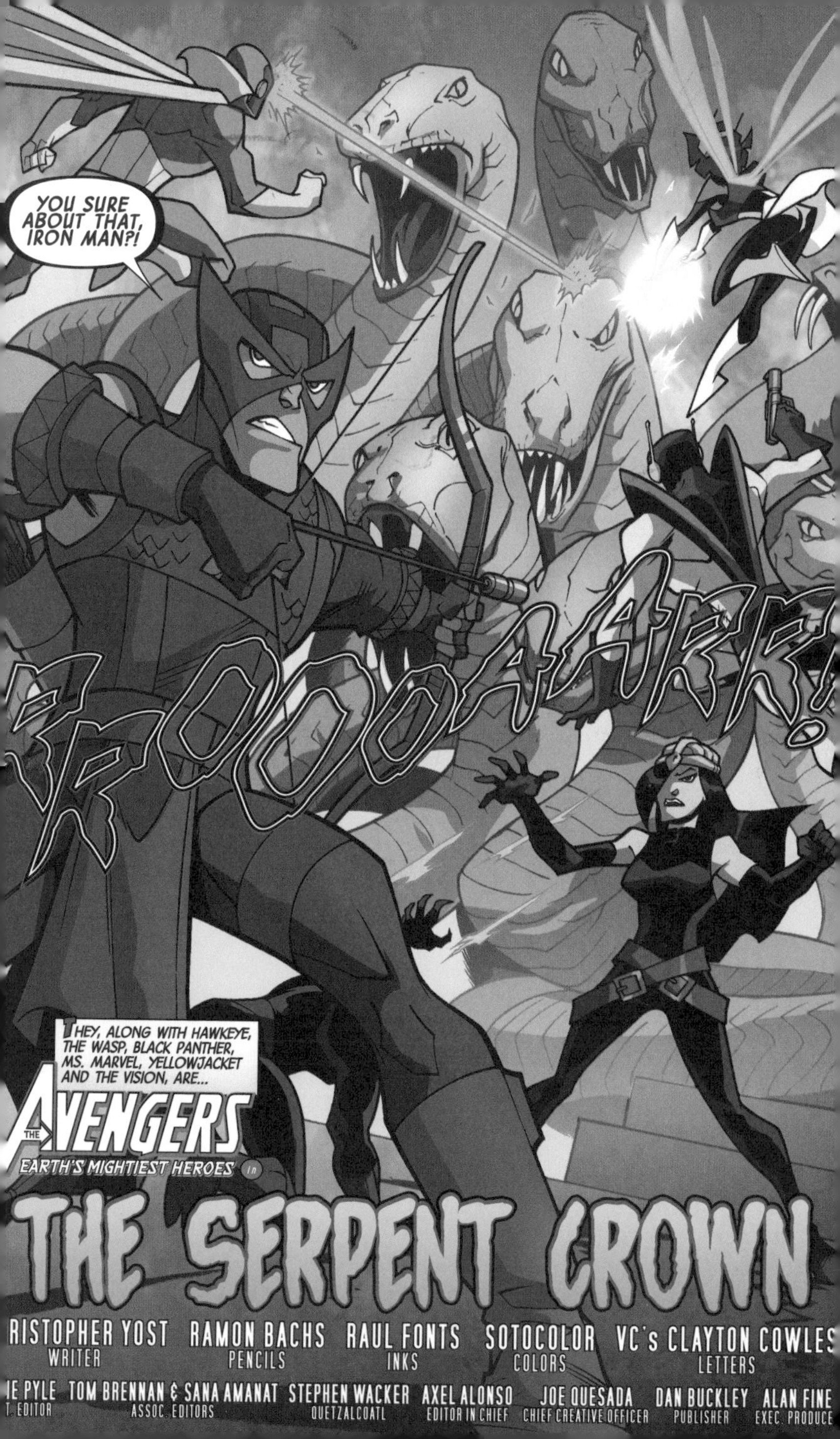

YOU SURE ABOUT THAT, IRON MAN?!
RROOOAARR!
THEY, ALONG WITH HAWKEYE, THE WASP, BLACK PANTHER, MS. MARVEL, YELLOWJACKET AND THE VISION, ARE...
THE AVENGERS
EARTH'S MIGHTIEST HEROES in
THE SERPENT CROWN
RISTOPHER YOST WRITER
RAMON BACHS PENCILS
RAUL FONTS INKS
SOTOCOLOR COLORS
VC's CLAYTON COWLES LETTERS
IE PYLE T. EDITOR
TOM BRENNAN & SANA AMANAT ASSOC. EDITORS
STEPHEN WACKER QUETZALCOATL
AXEL ALONSO EDITOR IN CHIEF
JOE QUESADA CHIEF CREATIVE OFFICER
DAN BUCKLEY PUBLISHER
ALAN FINE EXEC. PRODUCE

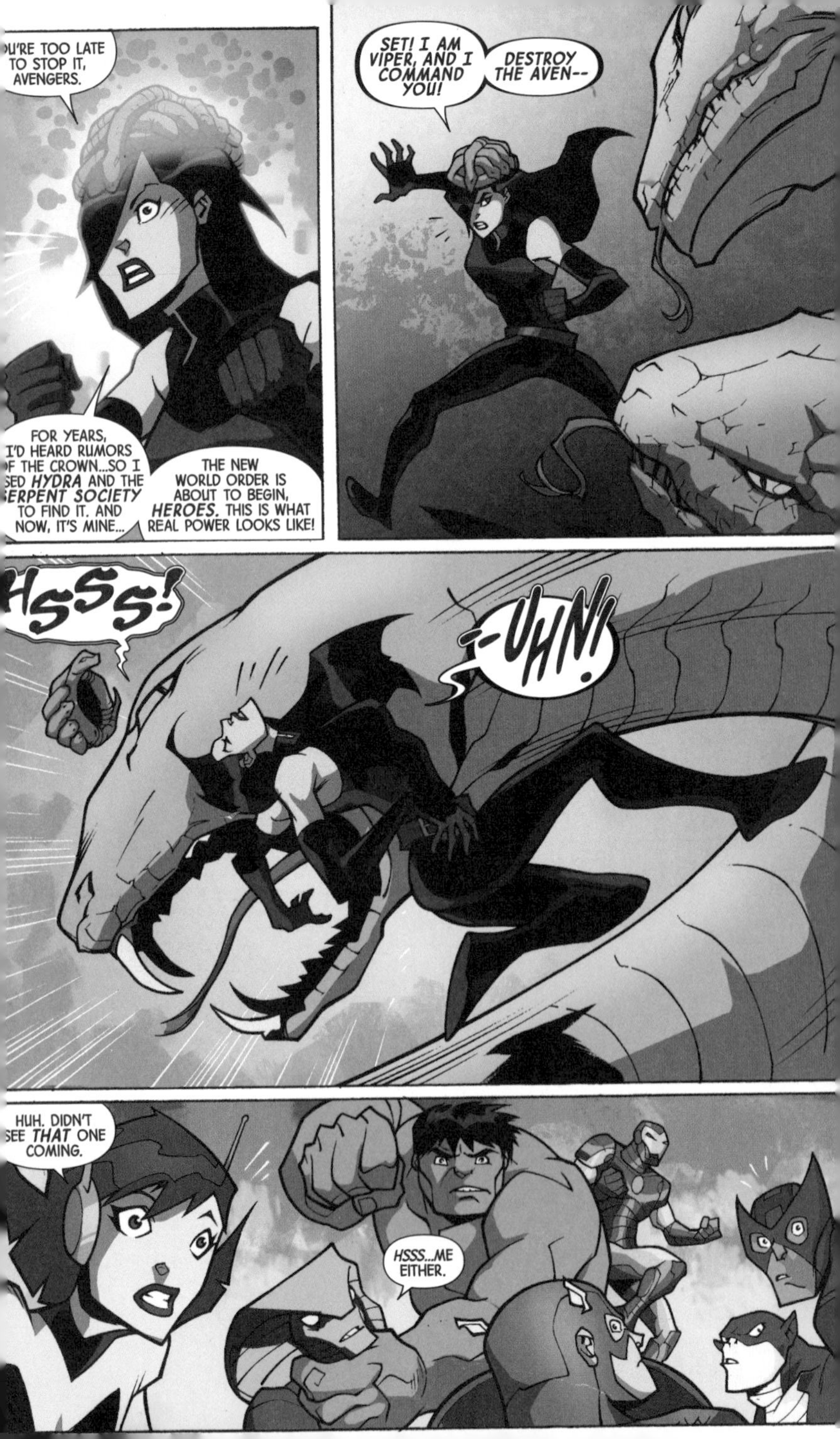

U'RE TOO LATE TO STOP IT, AVENGERS.
FOR YEARS, I'D HEARD RUMORS OF THE CROWN...SO I SED HYDRA AND THE ERPENT SOCIETY TO FIND IT. AND NOW, IT'S MINE...
THE NEW WORLD ORDER IS ABOUT TO BEGIN, HEROES. THIS IS WHAT REAL POWER LOOKS LIKE!
SET! I AM VIPER, AND I COMMAND YOU!
DESTROY THE AVEN--
HSSS!
--UHN!
HUH. DIDN'T SEE THAT ONE COMING.
HSSS...ME EITHER.

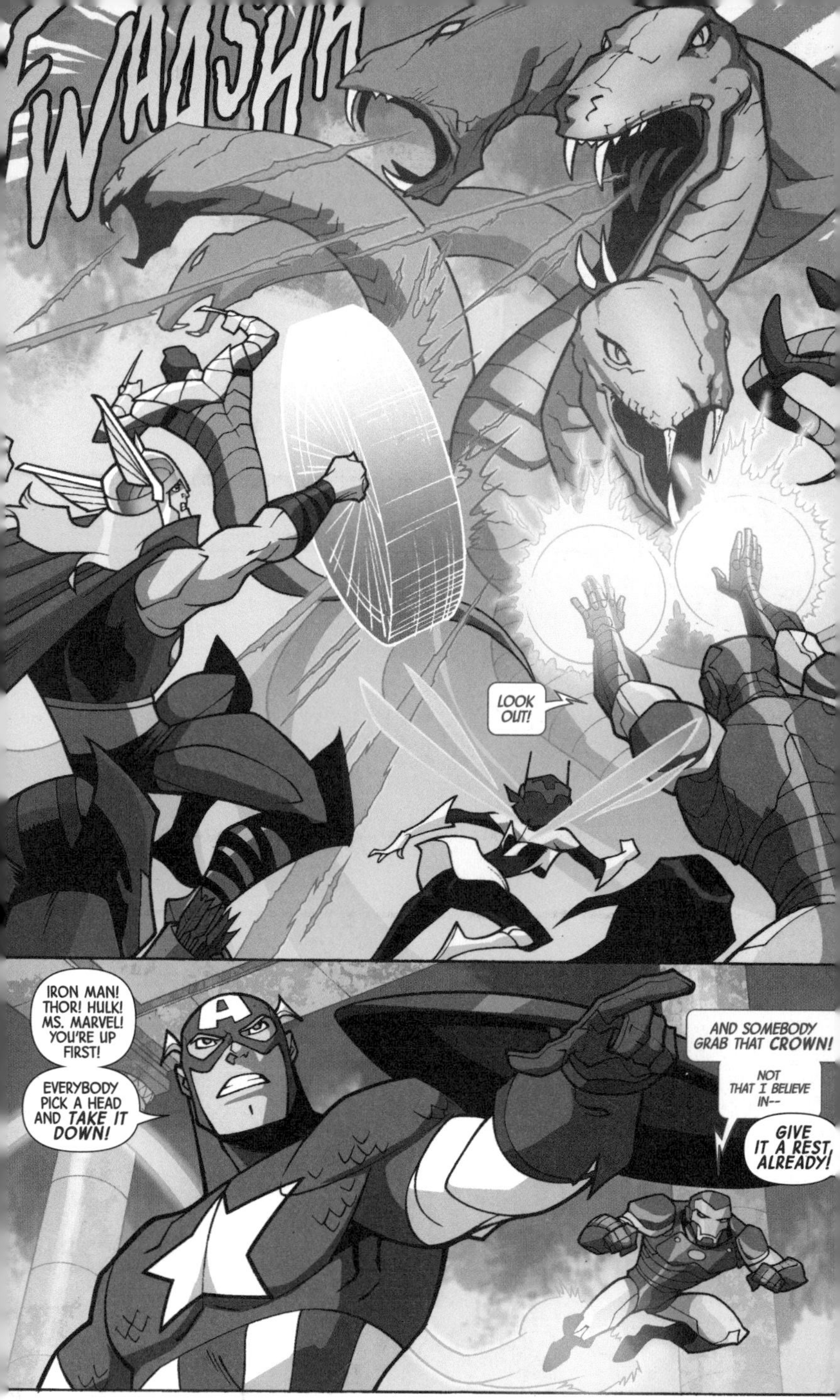
WHOOSH
LOOK OUT!
IRON MAN! THOR! HULK! MS. MARVEL! YOU'RE UP FIRST!
EVERYBODY PICK A HEAD AND TAKE IT DOWN!
AND SOMEBODY GRAB THAT CROWN!
NOT THAT I BELIEVE IN--
GIVE IT A REST, ALREADY!

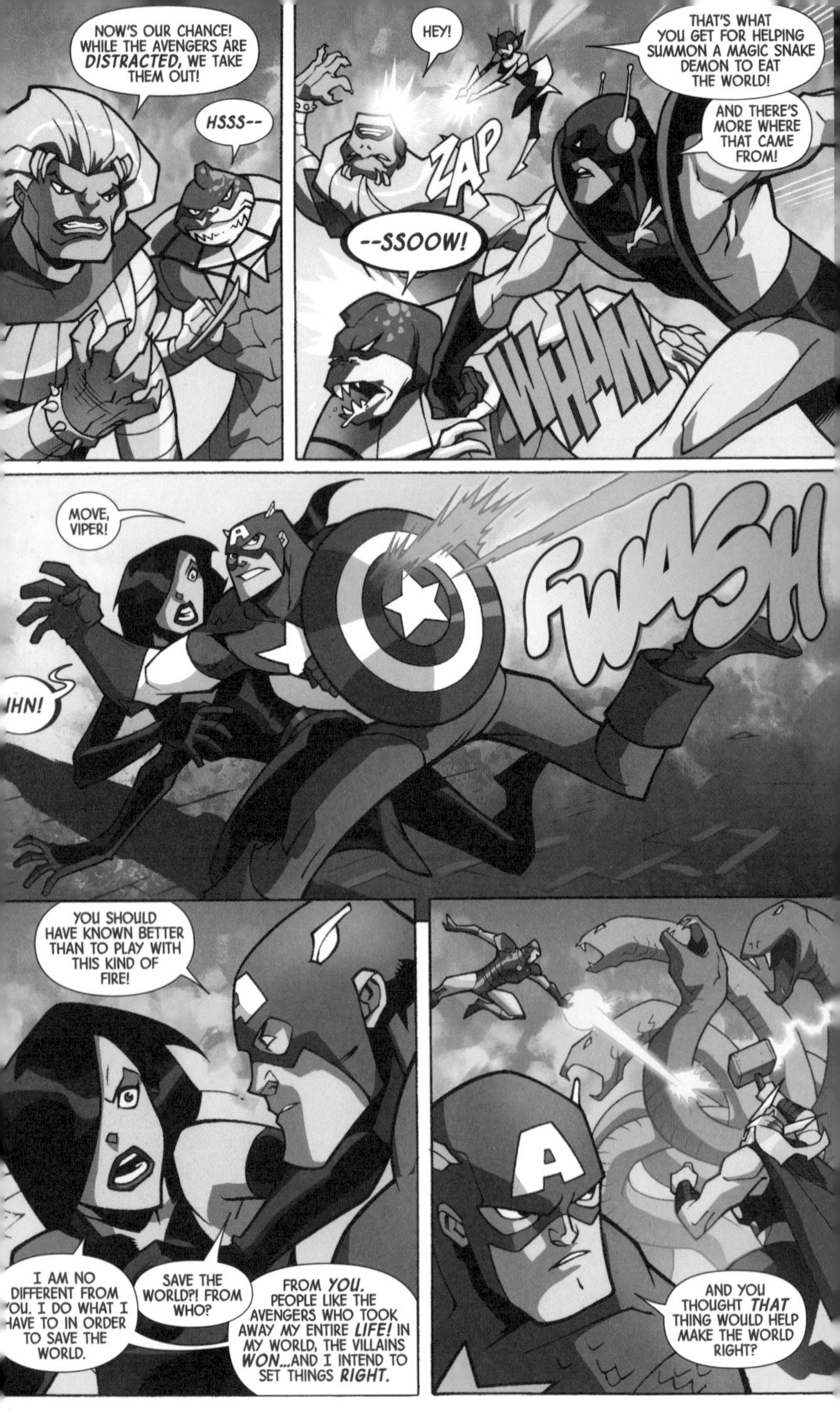
NOW'S OUR CHANCE! WHILE THE AVENGERS ARE DISTRACTED, WE TAKE THEM OUT!
HSSS--
HEY!
THAT'S WHAT YOU GET FOR HELPING SUMMON A MAGIC SNAKE DEMON TO EAT THE WORLD!
ZAP
AND THERE'S MORE WHERE THAT CAME FROM!
--SSOOW!
WHAM
MOVE, VIPER!
FWASH
HN!
YOU SHOULD HAVE KNOWN BETTER THAN TO PLAY WITH THIS KIND OF FIRE!
I AM NO DIFFERENT FROM YOU. I DO WHAT I HAVE TO IN ORDER TO SAVE THE WORLD.
SAVE THE WORLD?! FROM WHO?
FROM YOU. PEOPLE LIKE THE AVENGERS WHO TOOK AWAY MY ENTIRE LIFE! IN MY WORLD, THE VILLAINS WON...AND I INTEND TO SET THINGS RIGHT.
AND YOU THOUGHT THAT THING WOULD HELP MAKE THE WORLD RIGHT?

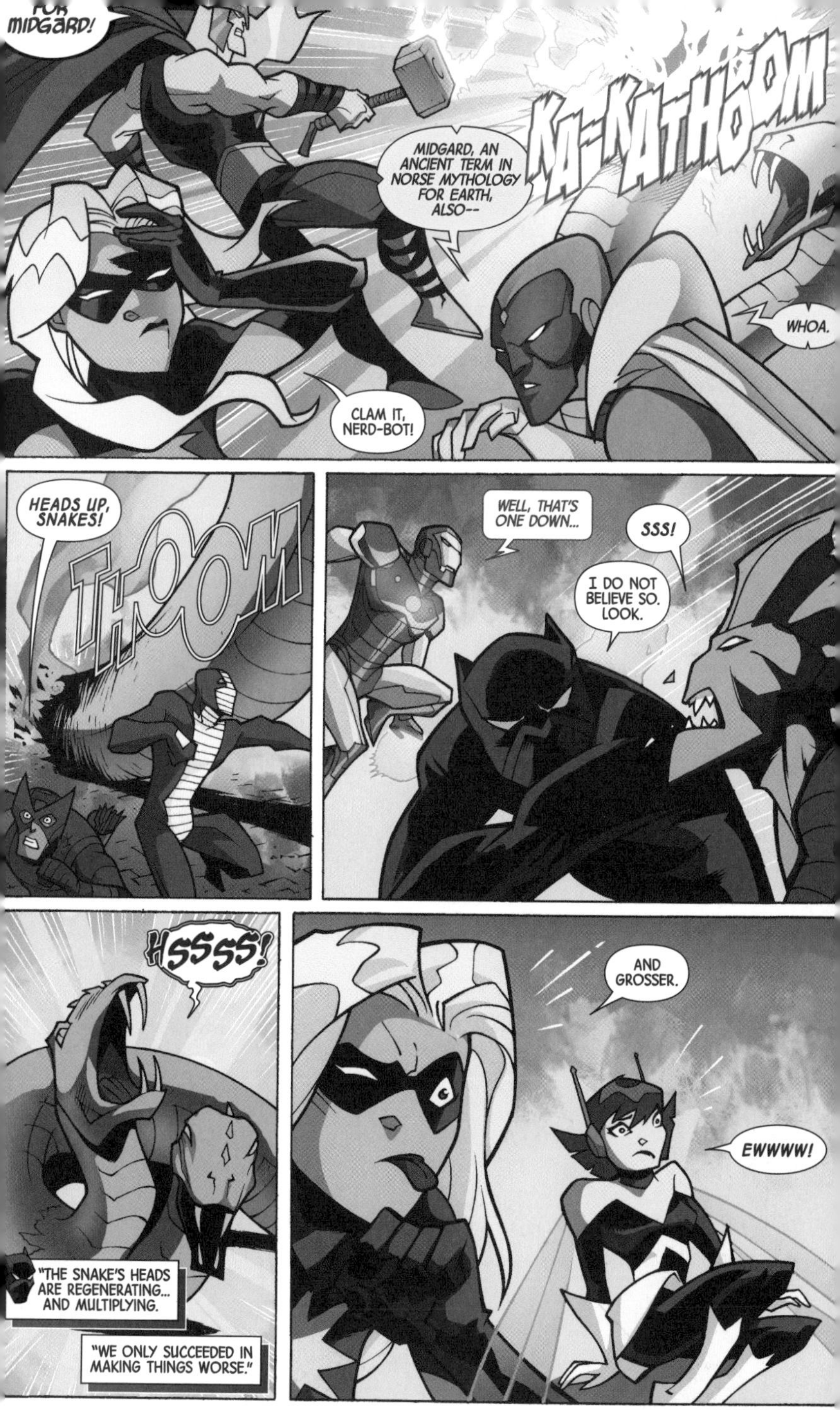

MIDGARD!
KA-KATHOOM
MIDGARD, AN ANCIENT TERM IN NORSE MYTHOLOGY FOR EARTH, ALSO--
WHOA.
CLAM IT, NERD-BOT!
HEADS UP, SNAKES!
THOOM
WELL, THAT'S ONE DOWN...
SSS!
I DO NOT BELIEVE SO. LOOK.
HSSSS!
AND GROSSER.
EWWWW!
"THE SNAKE'S HEADS ARE REGENERATING... AND MULTIPLYING.
"WE ONLY SUCCEEDED IN MAKING THINGS WORSE."

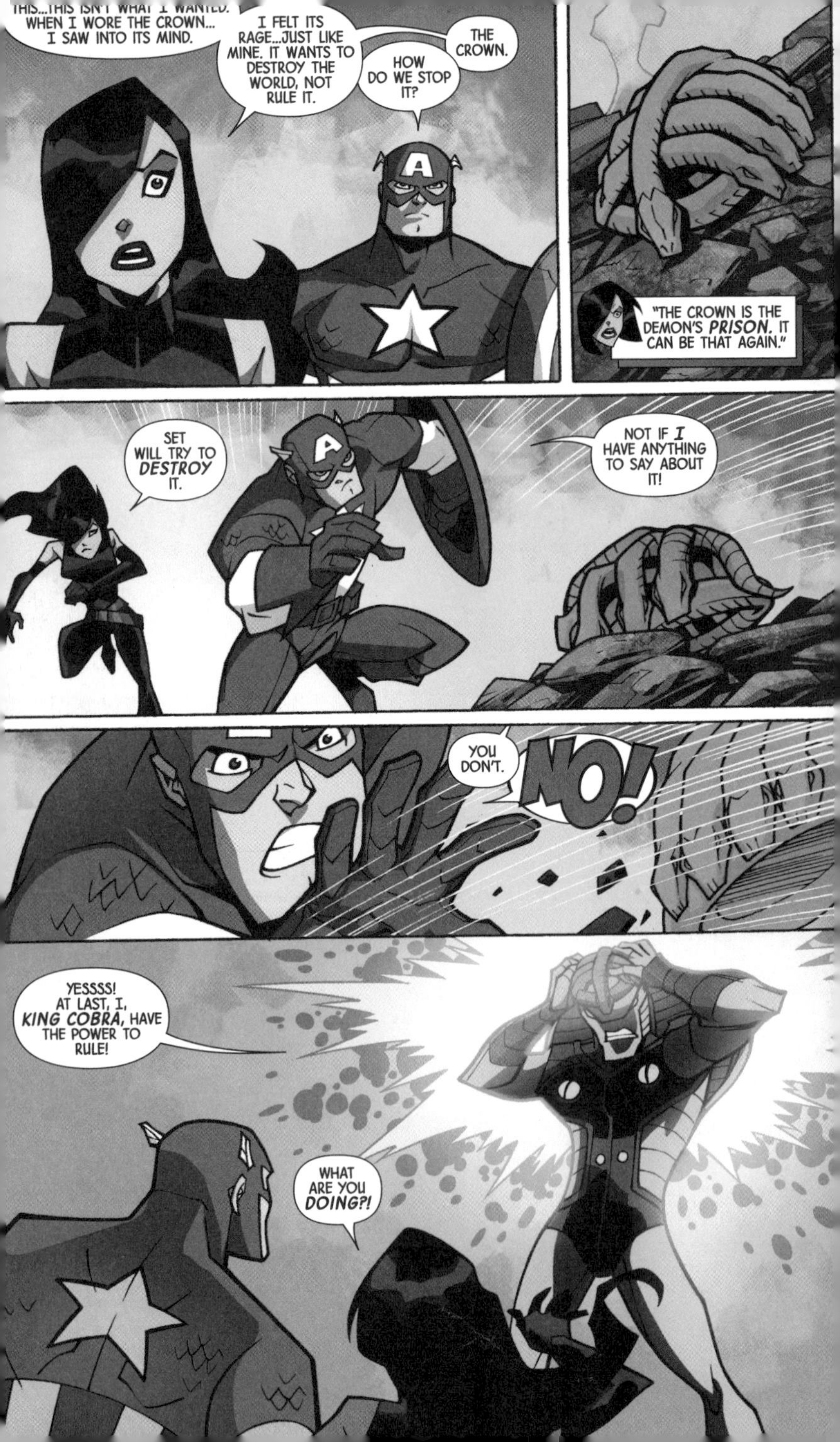
THIS...THIS ISN'T WHAT I WANTED. WHEN I WORE THE CROWN... I SAW INTO ITS MIND.
I FELT ITS RAGE...JUST LIKE MINE. IT WANTS TO DESTROY THE WORLD, NOT RULE IT.
HOW DO WE STOP IT?
THE CROWN.
"THE CROWN IS THE DEMON'S PRISON. IT CAN BE THAT AGAIN."
SET WILL TRY TO DESTROY IT.
NOT IF I HAVE ANYTHING TO SAY ABOUT IT!
YOU DON'T.
NO!
YESSSS! AT LAST, I, KING COBRA, HAVE THE POWER TO RULE!
WHAT ARE YOU DOING?!

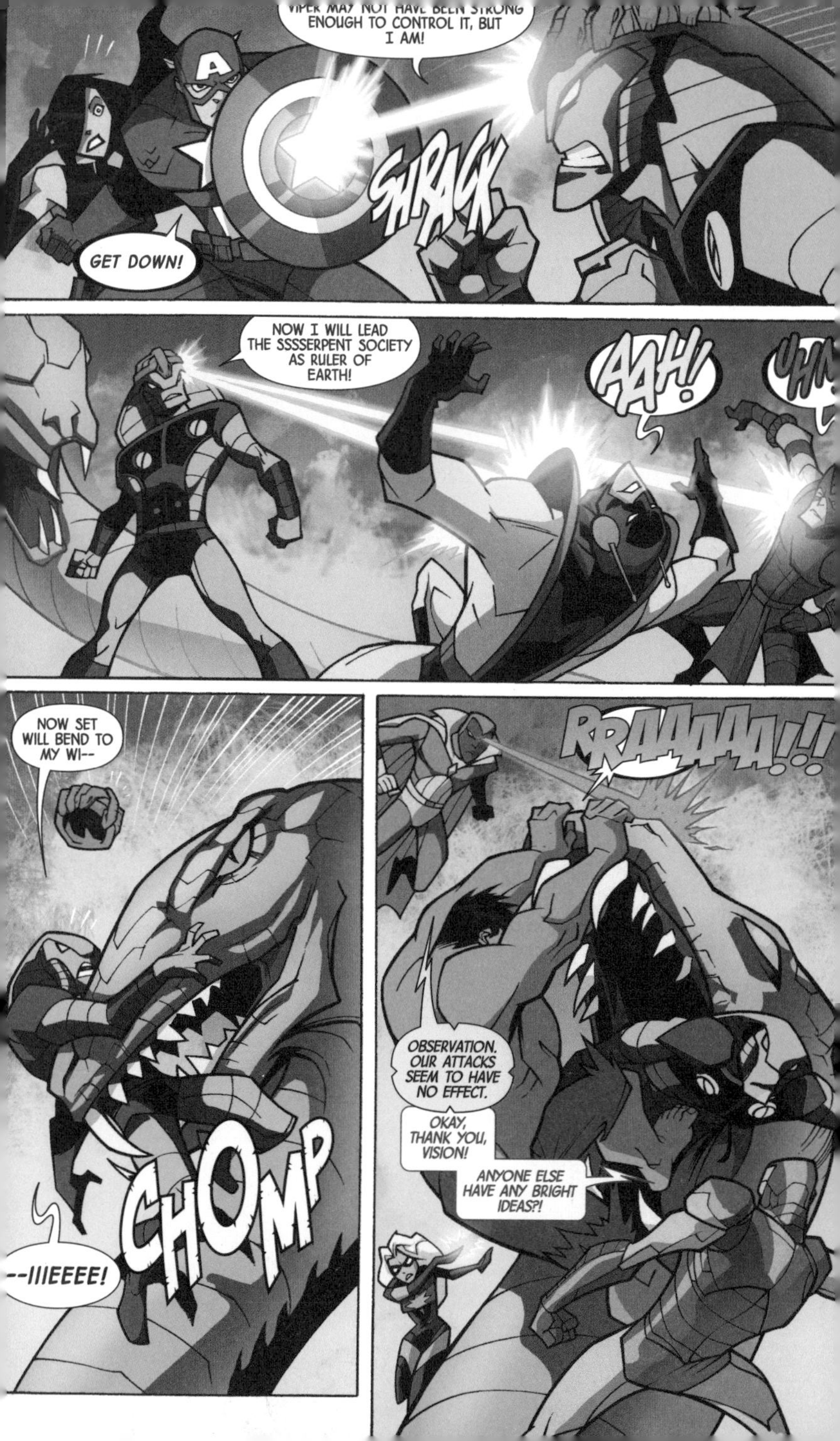
VIPER MAY NOT HAVE BEEN STRONG ENOUGH TO CONTROL IT, BUT I AM!
GET DOWN!
SHRACK
NOW I WILL LEAD THE SSSSERPENT SOCIETY AS RULER OF EARTH!
AAH!
NOW SET WILL BEND TO MY WI--
CHOMP
--IIIEEEE!
RRAAAAAA!!!
OBSERVATION. OUR ATTACKS SEEM TO HAVE NO EFFECT.
OKAY, THANK YOU, VISION!
ANYONE ELSE HAVE ANY BRIGHT IDEAS?!

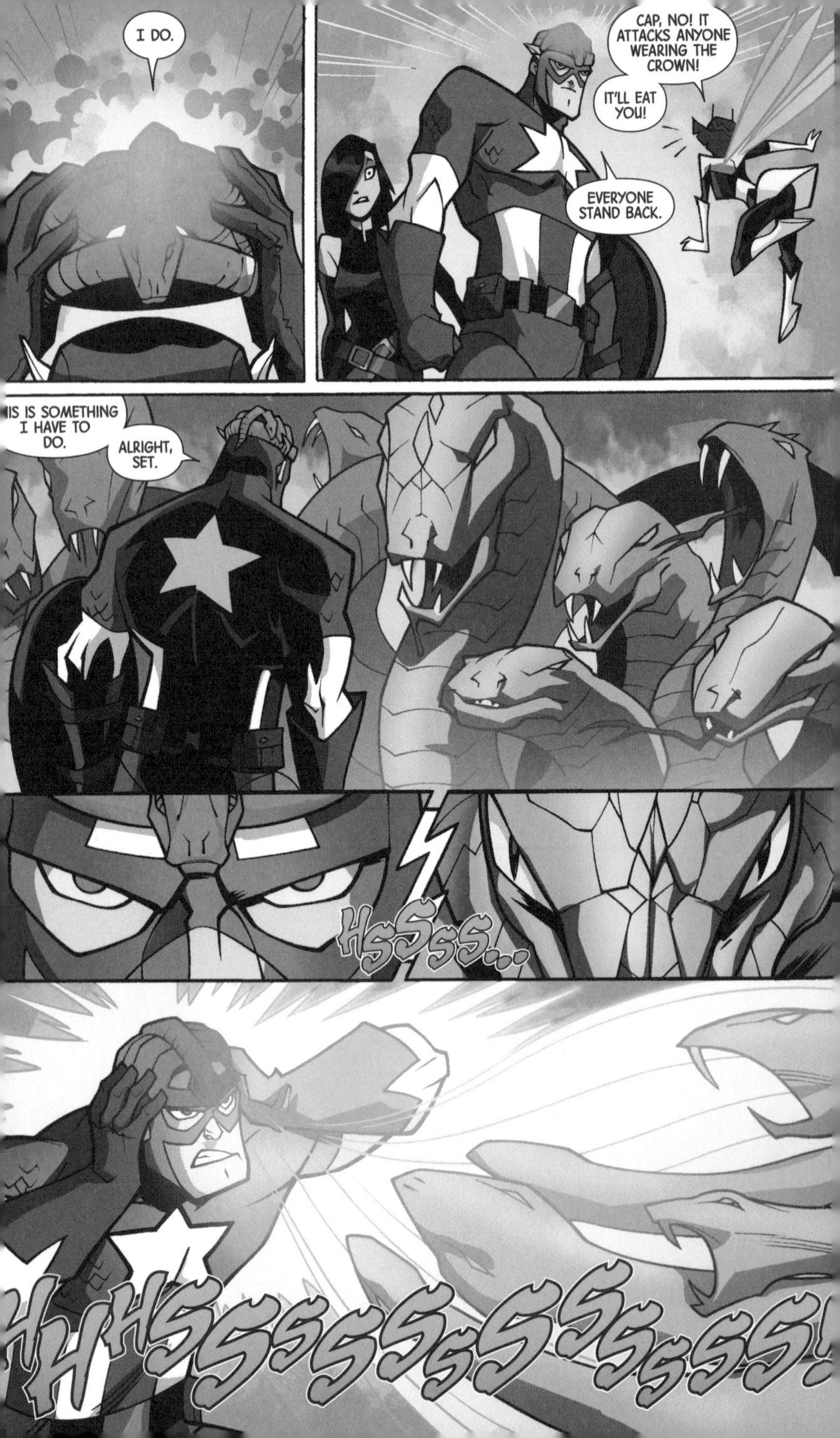
I DO.
CAP, NO! IT ATTACKS ANYONE WEARING THE CROWN!
IT'LL EAT YOU!
EVERYONE STAND BACK.
IS IS SOMETHING I HAVE TO DO.
ALRIGHT, SET.
HSSSSS...
HHHSSSSSSSSSSSSSSS!

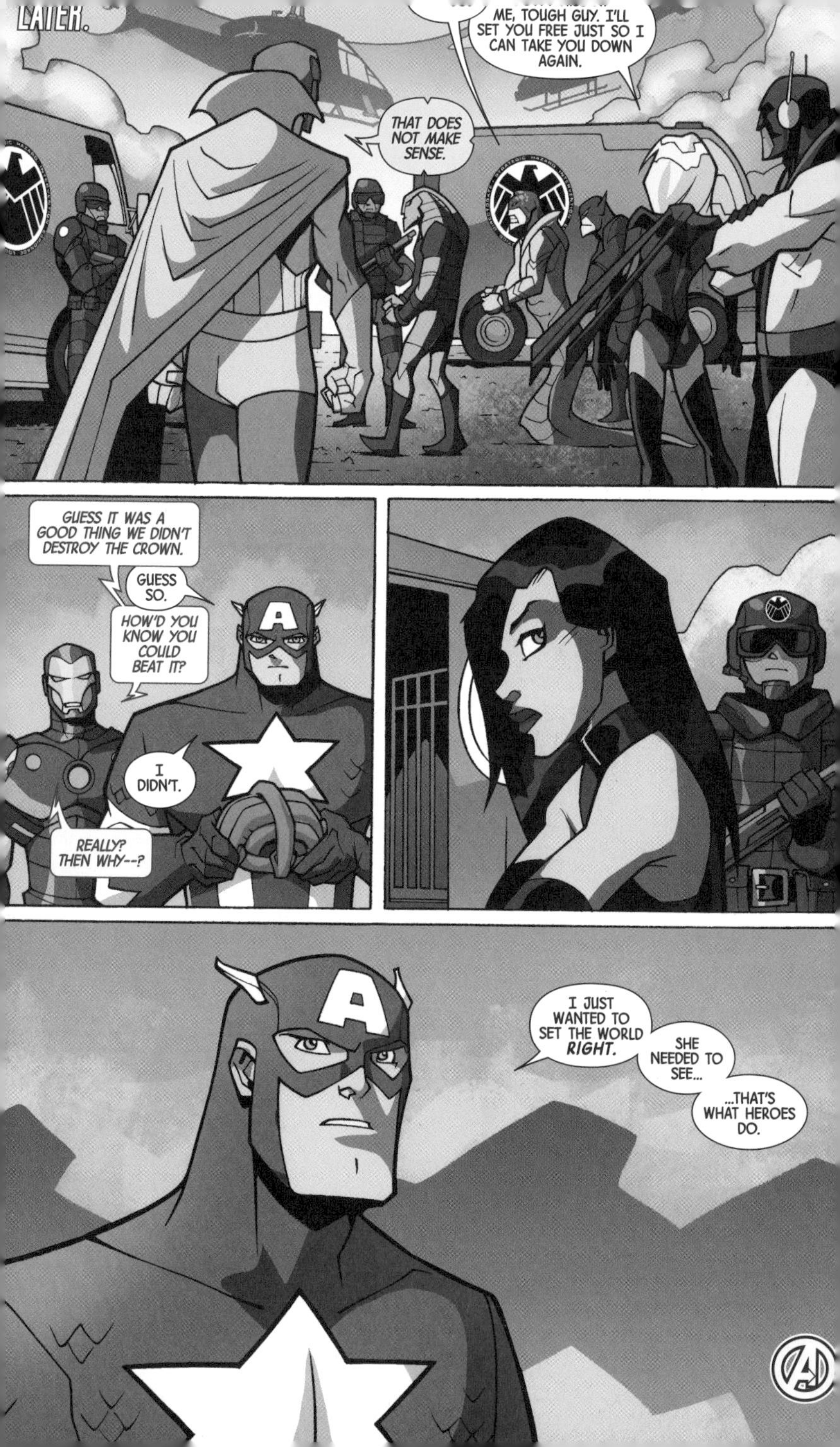
LATER.
ME, TOUGH GUY. I'LL SET YOU FREE JUST SO I CAN TAKE YOU DOWN AGAIN.
THAT DOES NOT MAKE SENSE.
GUESS IT WAS A GOOD THING WE DIDN'T DESTROY THE CROWN.
GUESS SO.
HOW'D YOU KNOW YOU COULD BEAT IT?
I DIDN'T.
REALLY? THEN WHY--?
I JUST WANTED TO SET THE WORLD RIGHT.
SHE NEEDED TO SEE...
...THAT'S WHAT HEROES DO.

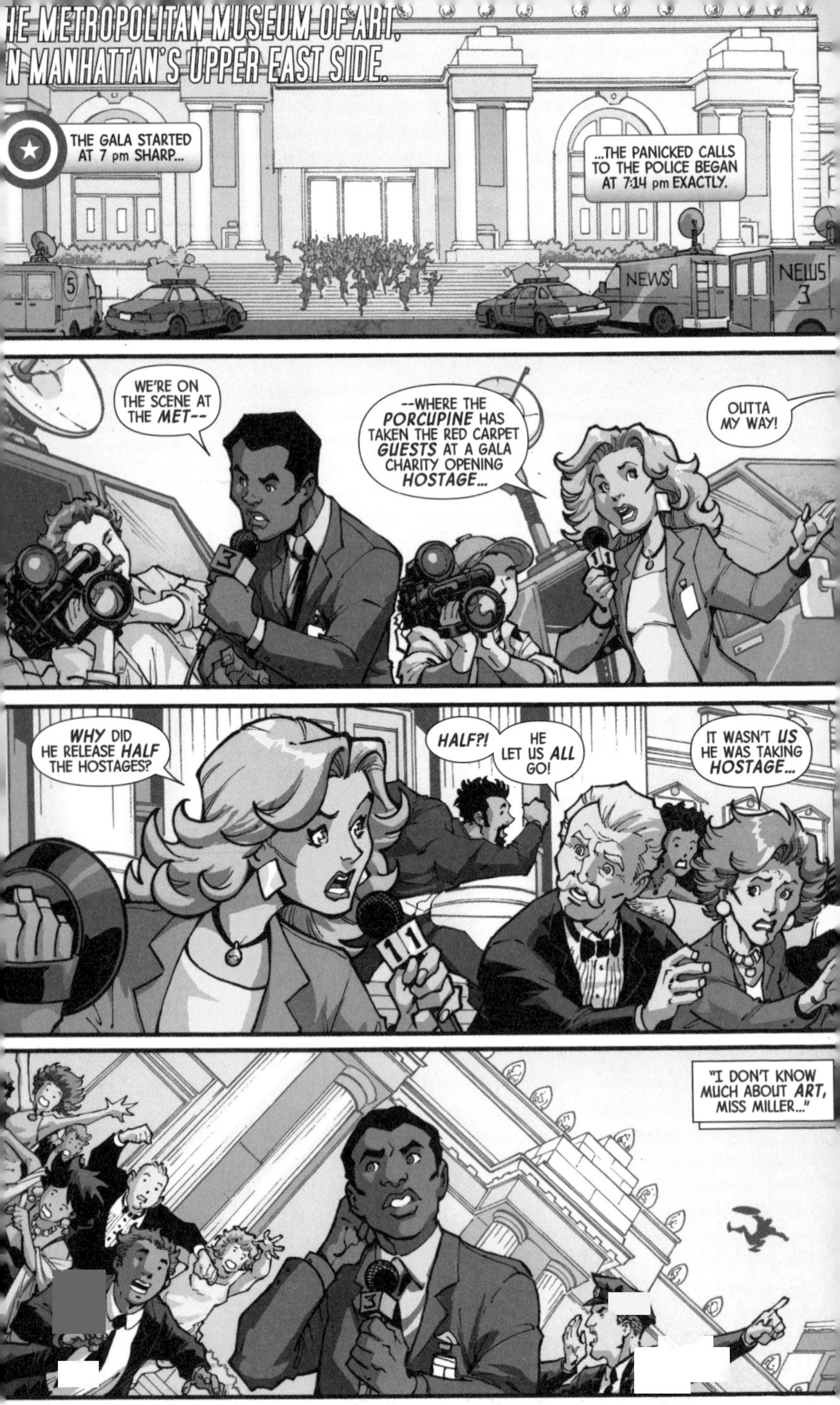
HE METROPOLITAN MUSEUM OF ART,
N MANHATTAN'S UPPER EAST SIDE.
THE GALA STARTED AT 7 pm SHARP...
...THE PANICKED CALLS TO THE POLICE BEGAN AT 7:14 pm EXACTLY.
NEWS 1
NEWS 3
WE'RE ON THE SCENE AT THE MET--
--WHERE THE PORCUPINE HAS TAKEN THE RED CARPET GUESTS AT A GALA CHARITY OPENING HOSTAGE...
OUTTA MY WAY!
WHY DID HE RELEASE HALF THE HOSTAGES?
HALF?!
HE LET US ALL GO!
IT WASN'T US HE WAS TAKING HOSTAGE...
"I DON'T KNOW MUCH ABOUT ART, MISS MILLER..."

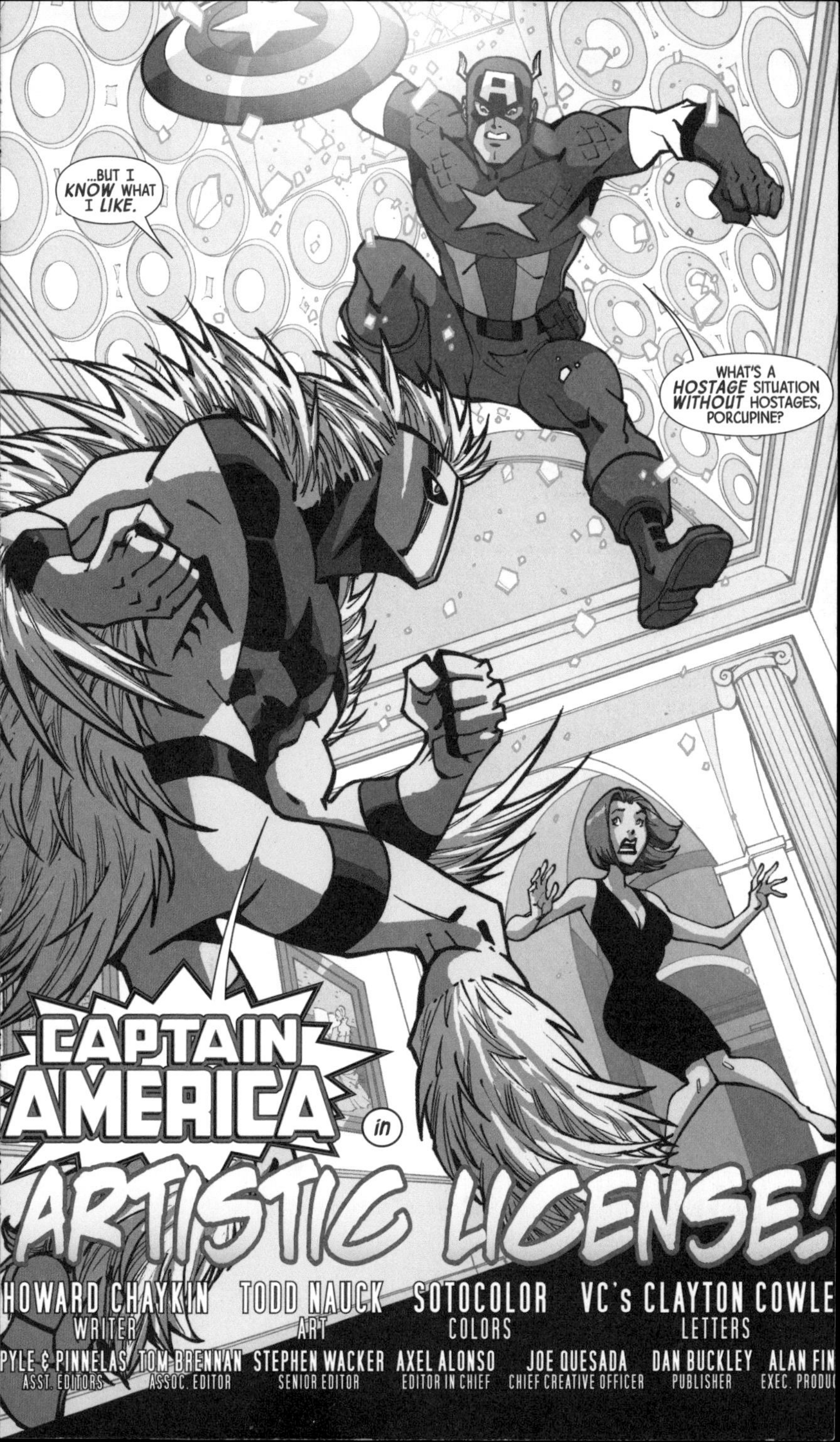
...BUT I KNOW WHAT I LIKE.
WHAT'S A HOSTAGE SITUATION WITHOUT HOSTAGES, PORCUPINE?
CAPTAIN AMERICA in
ARTISTIC LICENSE!
HOWARD CHAYKIN WRITER
TODD NAUCK ART
SOTOCOLOR COLORS
VC's CLAYTON COWLE LETTERS
PYLE & PINNELAS ASST. EDITORS
TOM BRENNAN ASSOC. EDITOR
STEPHEN WACKER SENIOR EDITOR
AXEL ALONSO EDITOR IN CHIEF
JOE QUESADA CHIEF CREATIVE OFFICER
DAN BUCKLEY PUBLISHER
ALAN FIN EXEC. PRODU

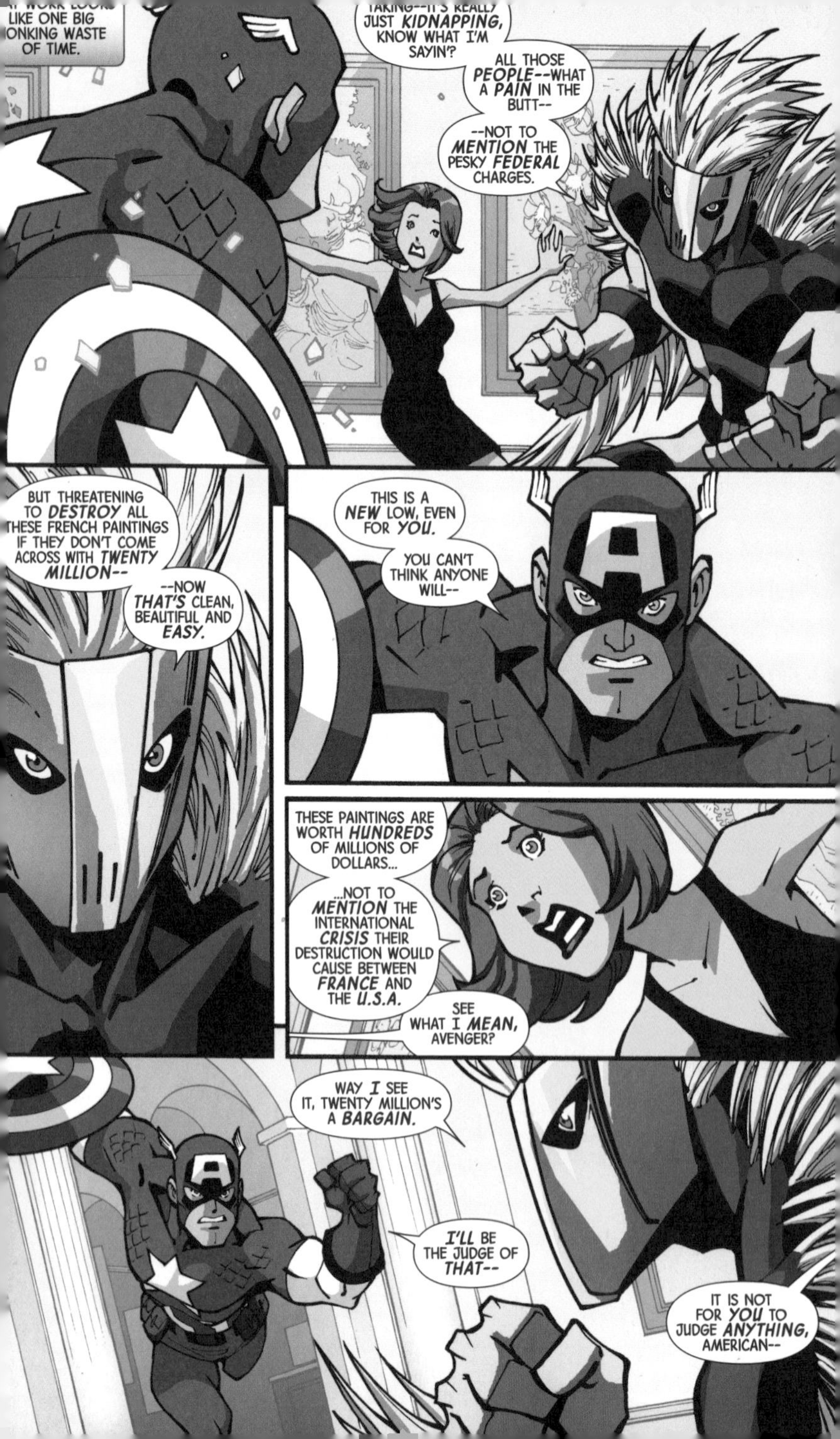
LIKE ONE BIG
ONKING WASTE
OF TIME.
JUST KIDNAPPING, KNOW WHAT I'M SAYIN'?
ALL THOSE PEOPLE--WHAT A PAIN IN THE BUTT--
--NOT TO MENTION THE PESKY FEDERAL CHARGES.
BUT THREATENING TO DESTROY ALL THESE FRENCH PAINTINGS IF THEY DON'T COME ACROSS WITH TWENTY MILLION--
--NOW THAT'S CLEAN, BEAUTIFUL AND EASY.
THIS IS A NEW LOW, EVEN FOR YOU.
YOU CAN'T THINK ANYONE WILL--
THESE PAINTINGS ARE WORTH HUNDREDS OF MILLIONS OF DOLLARS...
...NOT TO MENTION THE INTERNATIONAL CRISIS THEIR DESTRUCTION WOULD CAUSE BETWEEN FRANCE AND THE U.S.A.
SEE WHAT I MEAN, AVENGER?
WAY I SEE IT, TWENTY MILLION'S A BARGAIN.
I'LL BE THE JUDGE OF THAT--
IT IS NOT FOR YOU TO JUDGE ANYTHING, AMERICAN--

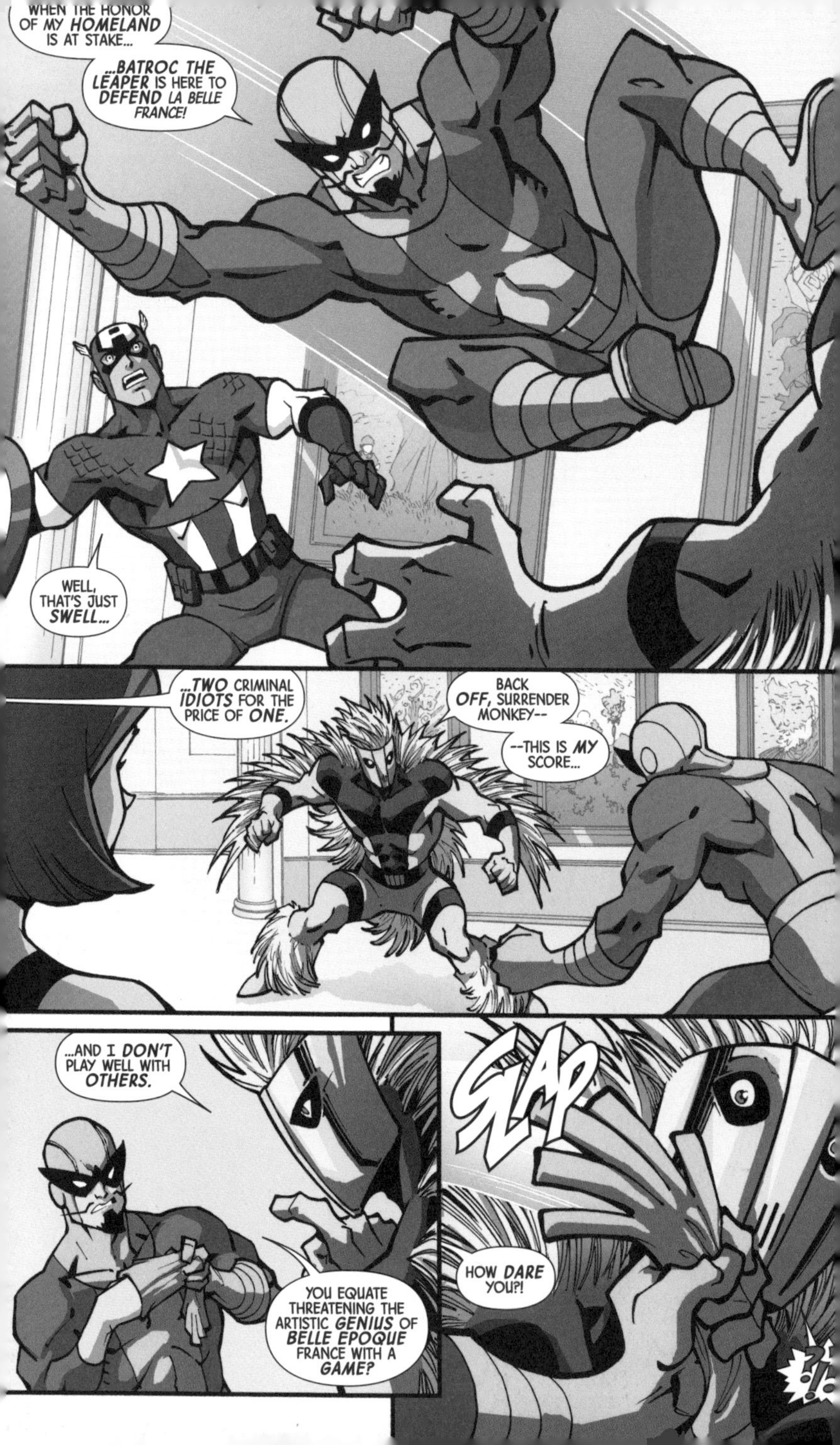
WHEN THE HONOR OF MY HOMELAND IS AT STAKE...
...BATROC THE LEAPER IS HERE TO DEFEND LA BELLE FRANCE!
WELL, THAT'S JUST SWELL...
...TWO CRIMINAL IDIOTS FOR THE PRICE OF ONE.
BACK OFF, SURRENDER MONKEY--
--THIS IS MY SCORE...
...AND I DON'T PLAY WELL WITH OTHERS.
YOU EQUATE THREATENING THE ARTISTIC GENIUS OF BELLE EPOQUE FRANCE WITH A GAME?
SLAP
HOW DARE YOU?!

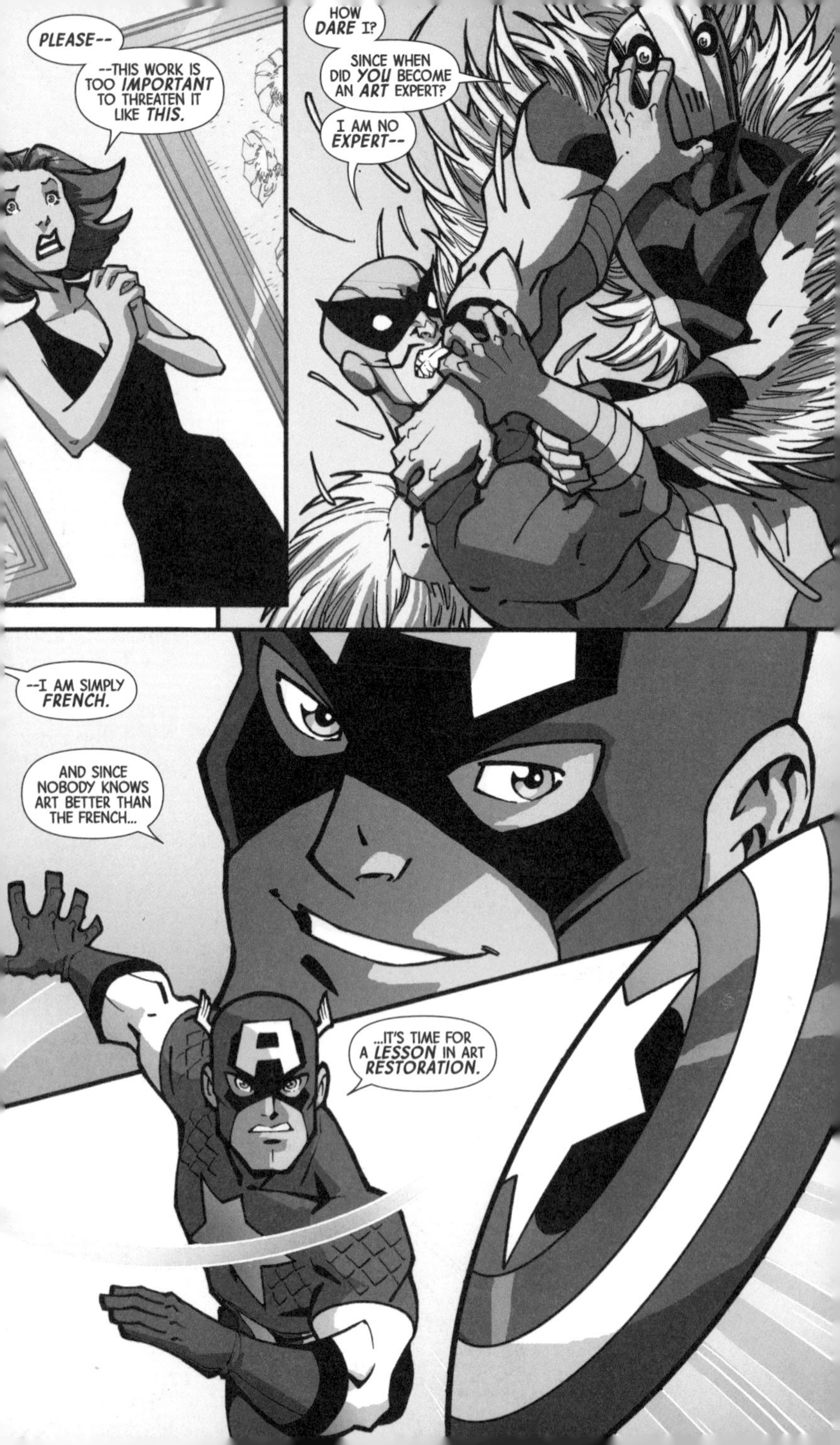
PLEASE--
--THIS WORK IS TOO IMPORTANT TO THREATEN IT LIKE THIS.
HOW DARE I?
SINCE WHEN DID YOU BECOME AN ART EXPERT?
I AM NO EXPERT--
--I AM SIMPLY FRENCH.
AND SINCE NOBODY KNOWS ART BETTER THAN THE FRENCH...
...IT'S TIME FOR A LESSON IN ART RESTORATION.

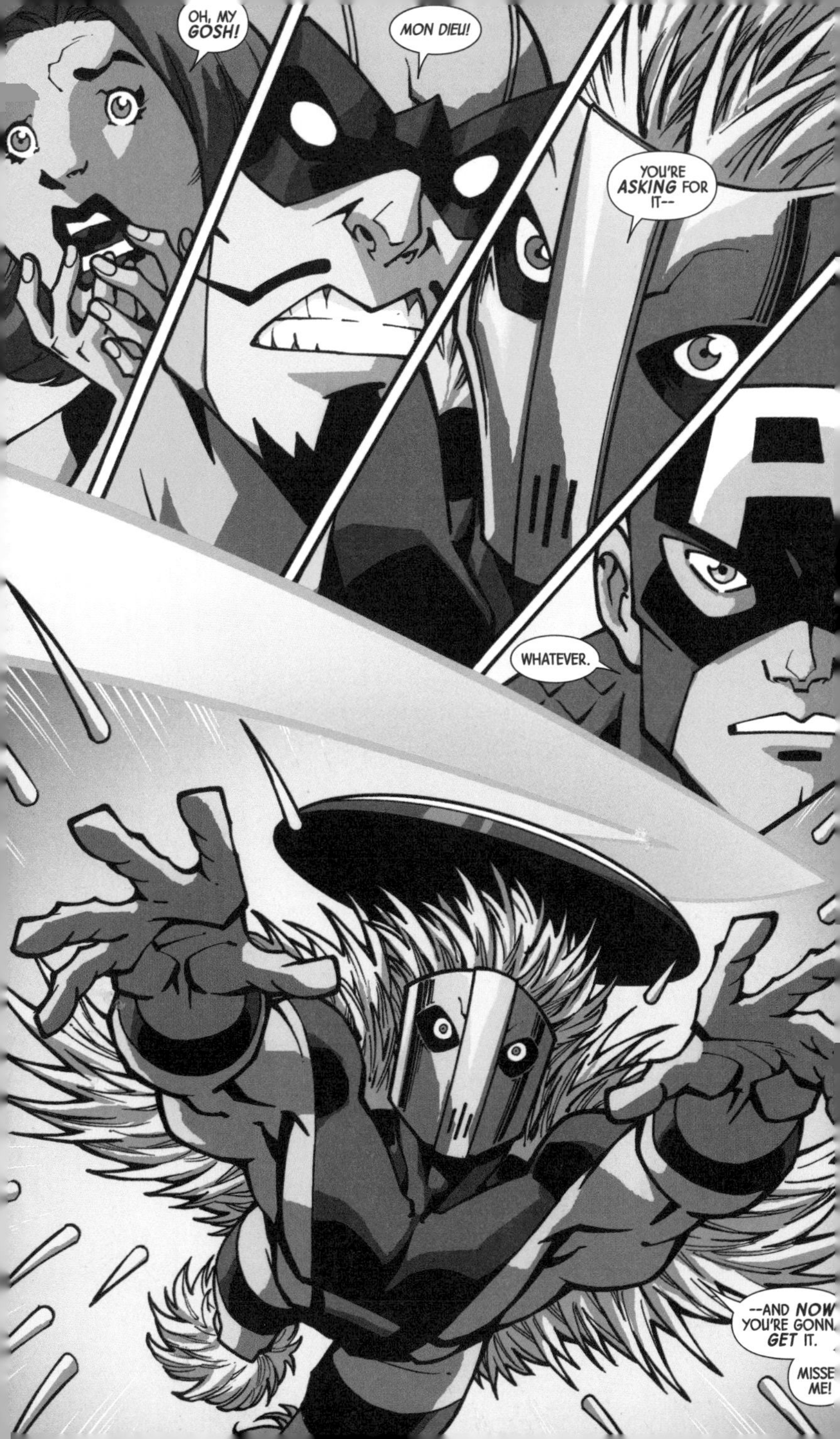

OH, MY GOSH!
MON DIEU!
YOU'RE ASKING FOR IT--
WHATEVER.
--AND NOW YOU'RE GONN GET IT.
MISSE ME!

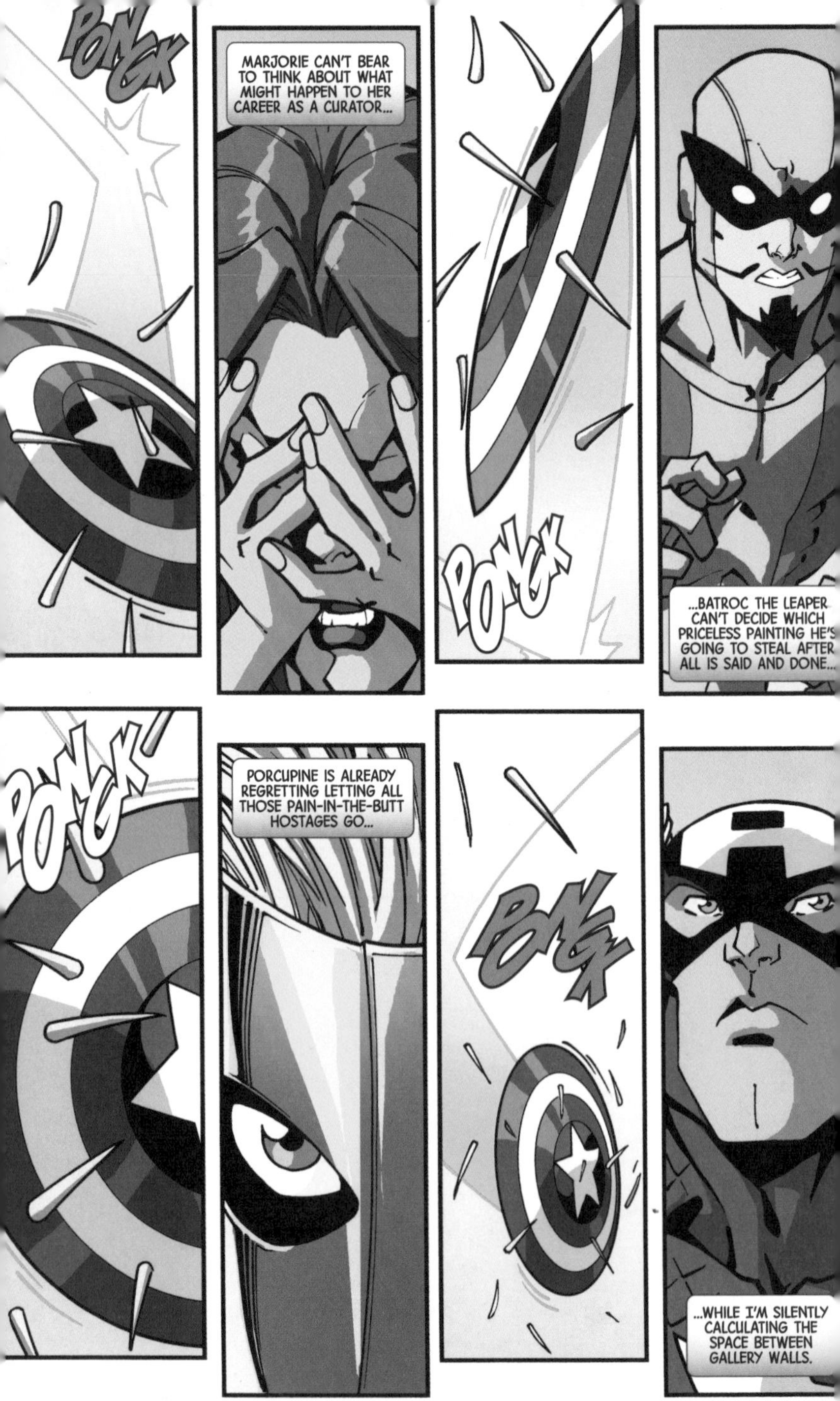
PONGK
MARJORIE CAN'T BEAR TO THINK ABOUT WHAT MIGHT HAPPEN TO HER CAREER AS A CURATOR...
PONGK
...BATROC THE LEAPER CAN'T DECIDE WHICH PRICELESS PAINTING HE'S GOING TO STEAL AFTER ALL IS SAID AND DONE...
PONGK
PORCUPINE IS ALREADY REGRETTING LETTING ALL THOSE PAIN-IN-THE-BUTT HOSTAGES GO...
BONGK
...WHILE I'M SILENTLY CALCULATING THE SPACE BETWEEN GALLERY WALLS.

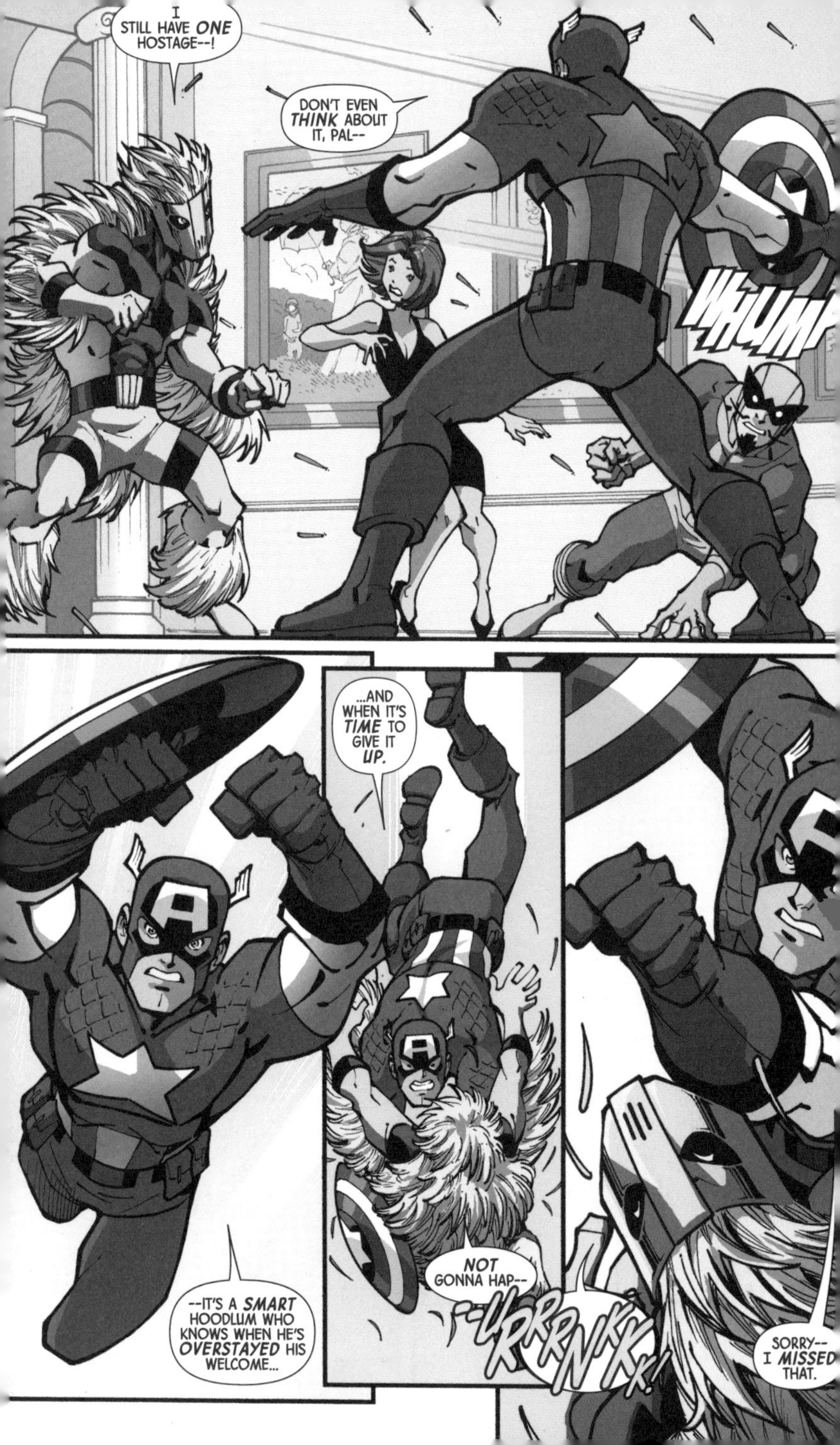

I STILL HAVE ONE HOSTAGE--!
DON'T EVEN THINK ABOUT IT, PAL--
WHUMP
--IT'S A SMART HOODLUM WHO KNOWS WHEN HE'S OVERSTAYED HIS WELCOME...
...AND WHEN IT'S TIME TO GIVE IT UP.
NOT GONNA HAP--
K-LRRRNKK!
SORRY-- I MISSED THAT.

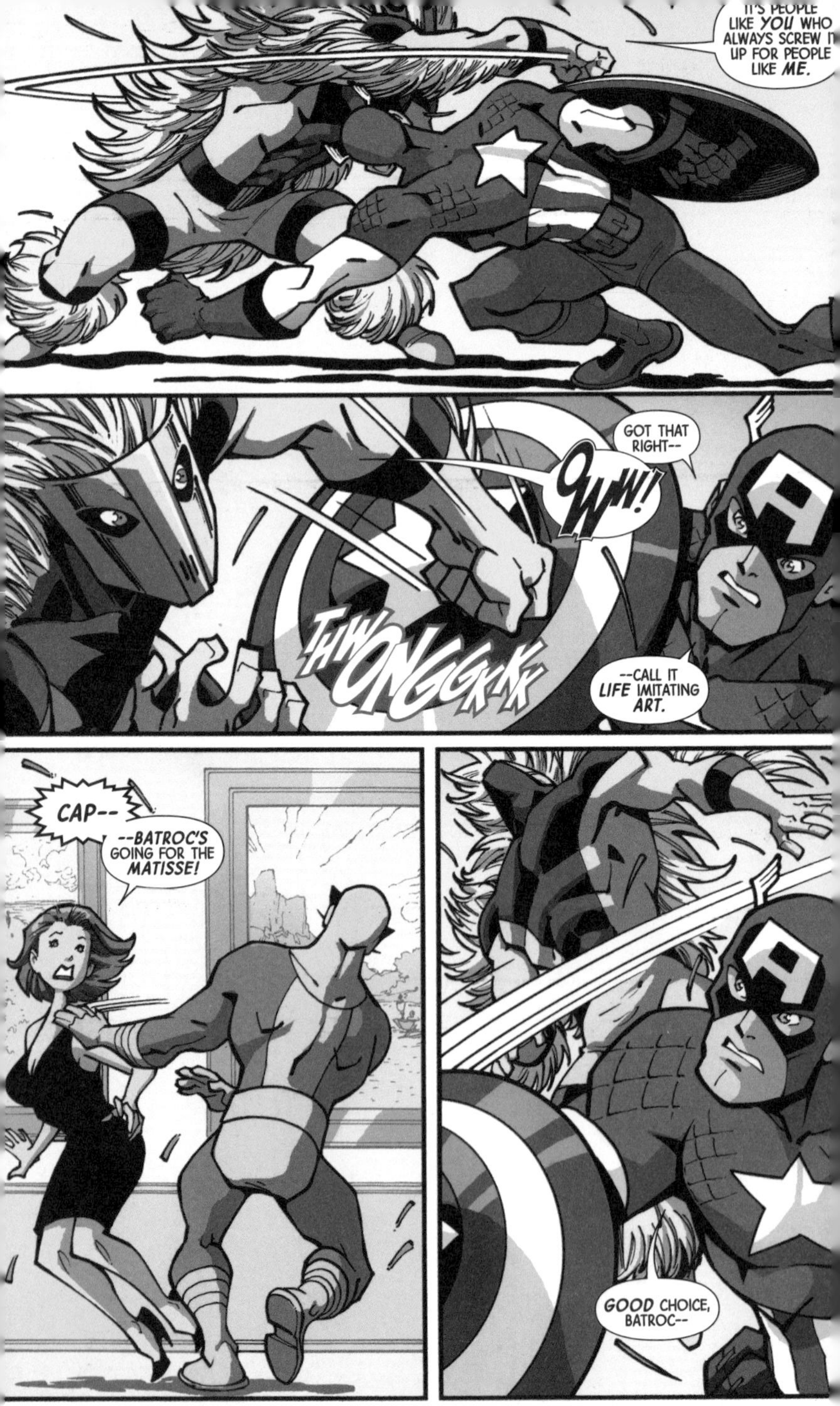
IT'S PEOPLE LIKE YOU WHO ALWAYS SCREW IT UP FOR PEOPLE LIKE ME.
GOT THAT RIGHT--
OWW!
THWONGGKKK
--CALL IT LIFE IMITATING ART.
CAP--
--BATROC'S GOING FOR THE MATISSE!
GOOD CHOICE, BATROC--

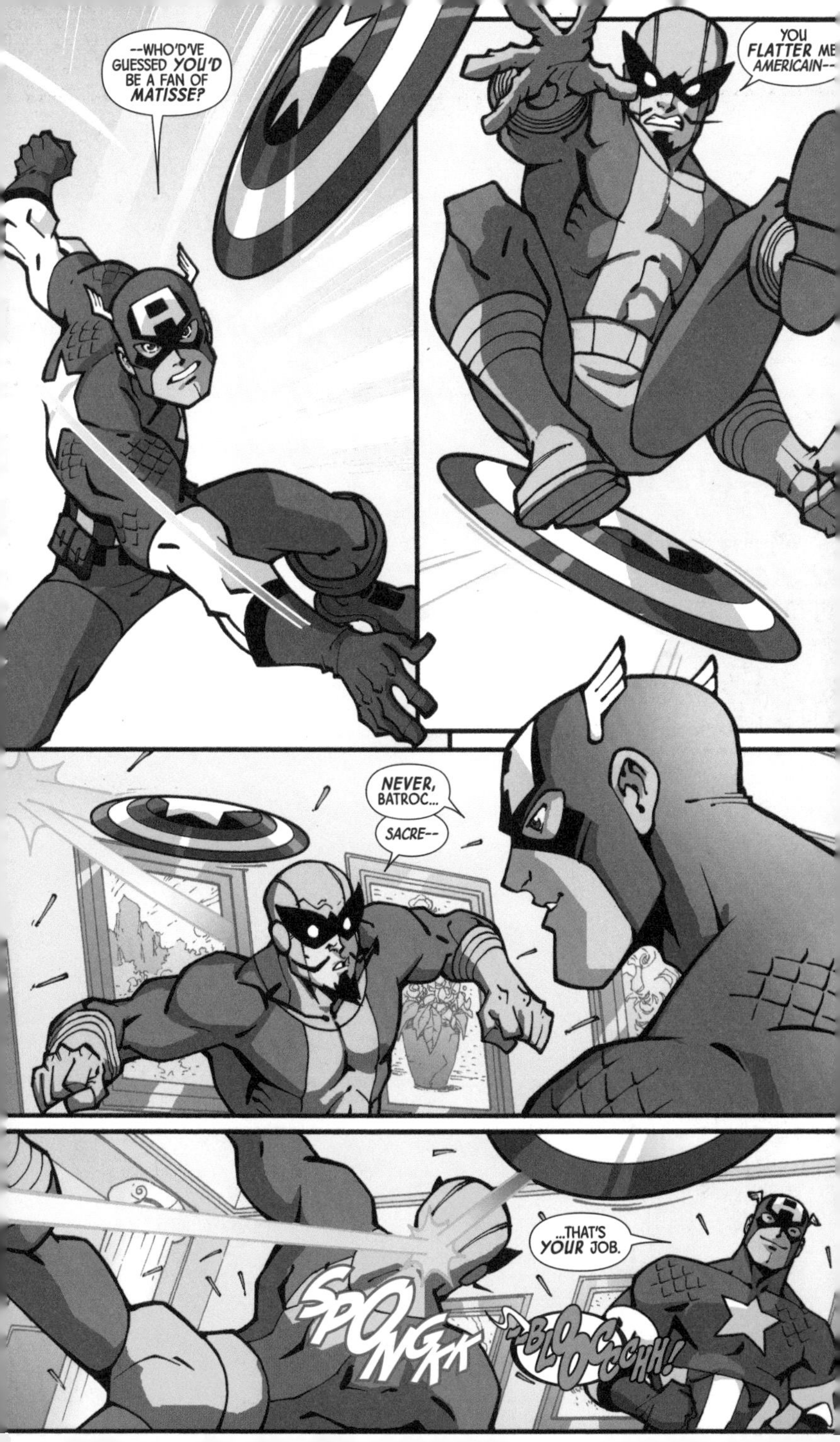
--WHO'D'VE GUESSED YOU'D BE A FAN OF MATISSE?
YOU FLATTER ME AMERICAIN--
NEVER, BATROC...
SACRE--
...THAT'S YOUR JOB.
SPONGKK
BLOOCCHH!

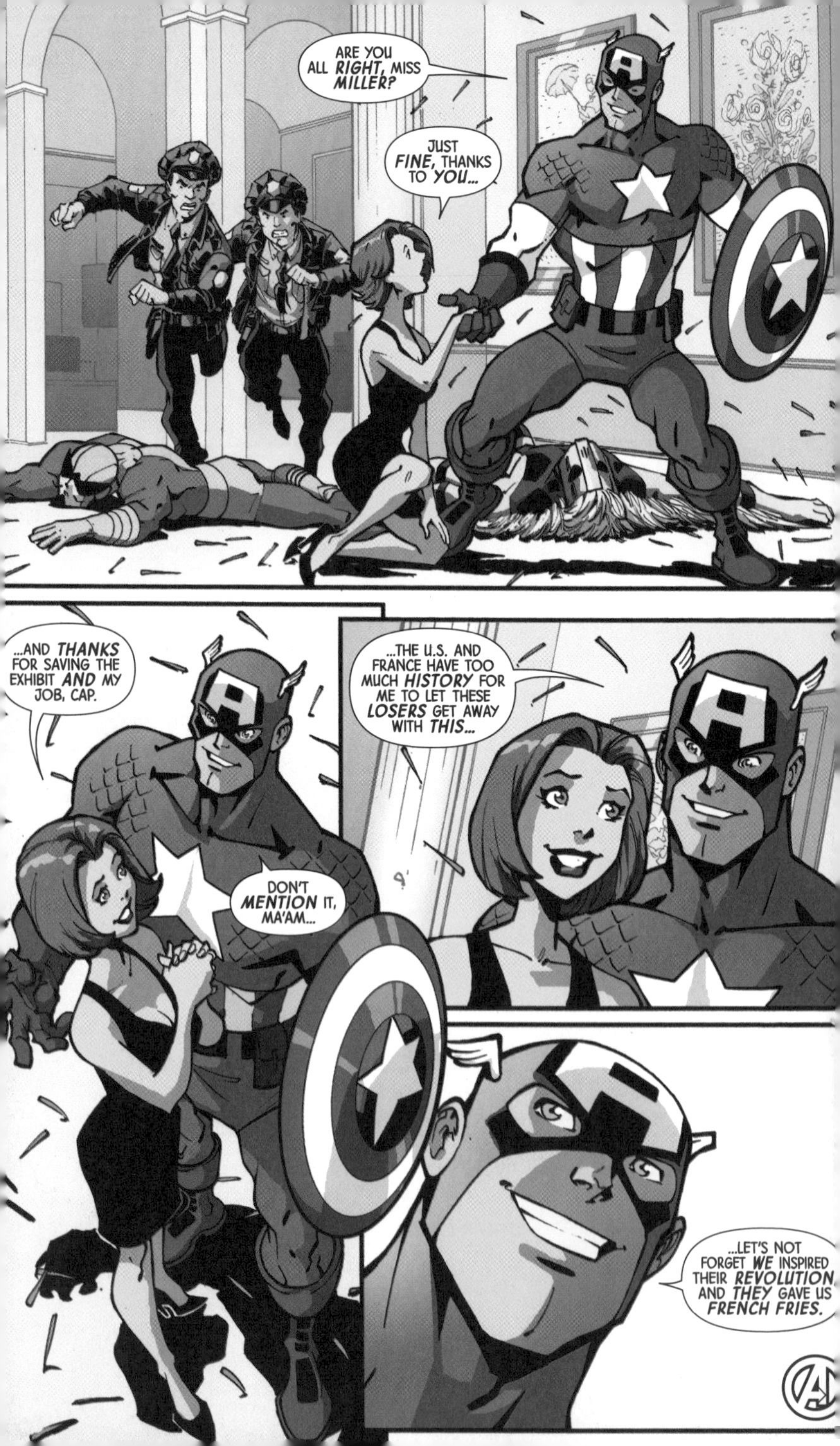
ARE YOU ALL RIGHT, MISS MILLER?
JUST FINE, THANKS TO YOU...
...AND THANKS FOR SAVING THE EXHIBIT AND MY JOB, CAP.
DON'T MENTION IT, MA'AM...
...THE U.S. AND FRANCE HAVE TOO MUCH HISTORY FOR ME TO LET THESE LOSERS GET AWAY WITH THIS...
...LET'S NOT FORGET WE INSPIRED THEIR REVOLUTION, AND THEY GAVE US FRENCH FRIES.

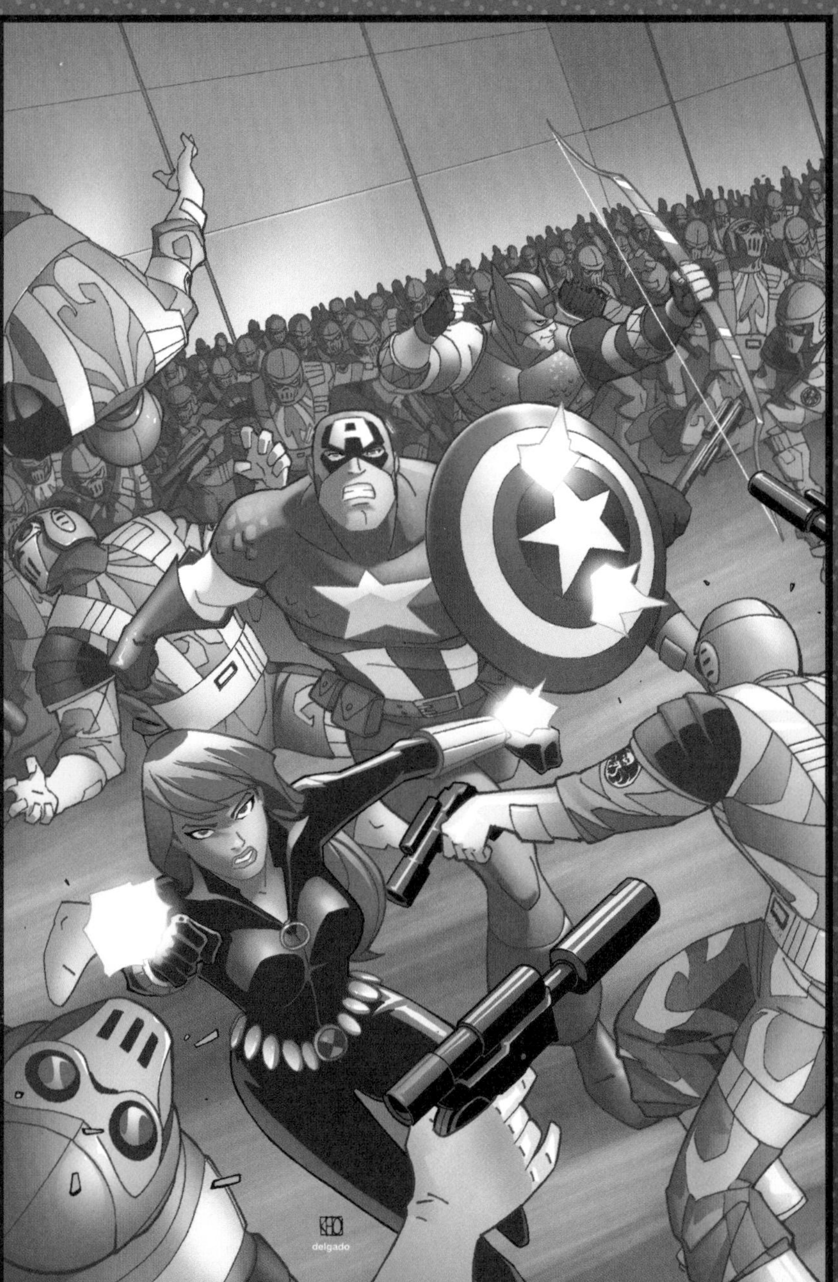
delgado

6

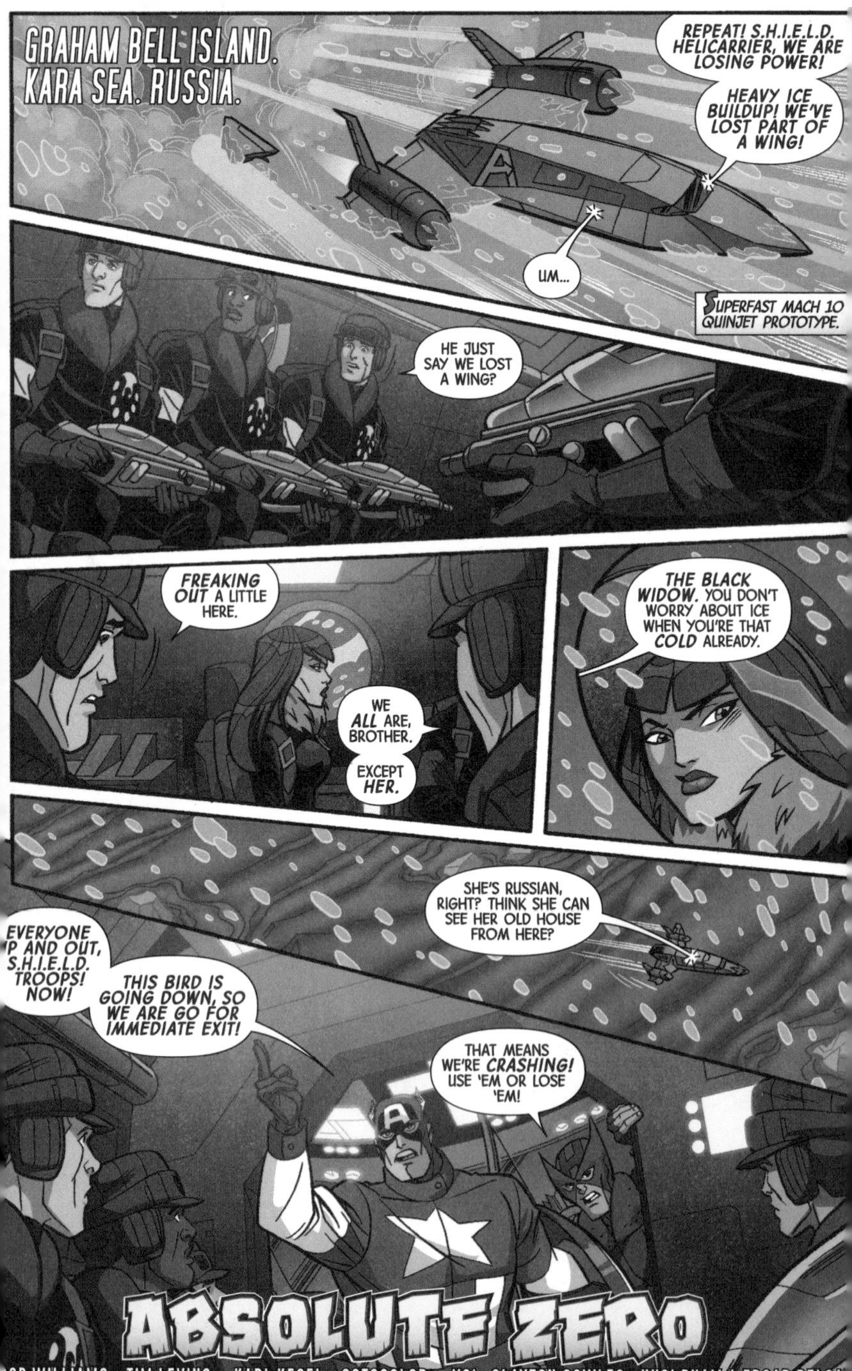
GRAHAM BELL ISLAND. KARA SEA. RUSSIA.
REPEAT! S.H.I.E.L.D. HELICARRIER, WE ARE LOSING POWER!
HEAVY ICE BUILDUP! WE'VE LOST PART OF A WING!
UM...
SUPERFAST MACH 10 QUINJET PROTOTYPE.
HE JUST SAY WE LOST A WING?
FREAKING OUT A LITTLE HERE.
WE ALL ARE, BROTHER.
EXCEPT HER.
THE BLACK WIDOW. YOU DON'T WORRY ABOUT ICE WHEN YOU'RE THAT COLD ALREADY.
SHE'S RUSSIAN, RIGHT? THINK SHE CAN SEE HER OLD HOUSE FROM HERE?
EVERYONE P AND OUT, S.H.I.E.L.D. TROOPS! NOW!
THIS BIRD IS GOING DOWN, SO WE ARE GO FOR IMMEDIATE EXIT!
THAT MEANS WE'RE CRASHING! USE 'EM OR LOSE 'EM!
ABSOLUTE ZERO

OB WILLIAMS WRITER · TIM LEVINS PENCILS · KARL KESEL INKS · SOTOCOLOR COLORS · VC's CLAYTON COWLES LETTERS · KHOI PHAM & EDGAR DELGA COVER ART

LLIE PYLE ASST. EDITOR · TOM BRENNAN EDITOR · STEPHEN WACKER CHILLY · AXEL ALONSO EDITOR IN CHIEF · JOE QUESADA CHIEF CREATIVE OFFICER · DAN BUCKLEY PUBLISHER · ALAN FIN EXEC. PRODU

YOU KNOW WHY WE'RE HERE! HYDRA ARE EN ROUTE AND COULD BE ON SITE ALREADY!

SO OPEN YOUR CHUTES AS LATE AS POSSIBLE AND DON'T GIVE THEM A FLOATING TARGET!

THIS IS THE ARCTIC CIRCLE, PEOPLE! WE ARE ON OUR OWN! BACKUP IS COMING, BUT IT WILL NOT GET HERE IN TIME!

HIT WATER THROUGH THE ICE AND THOSE SPECIAL SUITS YOU'RE WEARING WILL PROTECT YOU FOR TWO MINUTES MAX. THEN YOU DIE!

CAPTAIN, THIS PLACE WAS A TOP SECRET SOVIET MILITARY AIRFIELD IN THE COLD WAR. DEATH IS ALL IT HAS EVER OFFERED.

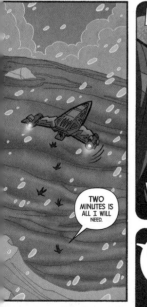

TWO MINUTES IS ALL I WILL NEED.

EARLIER.

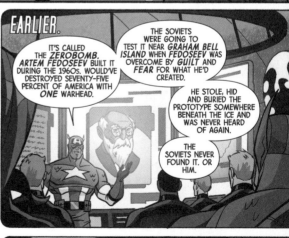

IT'S CALLED THE ZEROBOMB. ARTEM FEDOSEEV BUILT IT DURING THE 1960s. WOULD'VE DESTROYED SEVENTY-FIVE PERCENT OF AMERICA WITH ONE WARHEAD.

THE SOVIETS WERE GOING TO TEST IT NEAR GRAHAM BELL ISLAND WHEN FEDOSEEV WAS OVERCOME BY GUILT AND FEAR FOR WHAT HE'D CREATED.

HE STOLE, HID AND BURIED THE PROTOTYPE SOMEWHERE BENEATH THE ICE AND WAS NEVER HEARD OF AGAIN.

THE SOVIETS NEVER FOUND IT. OR HIM.

FEDOSEEV LEFT A LETTER WITH ONE OF HIS ASSISTANTS DETAILING THE ZEROBOMB'S LOCATION. THE ASSISTANT REVEALED THIS ON HIS DEATHBED. YESTERDAY.

THE LOCATION OF THE ZEROBOMB IS NOW OUT IN THE OPEN, AND YOU KNOW WHAT THAT MEANS...

THOOM THOOM THOOM
HYDRA!
HYDRA ARE ALREADY HERE! THEY'RE ALREADY... AAHHH!
THEY BEAT US TO IT!
CAP TO ATTACK TEAM. THEY'RE ALREADY DRILLING. HYDRA HAVE THE LOCATION OF THE ZEROBOMB!
GET ON THE GROUND FAST AND STOP THEM.
NATASHA! YOU'RE CUTTING IT TOO CLOSE...PULL THE CHUTE!
PULL THE CHUTE!

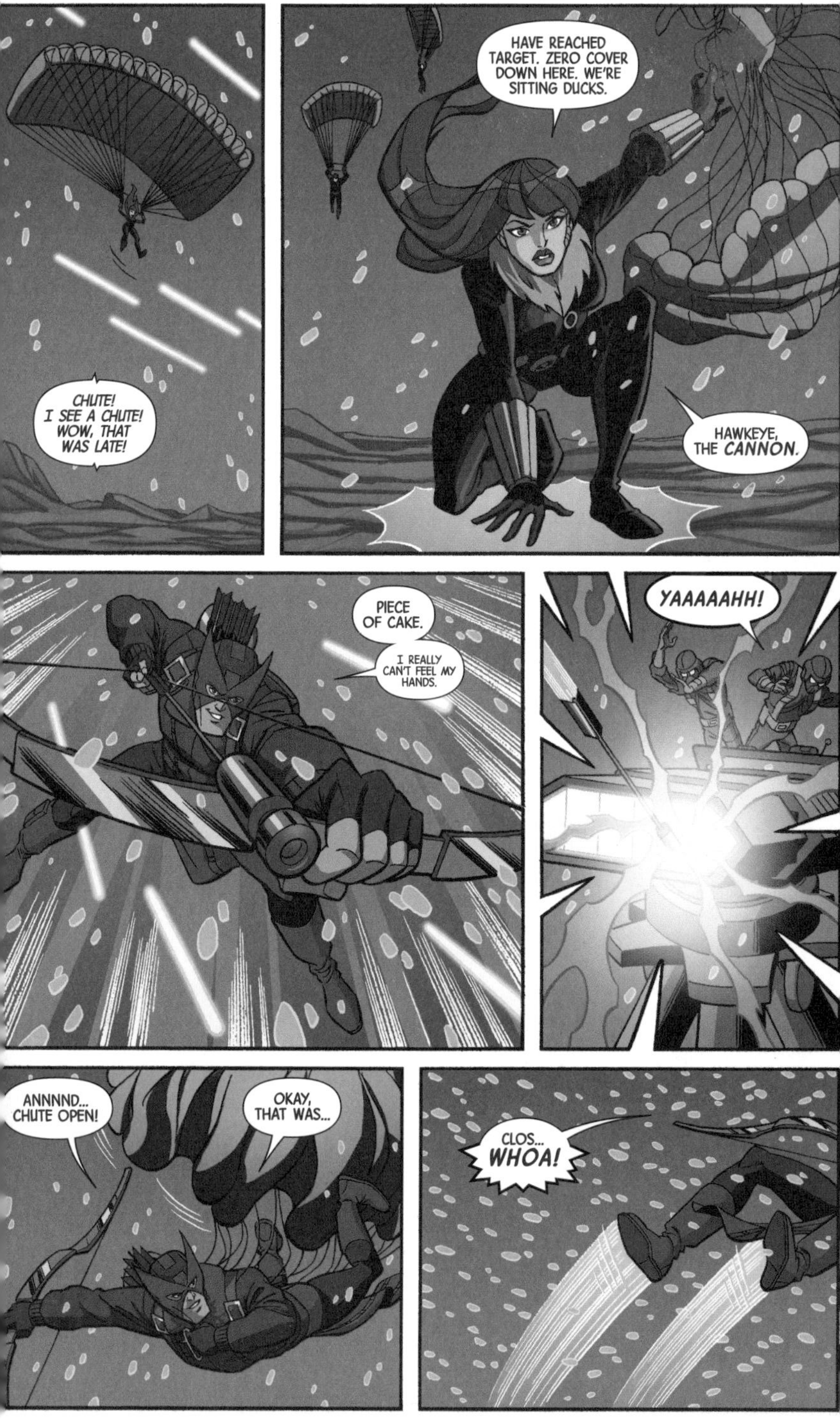
CHUTE! I SEE A CHUTE! WOW, THAT WAS LATE!
HAVE REACHED TARGET. ZERO COVER DOWN HERE. WE'RE SITTING DUCKS.
HAWKEYE, THE CANNON.
PIECE OF CAKE.
I REALLY CAN'T FEEL MY HANDS.
YAAAAAHH!
ANNNND... CHUTE OPEN!
OKAY, THAT WAS...
CLOS... WHOA!

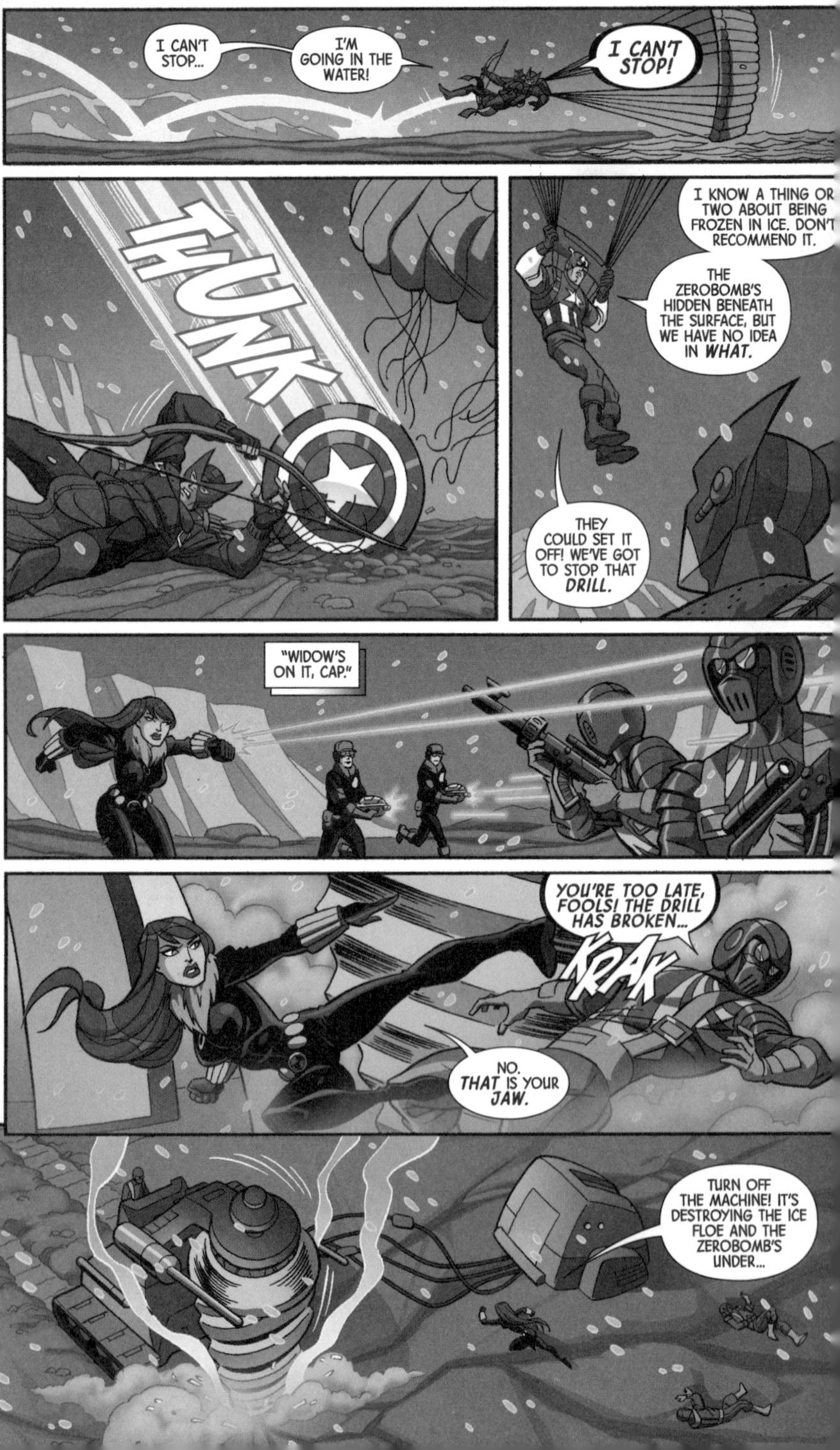
I CAN'T STOP...
I'M GOING IN THE WATER!
I CAN'T STOP!
THUNK
I KNOW A THING OR TWO ABOUT BEING FROZEN IN ICE. DON'T RECOMMEND IT.
THE ZEROBOMB'S HIDDEN BENEATH THE SURFACE, BUT WE HAVE NO IDEA IN WHAT.
THEY COULD SET IT OFF! WE'VE GOT TO STOP THAT DRILL.
"WIDOW'S ON IT, CAP."
YOU'RE TOO LATE, FOOLS! THE DRILL HAS BROKEN...
KRAK
NO. THAT IS YOUR JAW.
TURN OFF THE MACHINE! IT'S DESTROYING THE ICE FLOE AND THE ZEROBOMB'S UNDER...

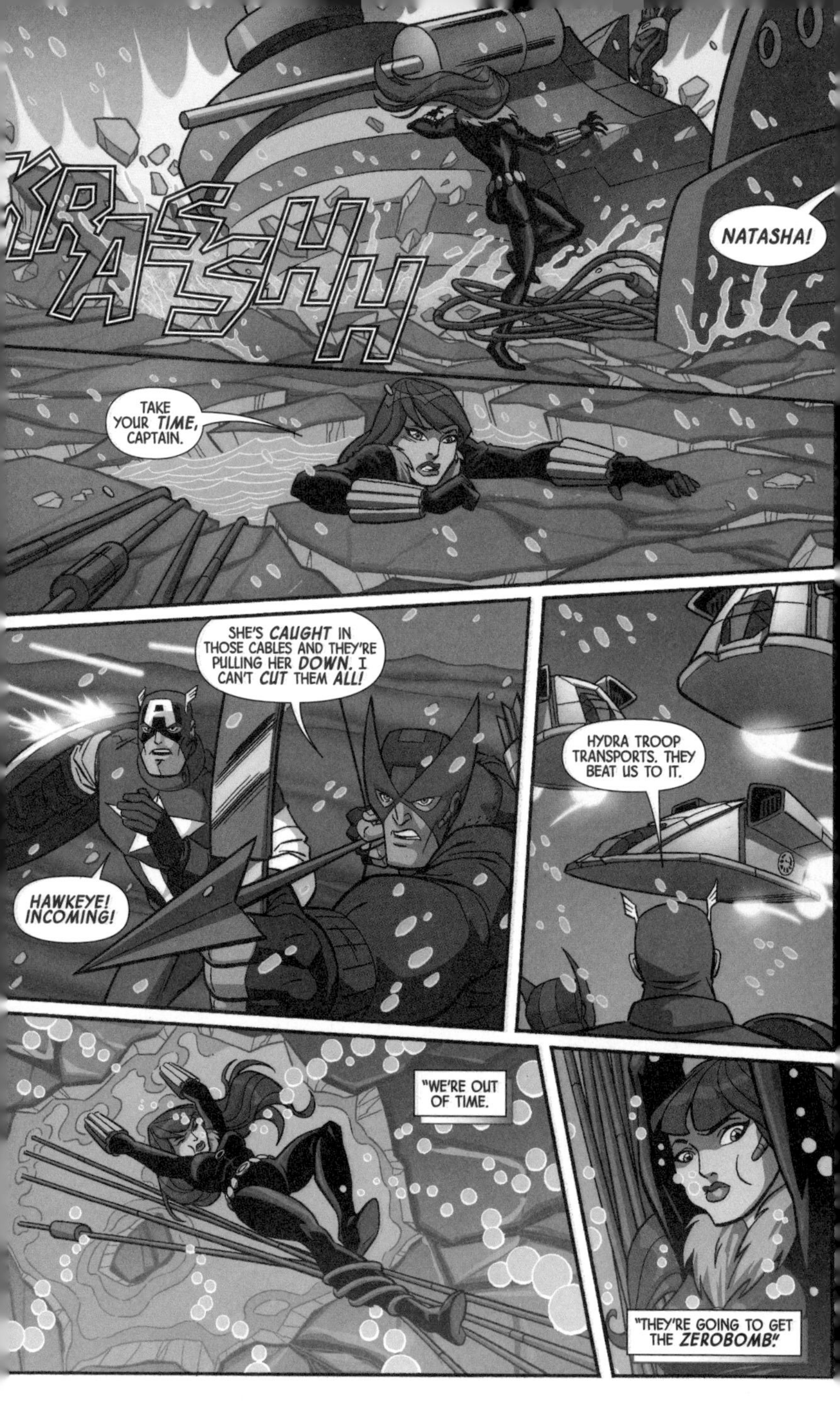
KRASSHH
NATASHA!
TAKE YOUR TIME, CAPTAIN.
SHE'S CAUGHT IN THOSE CABLES AND THEY'RE PULLING HER DOWN. I CAN'T CUT THEM ALL!
HAWKEYE! INCOMING!
HYDRA TROOP TRANSPORTS. THEY BEAT US TO IT.
"WE'RE OUT OF TIME.
"THEY'RE GOING TO GET THE ZEROBOMB."

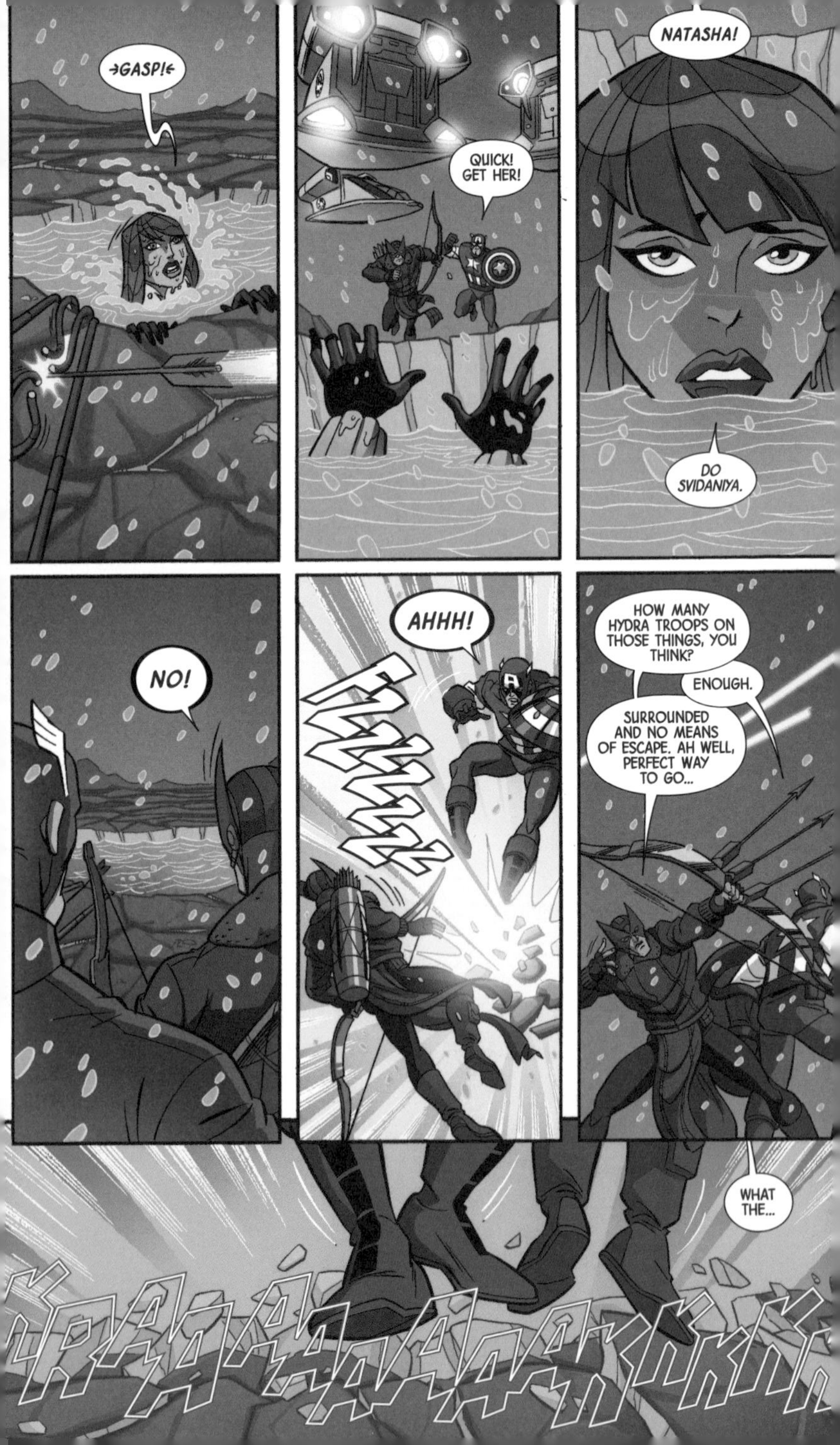

→GASP!←
QUICK! GET HER!
NATASHA!
DO SVIDANIYA.
NO!
AHHH!
FZZZZZ!
HOW MANY HYDRA TROOPS ON THOSE THINGS, YOU THINK?
ENOUGH.
SURROUNDED AND NO MEANS OF ESCAPE. AH WELL, PERFECT WAY TO GO...
WHAT THE...
KRAAAAAAAAAAKKK

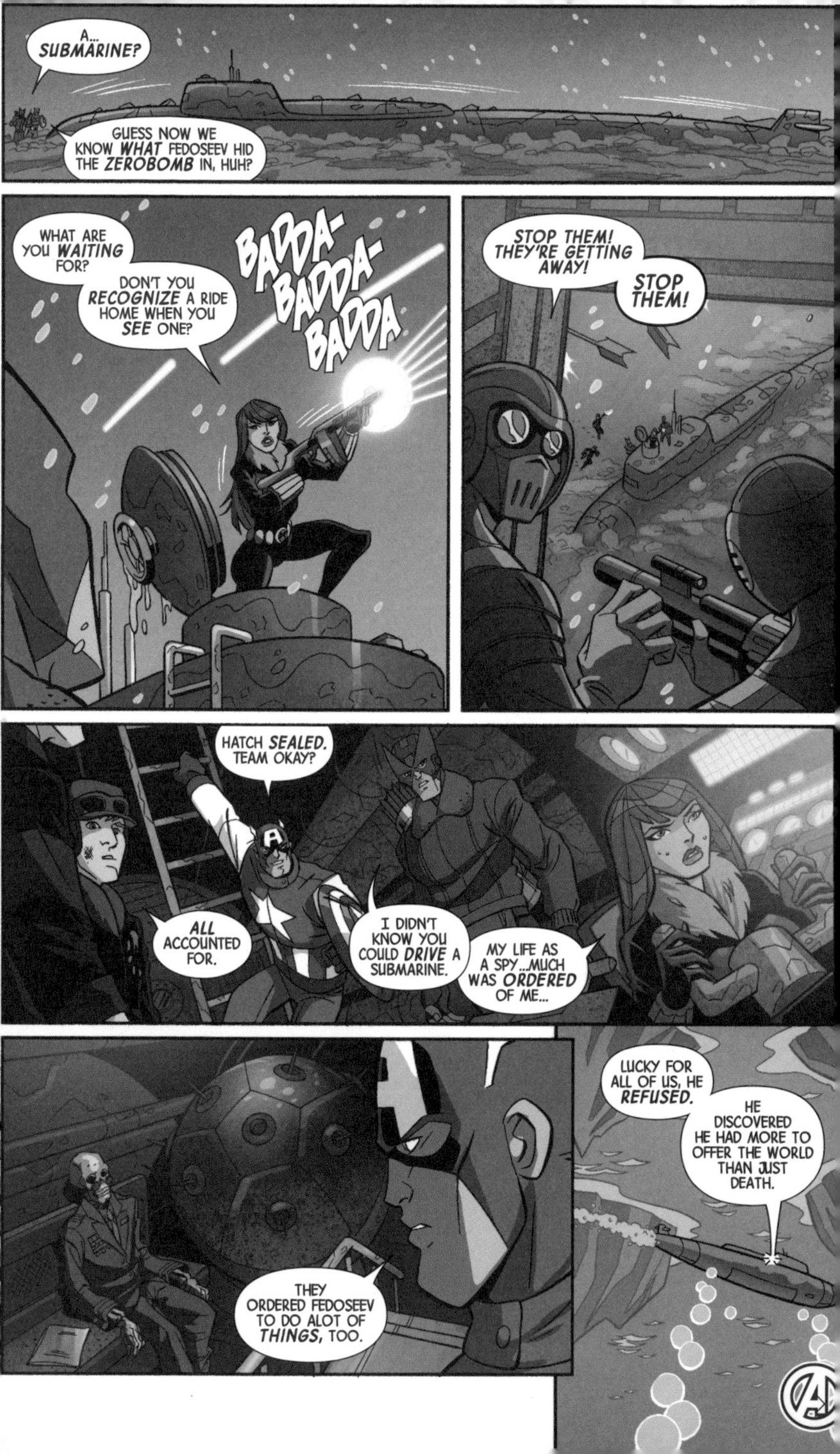

A... SUBMARINE?
GUESS NOW WE KNOW WHAT FEDOSEEV HID THE ZEROBOMB IN, HUH?
WHAT ARE YOU WAITING FOR?
DON'T YOU RECOGNIZE A RIDE HOME WHEN YOU SEE ONE?
BADDA-BADDA-BADDA
STOP THEM! THEY'RE GETTING AWAY!
STOP THEM!
HATCH SEALED. TEAM OKAY?
ALL ACCOUNTED FOR.
I DIDN'T KNOW YOU COULD DRIVE A SUBMARINE.
MY LIFE AS A SPY...MUCH WAS ORDERED OF ME...
THEY ORDERED FEDOSEEV TO DO ALOT OF THINGS, TOO.
LUCKY FOR ALL OF US, HE REFUSED.
HE DISCOVERED HE HAD MORE TO OFFER THE WORLD THAN JUST DEATH.

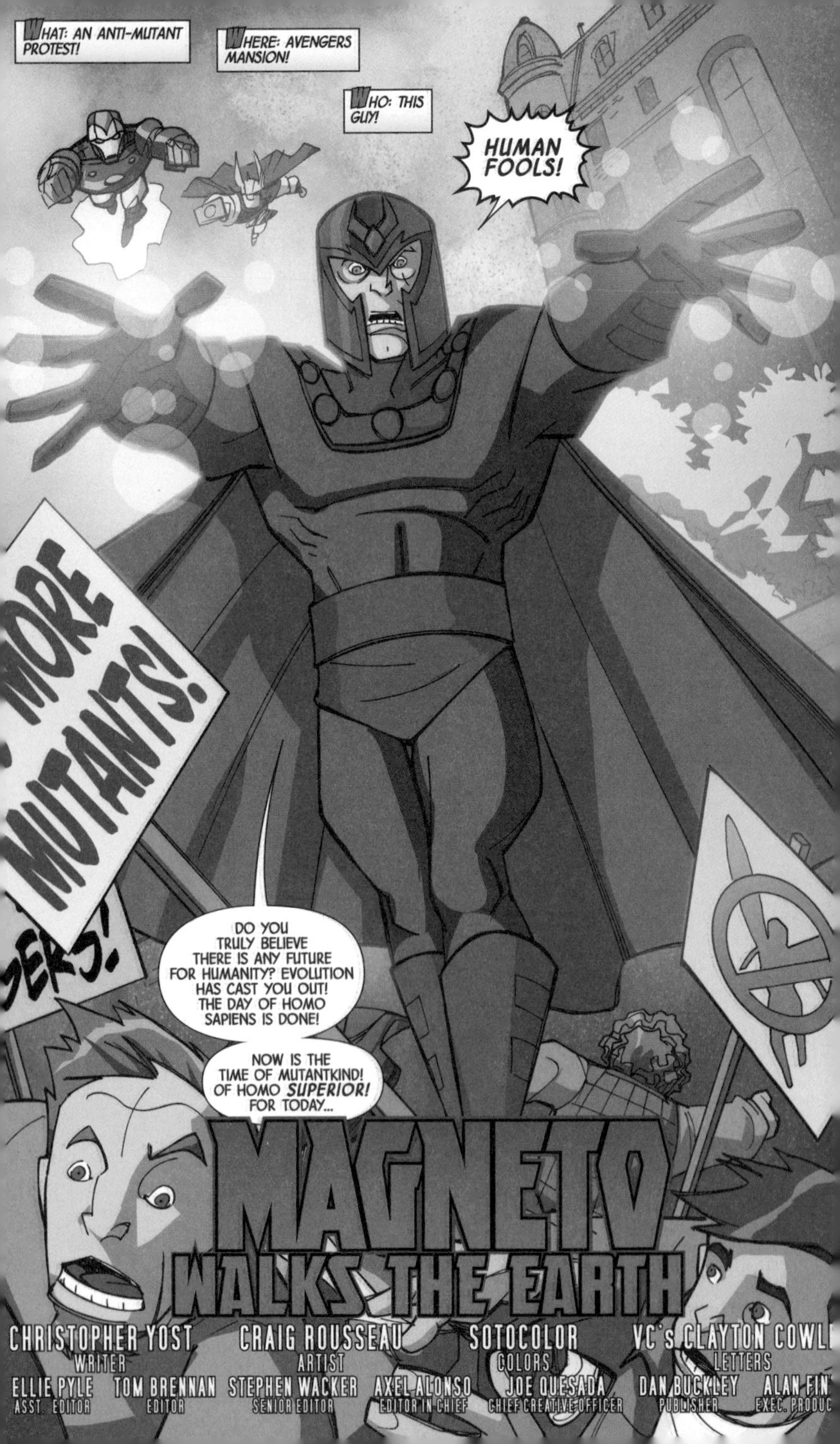
WHAT: AN ANTI-MUTANT PROTEST!
WHERE: AVENGERS MANSION!
WHO: THIS GUY!
HUMAN FOOLS!
MORE MUTANTS!
DO YOU TRULY BELIEVE THERE IS ANY FUTURE FOR HUMANITY? EVOLUTION HAS CAST YOU OUT! THE DAY OF HOMO SAPIENS IS DONE!
NOW IS THE TIME OF MUTANTKIND! OF HOMO *SUPERIOR!* FOR TODAY...
MAGNETO WALKS THE EARTH
CHRISTOPHER YOST WRITER
CRAIG ROUSSEAU ARTIST
SOTOCOLOR COLORS
VC's CLAYTON COWL LETTERS
ELLIE PYLE ASST. EDITOR
TOM BRENNAN EDITOR
STEPHEN WACKER SENIOR EDITOR
AXEL ALONSO EDITOR IN CHIEF
JOE QUESADA CHIEF CREATIVE OFFICER
DAN BUCKLEY PUBLISHER
ALAN FIN EXEC. PRODUC

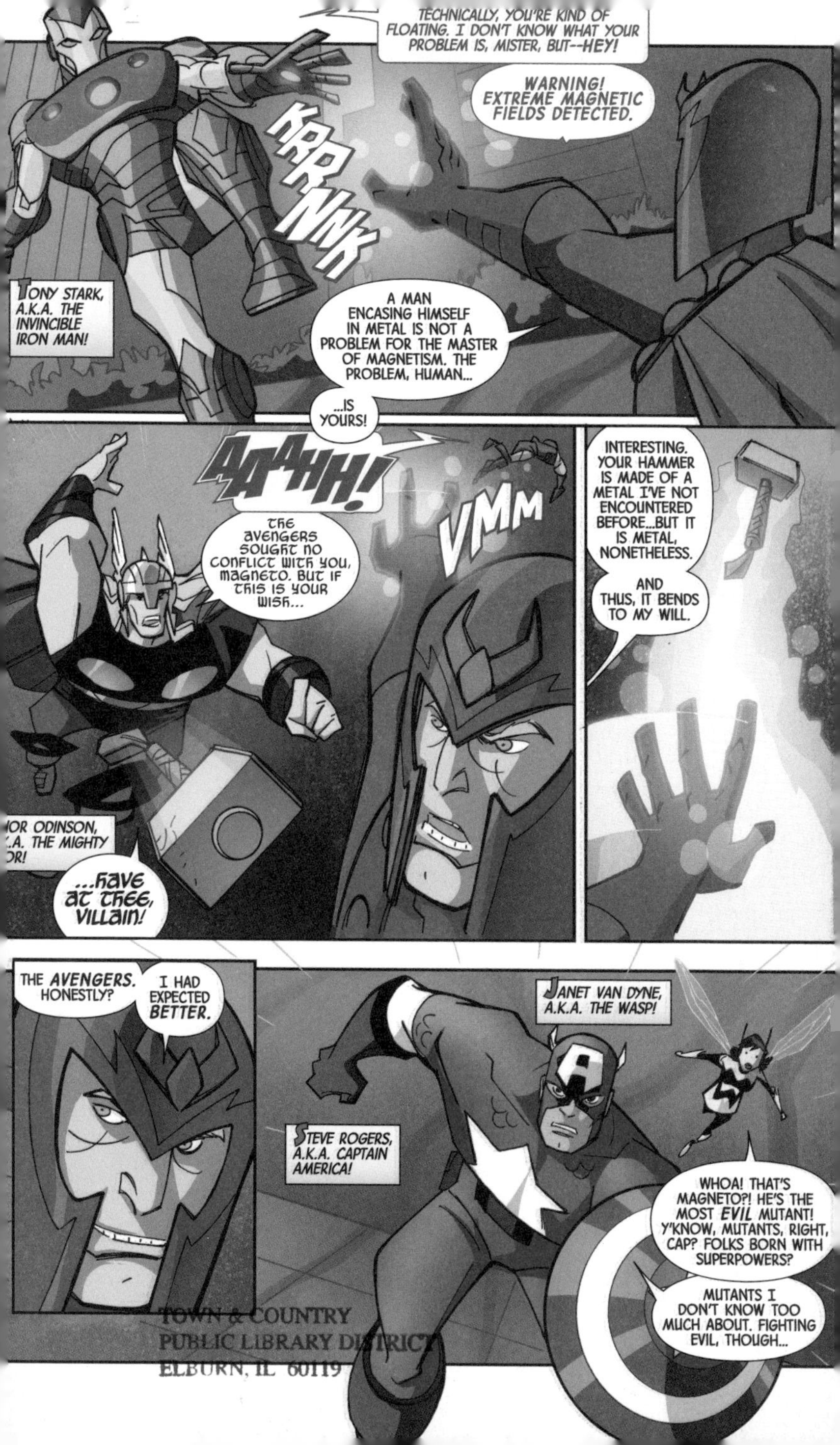
TECHNICALLY, YOU'RE KIND OF FLOATING. I DON'T KNOW WHAT YOUR PROBLEM IS, MISTER, BUT--HEY!
WARNING! EXTREME MAGNETIC FIELDS DETECTED.
KRRNNK
TONY STARK, A.K.A. THE INVINCIBLE IRON MAN!
A MAN ENCASING HIMSELF IN METAL IS NOT A PROBLEM FOR THE MASTER OF MAGNETISM. THE PROBLEM, HUMAN...
...IS YOURS!
AAAHH!
THE AVENGERS SOUGHT NO CONFLICT WITH YOU, MAGNETO. BUT IF THIS IS YOUR WISH...
VMM
HOR ODINSON, .K.A. THE MIGHTY OR!
...HAVE AT THEE, VILLAIN!
INTERESTING. YOUR HAMMER IS MADE OF A METAL I'VE NOT ENCOUNTERED BEFORE...BUT IT IS METAL, NONETHELESS.
AND THUS, IT BENDS TO MY WILL.
THE AVENGERS. HONESTLY?
I HAD EXPECTED BETTER.
JANET VAN DYNE, A.K.A. THE WASP!
STEVE ROGERS, A.K.A. CAPTAIN AMERICA!
WHOA! THAT'S MAGNETO?! HE'S THE MOST EVIL MUTANT! Y'KNOW, MUTANTS, RIGHT, CAP? FOLKS BORN WITH SUPERPOWERS?
MUTANTS I DON'T KNOW TOO MUCH ABOUT. FIGHTING EVIL, THOUGH...

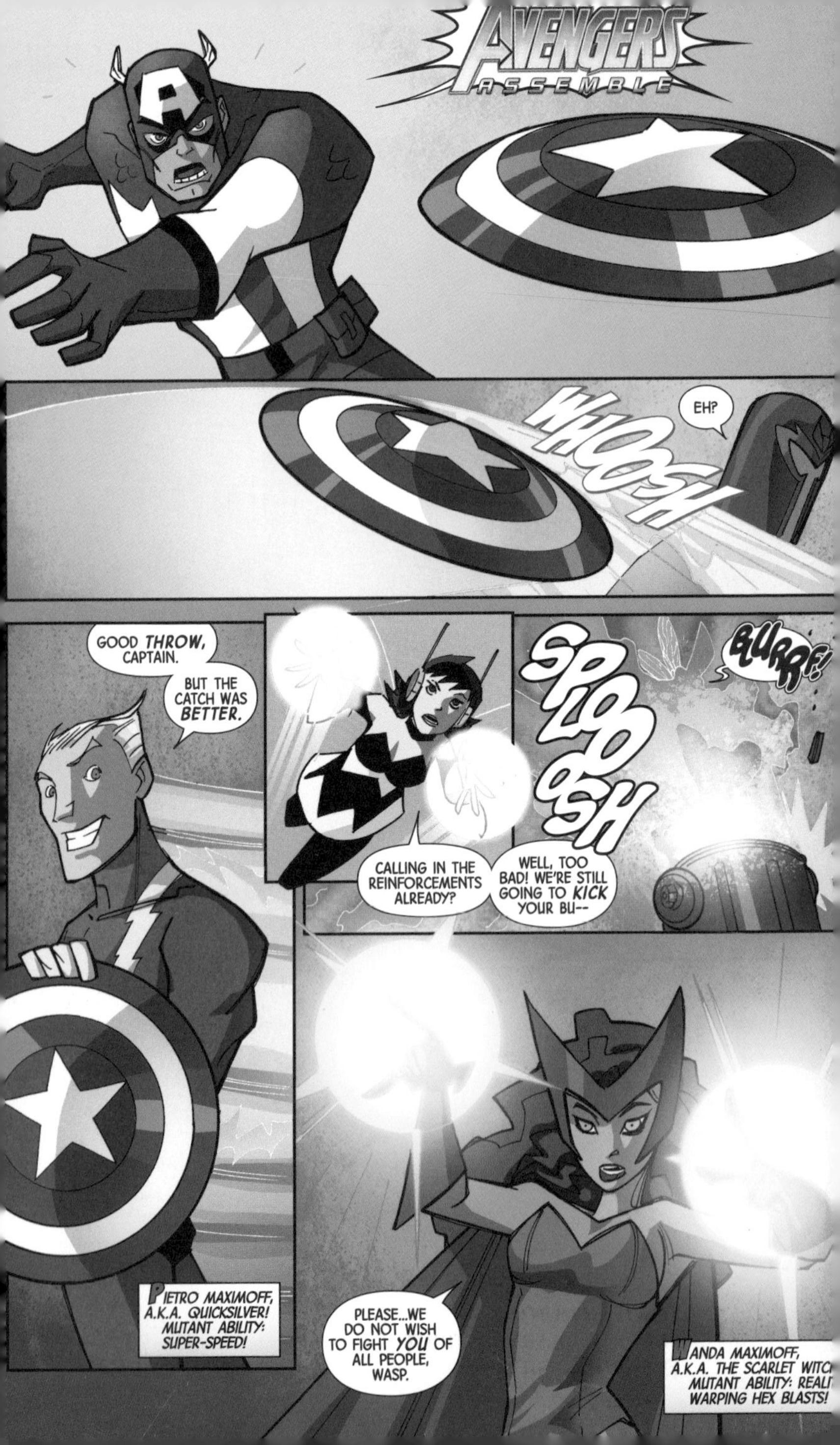
AVENGERS ASSEMBLE
WHOOSH
EH?
GOOD THROW, CAPTAIN.
BUT THE CATCH WAS BETTER.
SPLOOOSH
BLURRF!
CALLING IN THE REINFORCEMENTS ALREADY?
WELL, TOO BAD! WE'RE STILL GOING TO KICK YOUR BU--
PIETRO MAXIMOFF, A.K.A. QUICKSILVER! MUTANT ABILITY: SUPER-SPEED!
PLEASE...WE DO NOT WISH TO FIGHT YOU OF ALL PEOPLE, WASP.
WANDA MAXIMOFF, A.K.A. THE SCARLET WITC MUTANT ABILITY: REALI WARPING HEX BLASTS!

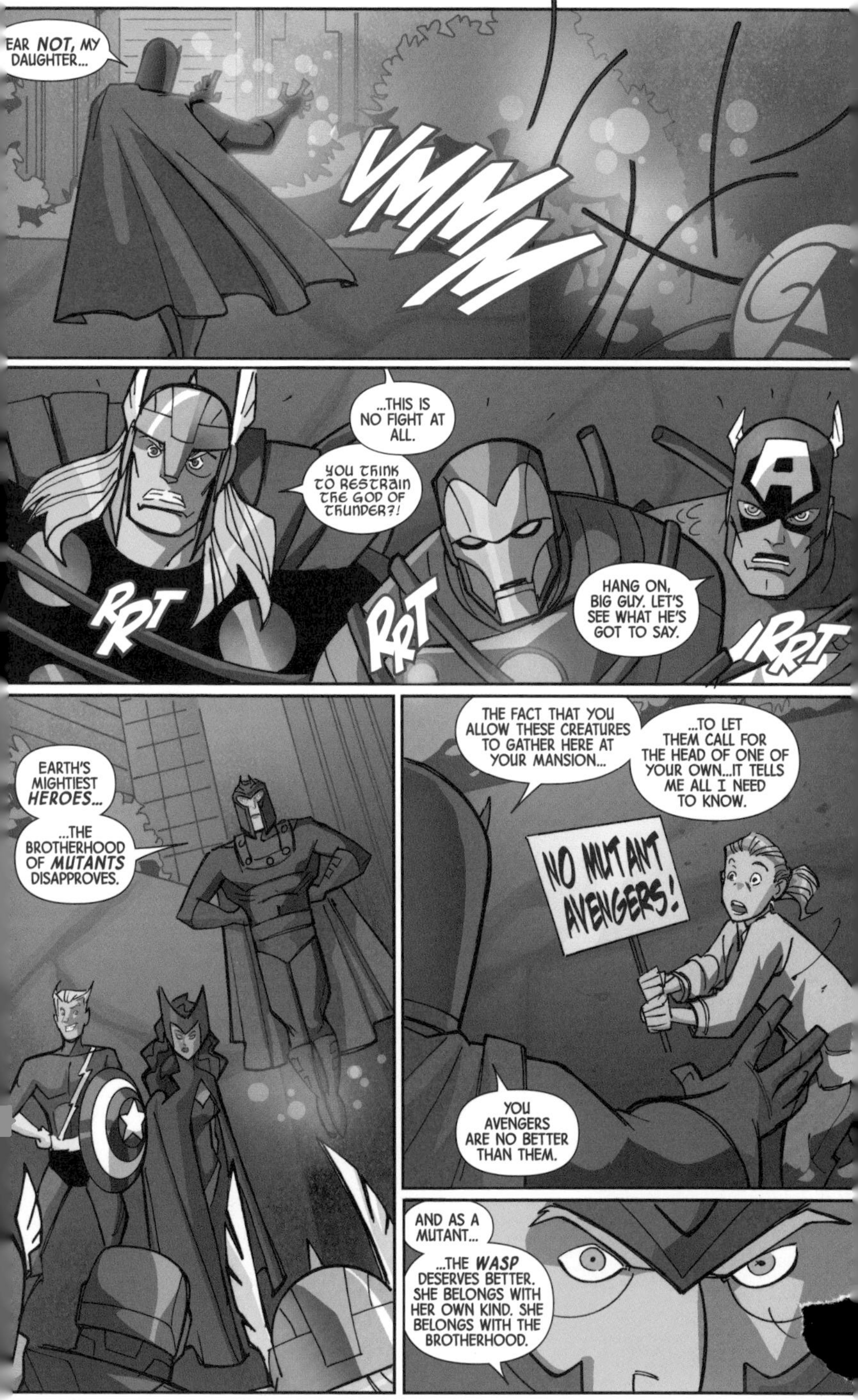
EAR NOT, MY DAUGHTER...
VMMM
...THIS IS NO FIGHT AT ALL.
YOU THINK TO RESTRAIN THE GOD OF THUNDER?!
RRT
RRT
HANG ON, BIG GUY. LET'S SEE WHAT HE'S GOT TO SAY.
RRT
EARTH'S MIGHTIEST HEROES...
...THE BROTHERHOOD OF MUTANTS DISAPPROVES.
THE FACT THAT YOU ALLOW THESE CREATURES TO GATHER HERE AT YOUR MANSION...
...TO LET THEM CALL FOR THE HEAD OF ONE OF YOUR OWN...IT TELLS ME ALL I NEED TO KNOW.
NO MUTANT AVENGERS!
YOU AVENGERS ARE NO BETTER THAN THEM.
AND AS A MUTANT...
...THE WASP DESERVES BETTER. SHE BELONGS WITH HER OWN KIND. SHE BELONGS WITH THE BROTHERHOOD.

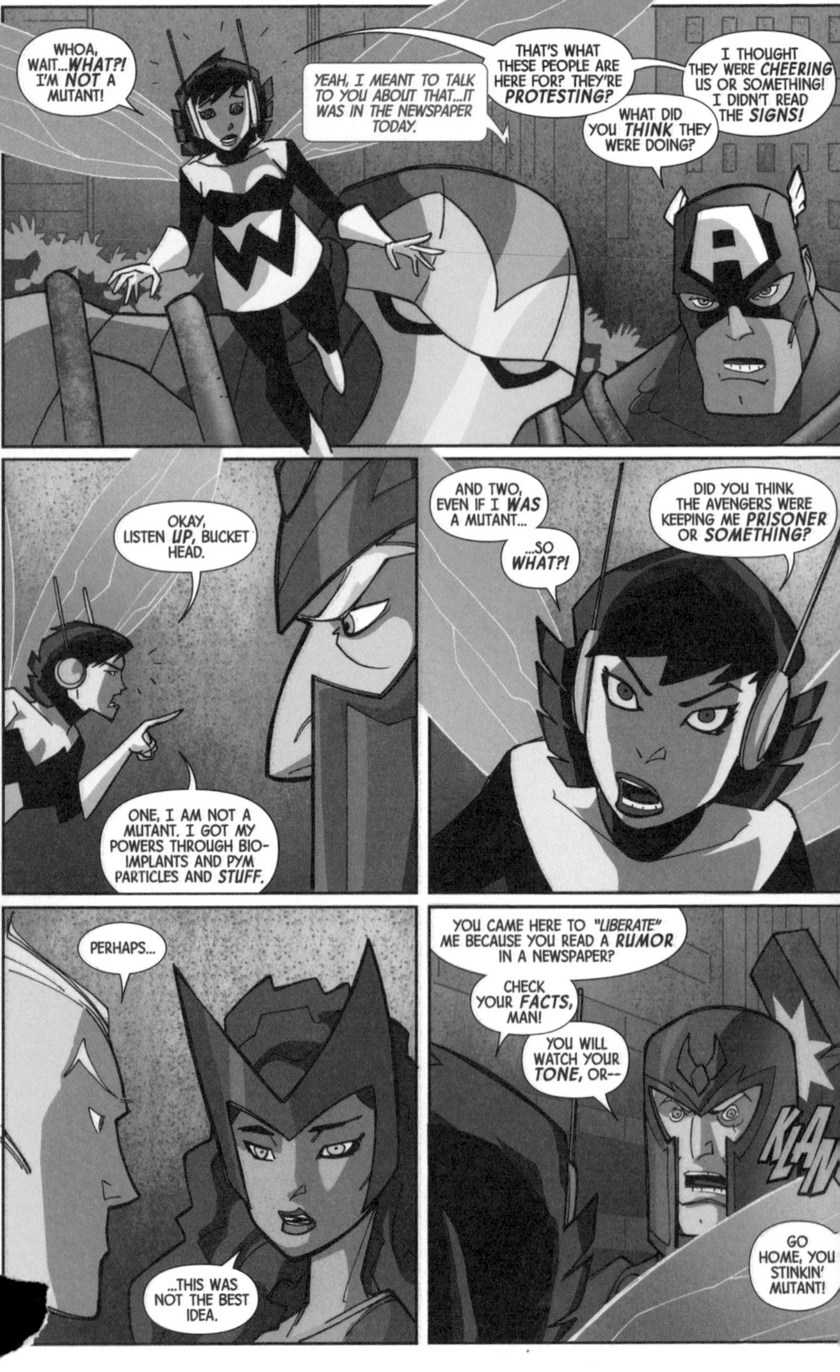
WHOA, WAIT...WHAT?! I'M NOT A MUTANT!
YEAH, I MEANT TO TALK TO YOU ABOUT THAT...IT WAS IN THE NEWSPAPER TODAY.
THAT'S WHAT THESE PEOPLE ARE HERE FOR? THEY'RE PROTESTING?
I THOUGHT THEY WERE CHEERING US OR SOMETHING! I DIDN'T READ THE SIGNS!
WHAT DID YOU THINK THEY WERE DOING?
OKAY, LISTEN UP, BUCKET HEAD.
ONE, I AM NOT A MUTANT. I GOT MY POWERS THROUGH BIO-IMPLANTS AND PYM PARTICLES AND STUFF.
AND TWO, EVEN IF I WAS A MUTANT...
...SO WHAT?!
DID YOU THINK THE AVENGERS WERE KEEPING ME PRISONER OR SOMETHING?
PERHAPS...
...THIS WAS NOT THE BEST IDEA.
YOU CAME HERE TO "LIBERATE" ME BECAUSE YOU READ A RUMOR IN A NEWSPAPER?
CHECK YOUR FACTS, MAN!
YOU WILL WATCH YOUR TONE, OR--
KLAN
GO HOME, YOU STINKIN' MUTANT!

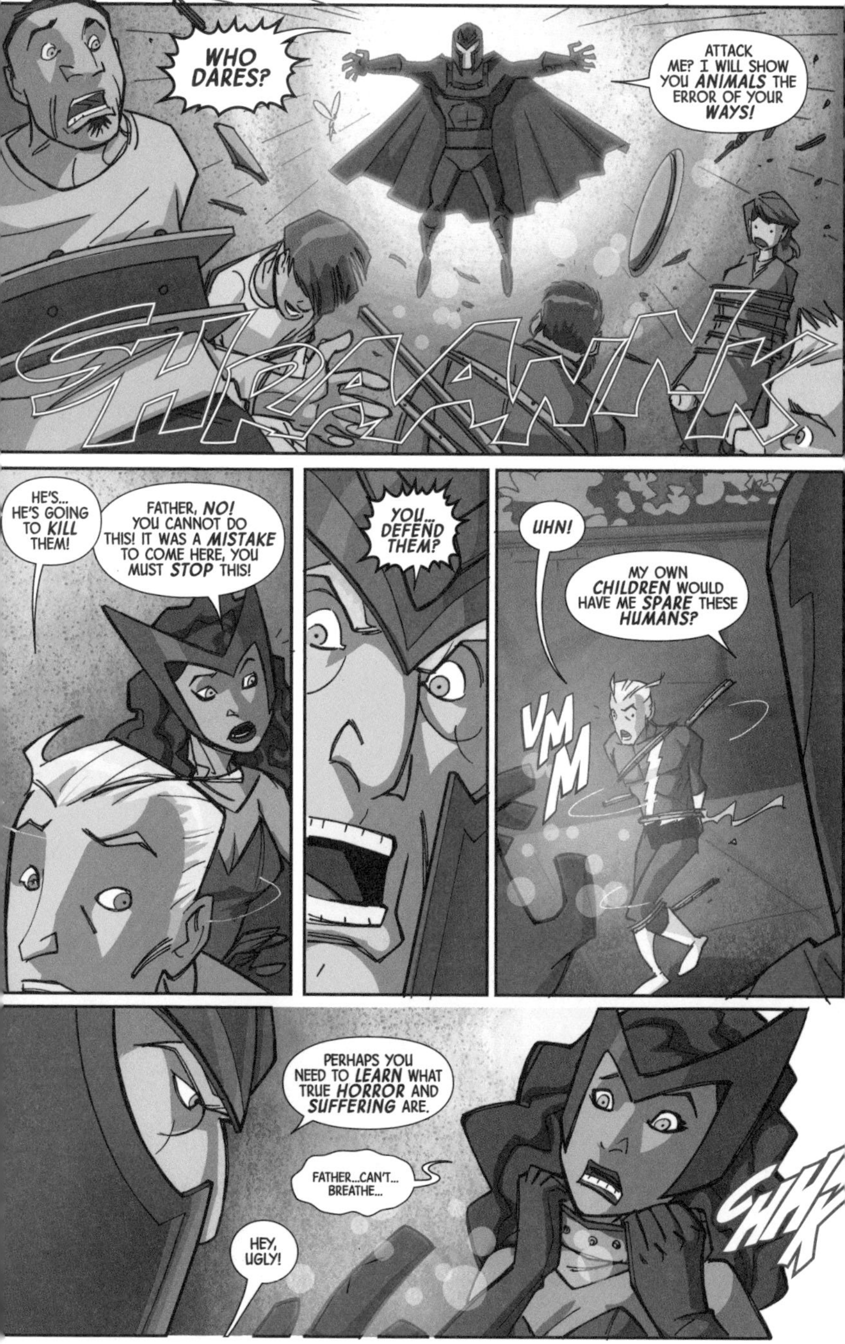
WHO DARES?
ATTACK ME? I WILL SHOW YOU ANIMALS THE ERROR OF YOUR WAYS!
SHRAANNK
HE'S... HE'S GOING TO KILL THEM!
FATHER, NO! YOU CANNOT DO THIS! IT WAS A MISTAKE TO COME HERE, YOU MUST STOP THIS!
YOU... DEFEND THEM?
UHN!
MY OWN CHILDREN WOULD HAVE ME SPARE THESE HUMANS?
VMM
PERHAPS YOU NEED TO LEARN WHAT TRUE HORROR AND SUFFERING ARE.
FATHER...CAN'T... BREATHE...
HEY, UGLY!
CHK

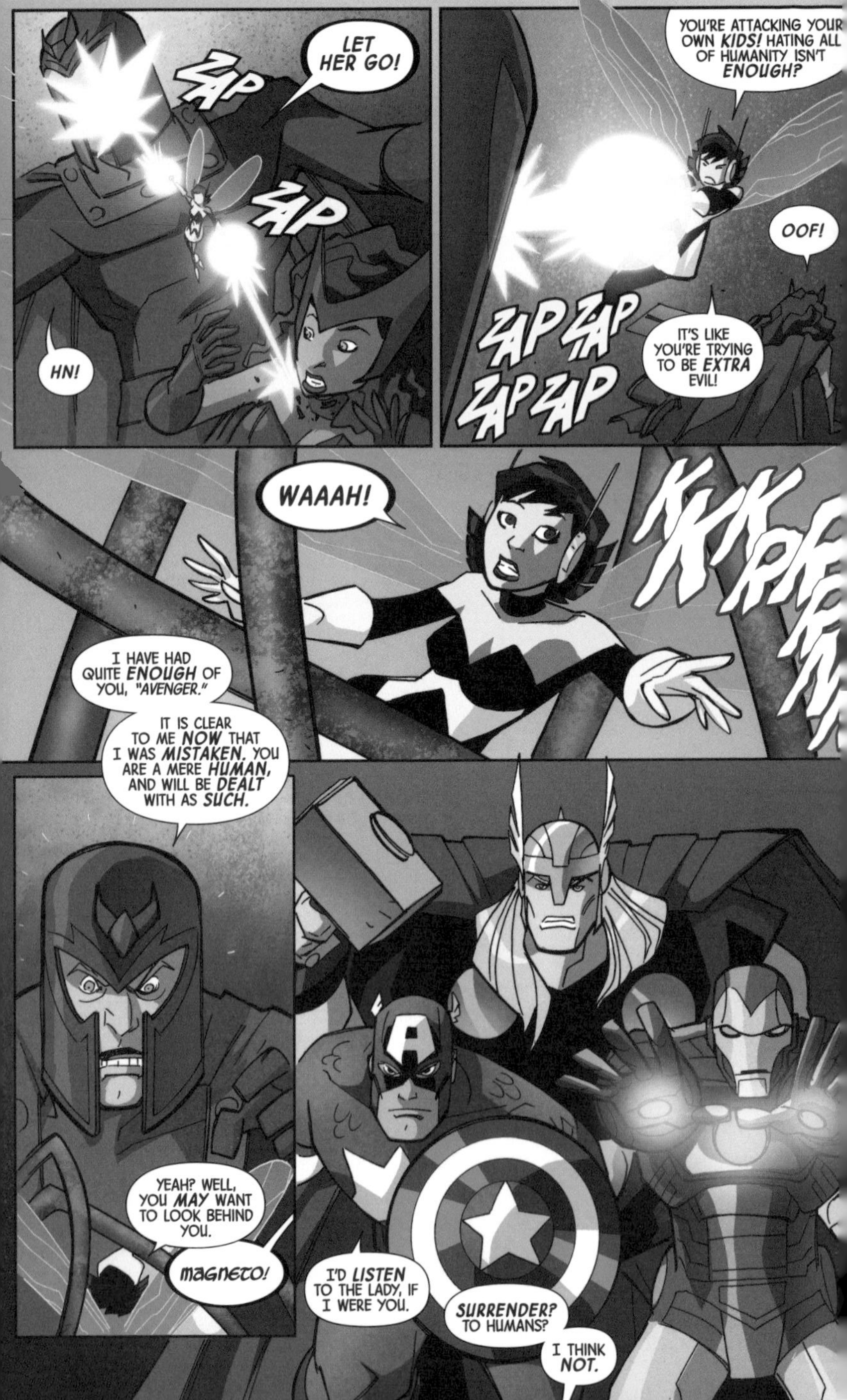

LET HER GO!
ZAP
ZAP
HN!
YOU'RE ATTACKING YOUR OWN KIDS! HATING ALL OF HUMANITY ISN'T ENOUGH?
ZAP ZAP ZAP ZAP
OOF!
IT'S LIKE YOU'RE TRYING TO BE EXTRA EVIL!
WAAAH!
I HAVE HAD QUITE ENOUGH OF YOU, "AVENGER."
IT IS CLEAR TO ME NOW THAT I WAS MISTAKEN. YOU ARE A MERE HUMAN, AND WILL BE DEALT WITH AS SUCH.
YEAH? WELL, YOU MAY WANT TO LOOK BEHIND YOU.
MAGNETO!
I'D LISTEN TO THE LADY, IF I WERE YOU.
SURRENDER? TO HUMANS?
I THINK NOT.

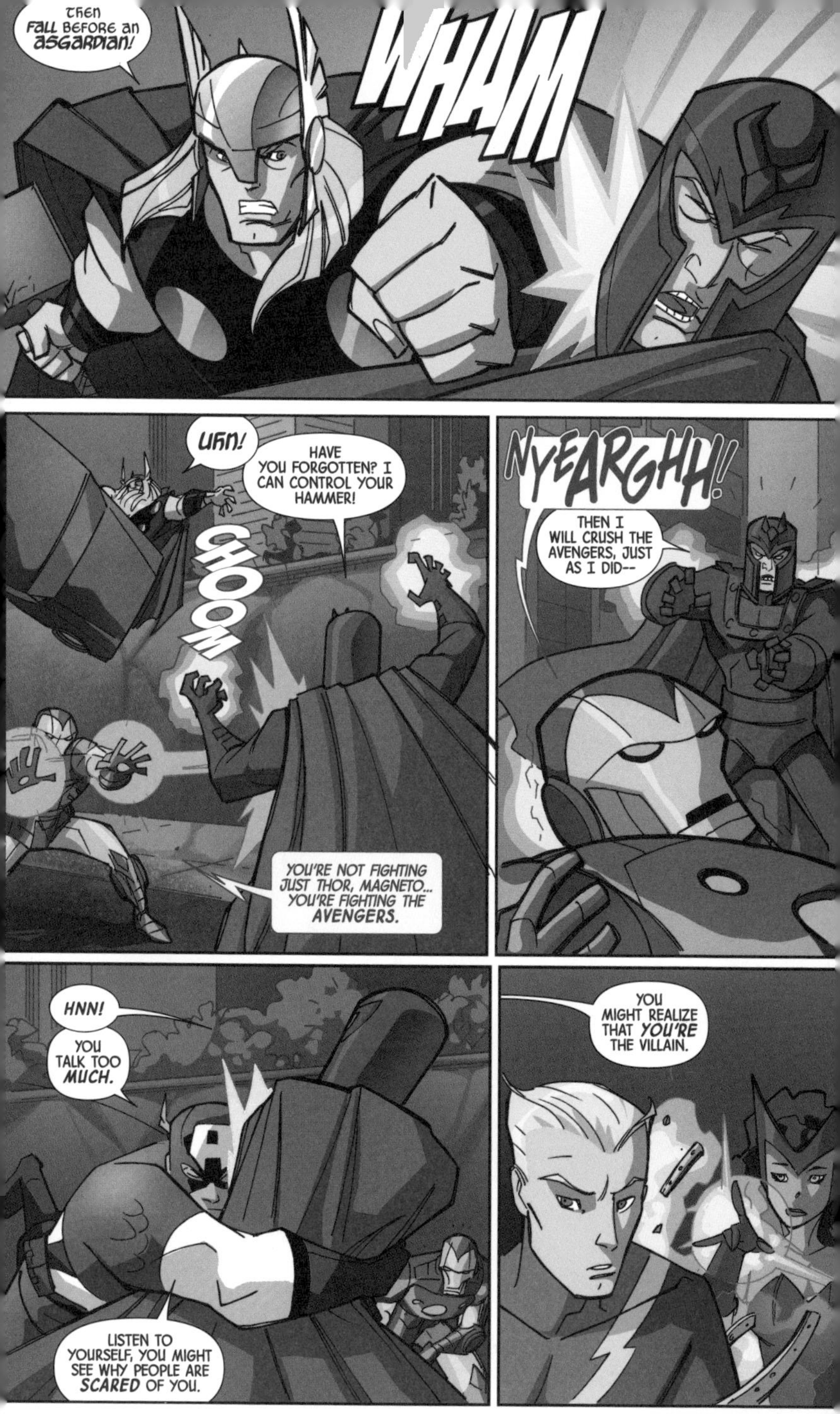
THEN FALL BEFORE AN ASGARDIAN!
WHAM
UHN!
HAVE YOU FORGOTTEN? I CAN CONTROL YOUR HAMMER!
CHOOOM
YOU'RE NOT FIGHTING JUST THOR, MAGNETO... YOU'RE FIGHTING THE AVENGERS.
NYEARGHH!!
THEN I WILL CRUSH THE AVENGERS, JUST AS I DID--
HNN!
YOU TALK TOO MUCH.
LISTEN TO YOURSELF, YOU MIGHT SEE WHY PEOPLE ARE SCARED OF YOU.
YOU MIGHT REALIZE THAT YOU'RE THE VILLAIN.

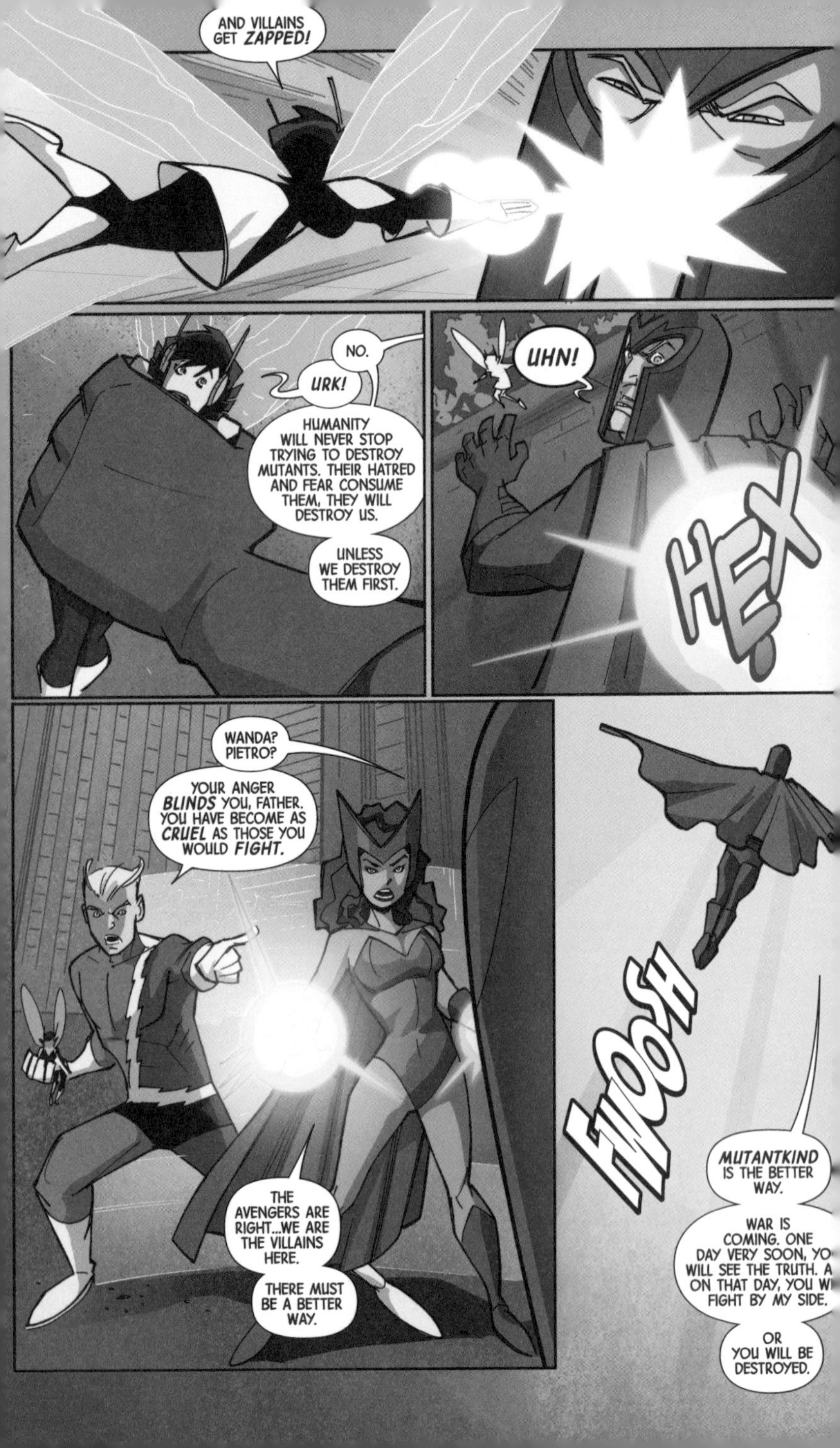
AND VILLAINS GET ZAPPED!
NO.
URK!
HUMANITY WILL NEVER STOP TRYING TO DESTROY MUTANTS. THEIR HATRED AND FEAR CONSUME THEM, THEY WILL DESTROY US.
UNLESS WE DESTROY THEM FIRST.
UHN!
HEX
WANDA? PIETRO?
YOUR ANGER BLINDS YOU, FATHER. YOU HAVE BECOME AS CRUEL AS THOSE YOU WOULD FIGHT.
THE AVENGERS ARE RIGHT...WE ARE THE VILLAINS HERE.
THERE MUST BE A BETTER WAY.
FWOOSH
MUTANTKIND IS THE BETTER WAY.
WAR IS COMING. ONE DAY VERY SOON, YO WILL SEE THE TRUTH. A ON THAT DAY, YOU WI FIGHT BY MY SIDE.
OR YOU WILL BE DESTROYED.

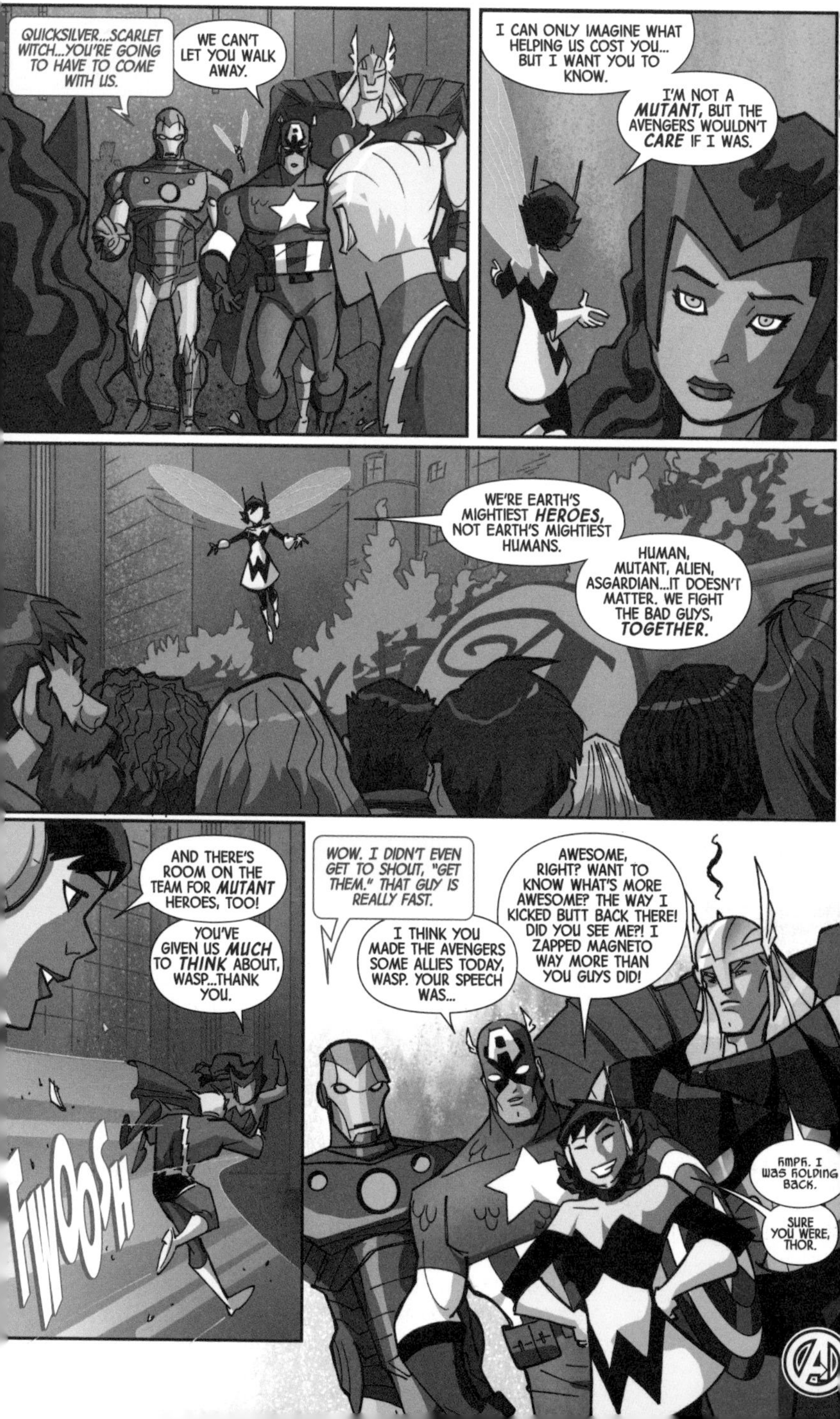

QUICKSILVER...SCARLET WITCH...YOU'RE GOING TO HAVE TO COME WITH US.
WE CAN'T LET YOU WALK AWAY.
I CAN ONLY IMAGINE WHAT HELPING US COST YOU... BUT I WANT YOU TO KNOW.
I'M NOT A MUTANT, BUT THE AVENGERS WOULDN'T CARE IF I WAS.
WE'RE EARTH'S MIGHTIEST HEROES, NOT EARTH'S MIGHTIEST HUMANS.
HUMAN, MUTANT, ALIEN, ASGARDIAN...IT DOESN'T MATTER. WE FIGHT THE BAD GUYS, TOGETHER.
AND THERE'S ROOM ON THE TEAM FOR MUTANT HEROES, TOO!
YOU'VE GIVEN US MUCH TO THINK ABOUT, WASP...THANK YOU.
FWOOSH
WOW. I DIDN'T EVEN GET TO SHOUT, "GET THEM." THAT GUY IS REALLY FAST.
I THINK YOU MADE THE AVENGERS SOME ALLIES TODAY, WASP. YOUR SPEECH WAS...
AWESOME, RIGHT? WANT TO KNOW WHAT'S MORE AWESOME? THE WAY I KICKED BUTT BACK THERE! DID YOU SEE ME?! I ZAPPED MAGNETO WAY MORE THAN YOU GUYS DID!
HMPH. I WAS HOLDING BACK.
SURE YOU WERE, THOR.

MARVEL UNIVERSE PRESENTS: MINI-HULKS IN HULK YOGA!

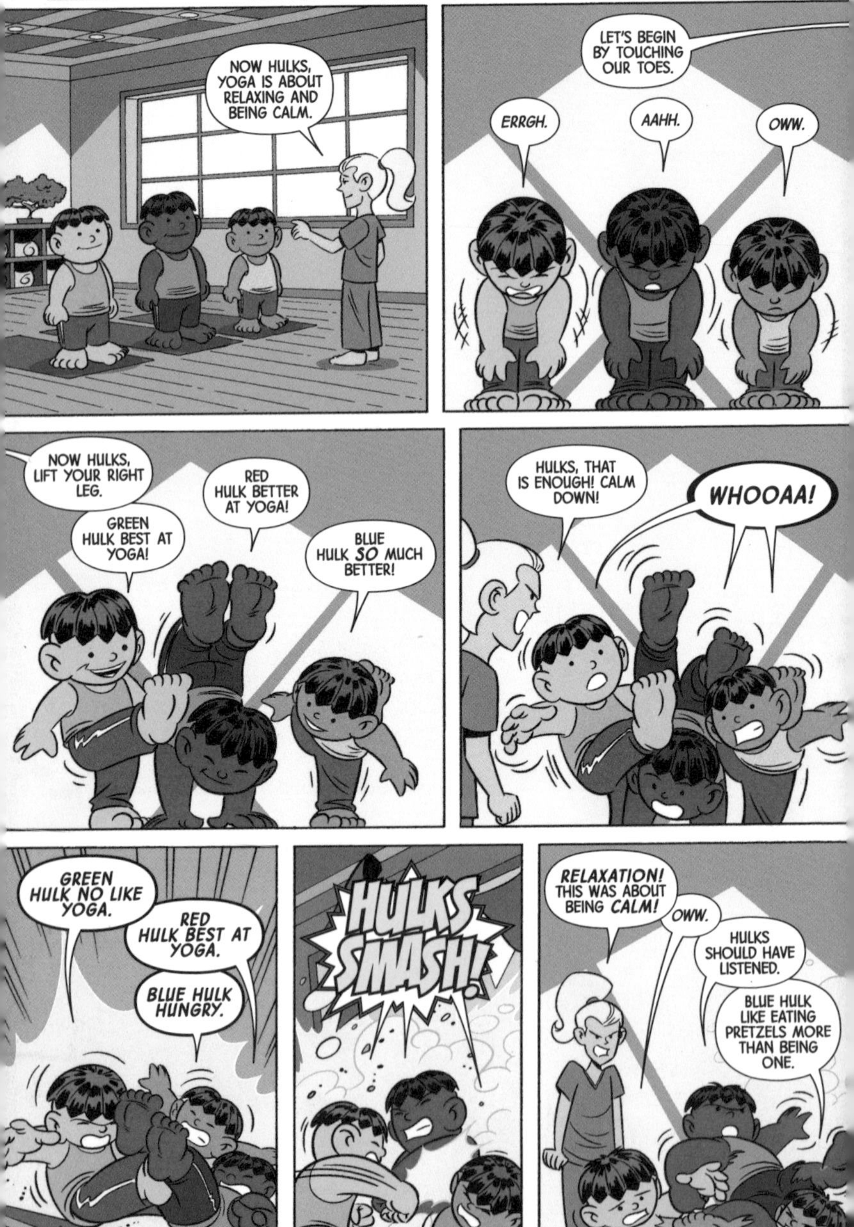

NOW HULKS, YOGA IS ABOUT RELAXING AND BEING CALM.
LET'S BEGIN BY TOUCHING OUR TOES.
ERRGH.
AAHH.
OWW.
NOW HULKS, LIFT YOUR RIGHT LEG.
GREEN HULK BEST AT YOGA!
RED HULK BETTER AT YOGA!
BLUE HULK SO MUCH BETTER!
HULKS, THAT IS ENOUGH! CALM DOWN!
WHOOAA!
GREEN HULK NO LIKE YOGA.
RED HULK BEST AT YOGA.
BLUE HULK HUNGRY.
HULKS SMASH!
RELAXATION! THIS WAS ABOUT BEING CALM!
OWW.
HULKS SHOULD HAVE LISTENED.
BLUE HULK LIKE EATING PRETZELS MORE THAN BEING ONE.

UDREY LOEB, WRITER DARIO BRIZUELA, ARTIST VC'S CLAYTON COWLES, LETTERE

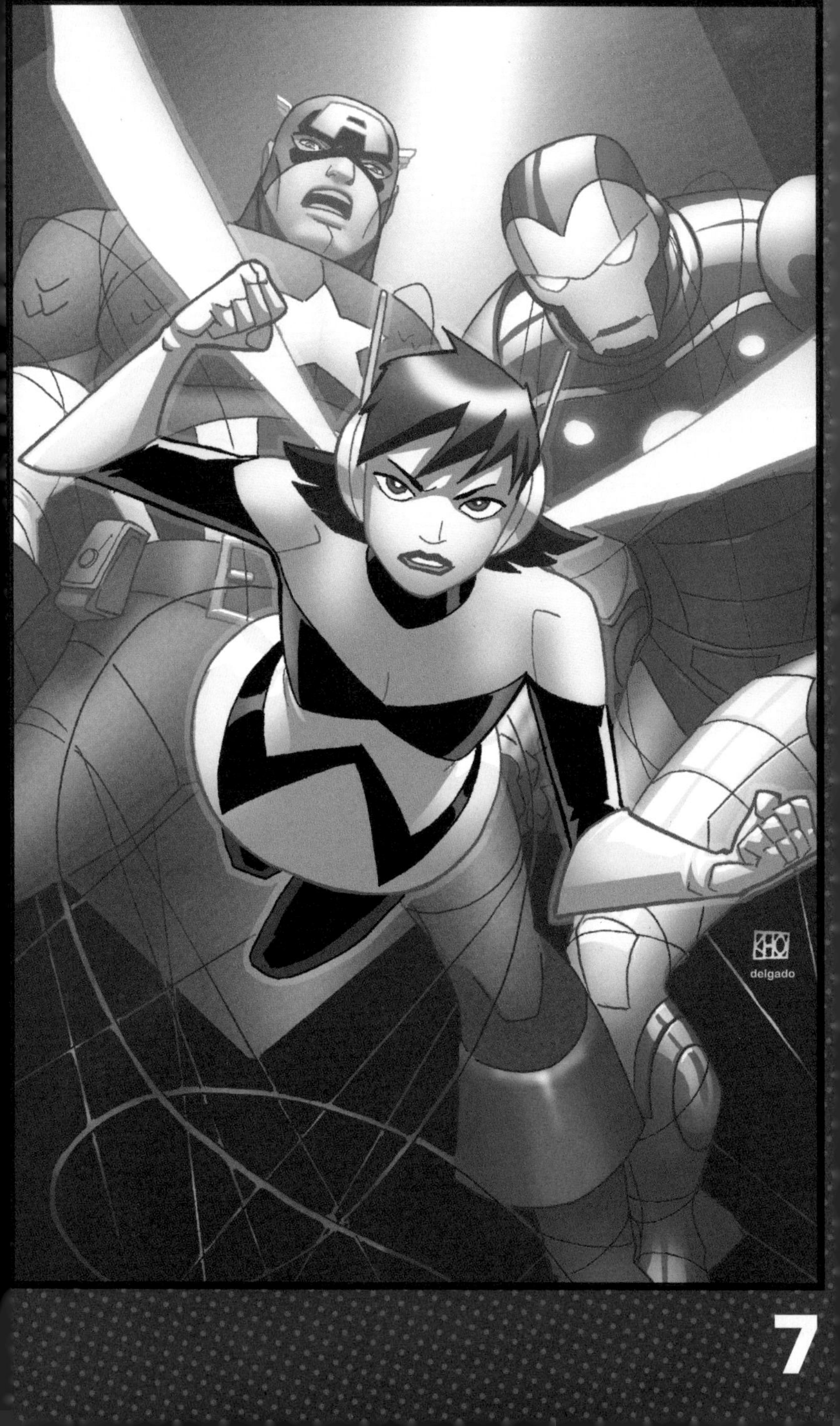

delgado

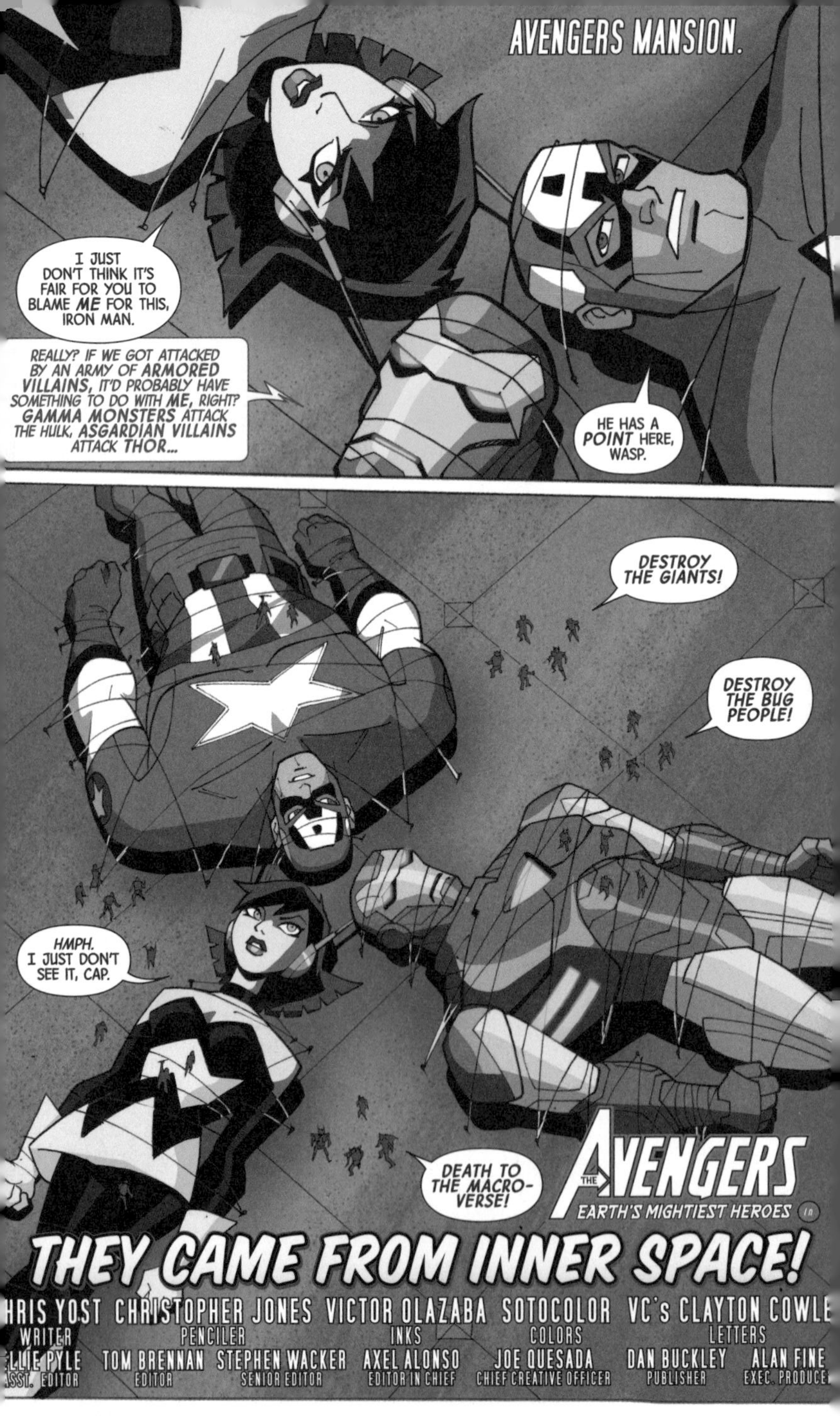
AVENGERS MANSION.
I JUST DON'T THINK IT'S FAIR FOR YOU TO BLAME ME FOR THIS, IRON MAN.
REALLY? IF WE GOT ATTACKED BY AN ARMY OF ARMORED VILLAINS, IT'D PROBABLY HAVE SOMETHING TO DO WITH ME, RIGHT? GAMMA MONSTERS ATTACK THE HULK, ASGARDIAN VILLAINS ATTACK THOR...
HE HAS A POINT HERE, WASP.
DESTROY THE GIANTS!
DESTROY THE BUG PEOPLE!
HMPH. I JUST DON'T SEE IT, CAP.
DEATH TO THE MACRO-VERSE!
THE AVENGERS EARTH'S MIGHTIEST HEROES in
THEY CAME FROM INNER SPACE!
HRIS YOST WRITER
CHRISTOPHER JONES PENCILER
VICTOR OLAZABA INKS
SOTOCOLOR COLORS
VC's CLAYTON COWLE LETTERS
ELLIE PYLE ASST. EDITOR
TOM BRENNAN EDITOR
STEPHEN WACKER SENIOR EDITOR
AXEL ALONSO EDITOR IN CHIEF
JOE QUESADA CHIEF CREATIVE OFFICER
DAN BUCKLEY PUBLISHER
ALAN FINE EXEC. PRODUCE

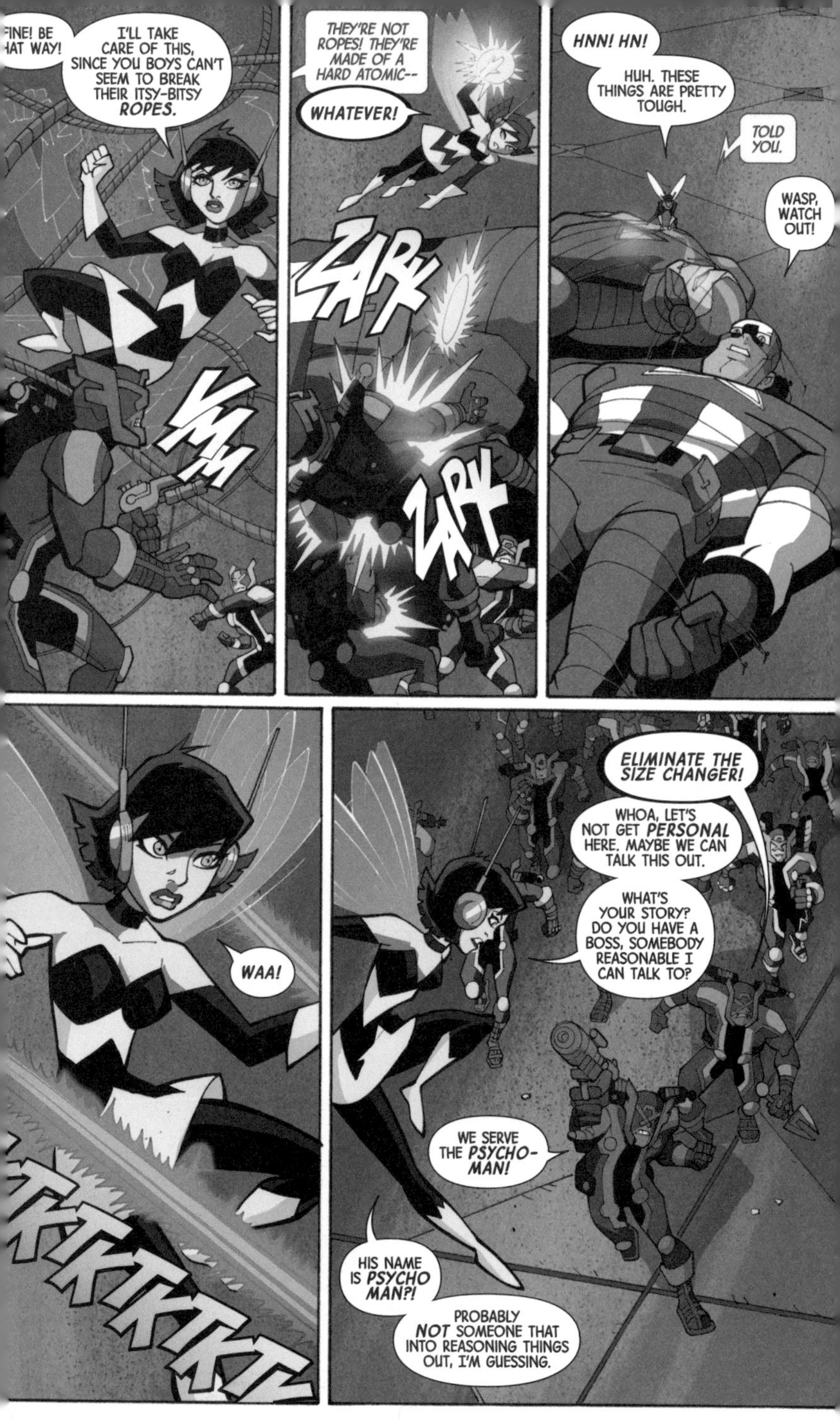
FINE! BE THAT WAY!
I'LL TAKE CARE OF THIS, SINCE YOU BOYS CAN'T SEEM TO BREAK THEIR ITSY-BITSY ROPES.
VMMM
THEY'RE NOT ROPES! THEY'RE MADE OF A HARD ATOMIC--
WHATEVER!
ZARK
ZARK
HNN! HN!
HUH. THESE THINGS ARE PRETTY TOUGH.
TOLD YOU.
WASP, WATCH OUT!
WAA!
TKTKTKTKTKTK
ELIMINATE THE SIZE CHANGER!
WHOA, LET'S NOT GET PERSONAL HERE. MAYBE WE CAN TALK THIS OUT.
WHAT'S YOUR STORY? DO YOU HAVE A BOSS, SOMEBODY REASONABLE I CAN TALK TO?
WE SERVE THE PSYCHO-MAN!
HIS NAME IS PSYCHO MAN?!
PROBABLY NOT SOMEONE THAT INTO REASONING THINGS OUT, I'M GUESSING.

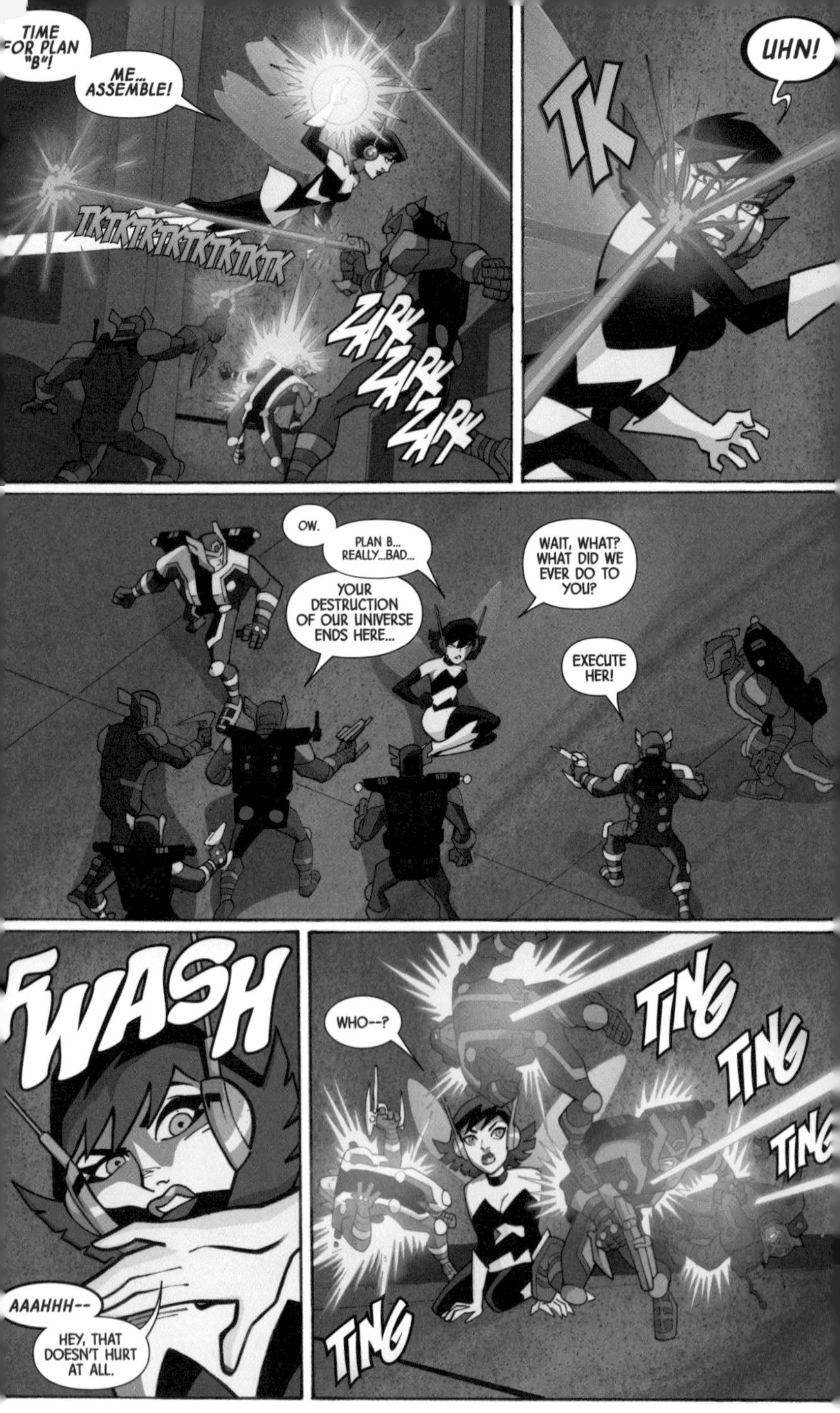
TIME FOR PLAN "B"!
ME... ASSEMBLE!
TKTKTKTKTKTKTKTKTK
ZARK ZARK ZARK
TK
UHN!
OW.
PLAN B... REALLY...BAD...
YOUR DESTRUCTION OF OUR UNIVERSE ENDS HERE...
WAIT, WHAT? WHAT DID WE EVER DO TO YOU?
EXECUTE HER!
FWASH
AAAHHH--
HEY, THAT DOESN'T HURT AT ALL.
WHO--?
TING
TING
TING
TING

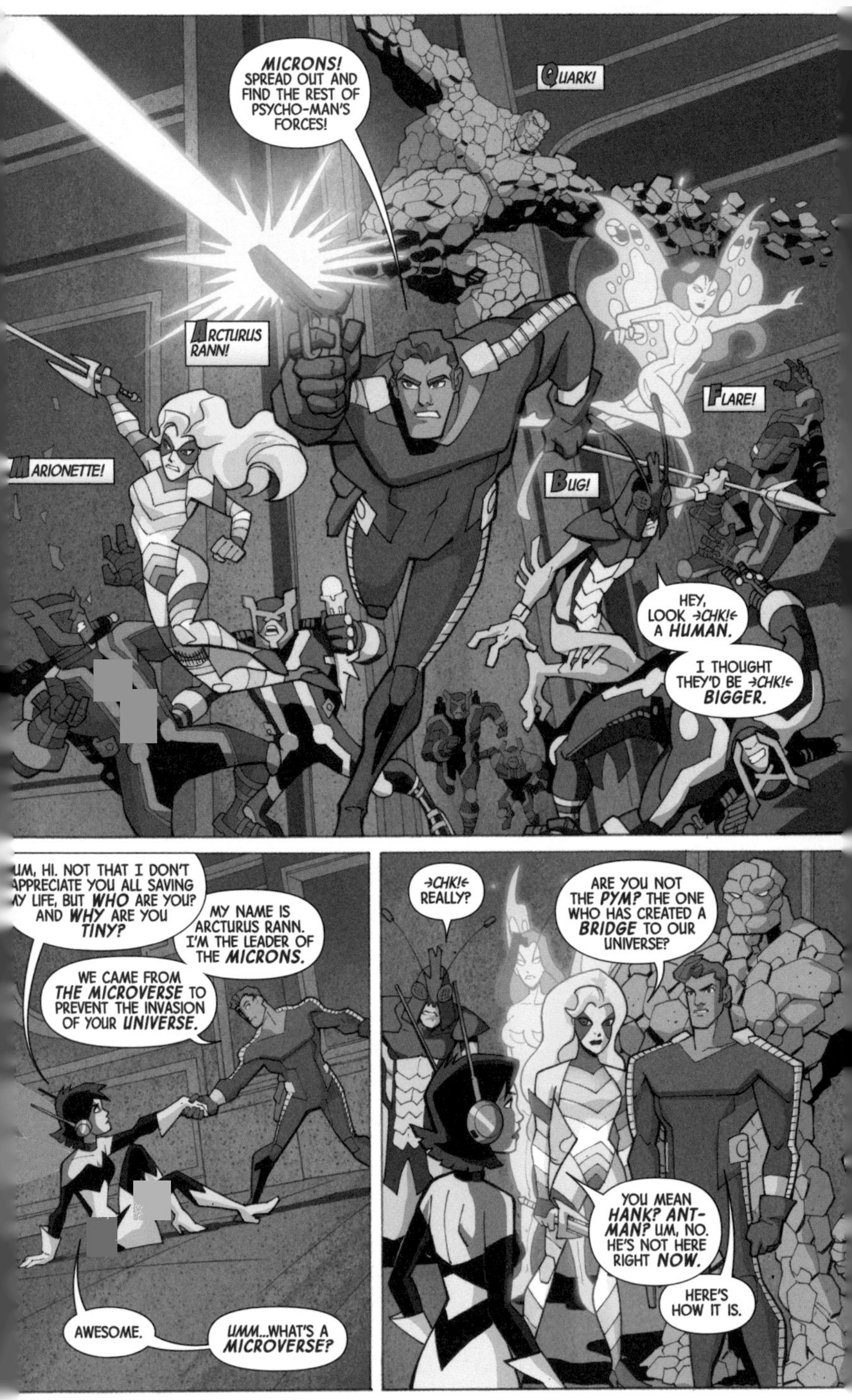
MICRONS! SPREAD OUT AND FIND THE REST OF PSYCHO-MAN'S FORCES!
QUARK!
ARCTURUS RANN!
FLARE!
MARIONETTE!
BUG!
HEY, LOOK →CHK!← A HUMAN.
I THOUGHT THEY'D BE →CHK!← BIGGER.
UM, HI. NOT THAT I DON'T APPRECIATE YOU ALL SAVING MY LIFE, BUT WHO ARE YOU? AND WHY ARE YOU TINY?
MY NAME IS ARCTURUS RANN. I'M THE LEADER OF THE MICRONS.
WE CAME FROM THE MICROVERSE TO PREVENT THE INVASION OF YOUR UNIVERSE.
AWESOME.
UMM...WHAT'S A MICROVERSE?
→CHK!← REALLY?
ARE YOU NOT THE PYM? THE ONE WHO HAS CREATED A BRIDGE TO OUR UNIVERSE?
YOU MEAN HANK? ANT-MAN? UM, NO. HE'S NOT HERE RIGHT NOW.
HERE'S HOW IT IS.

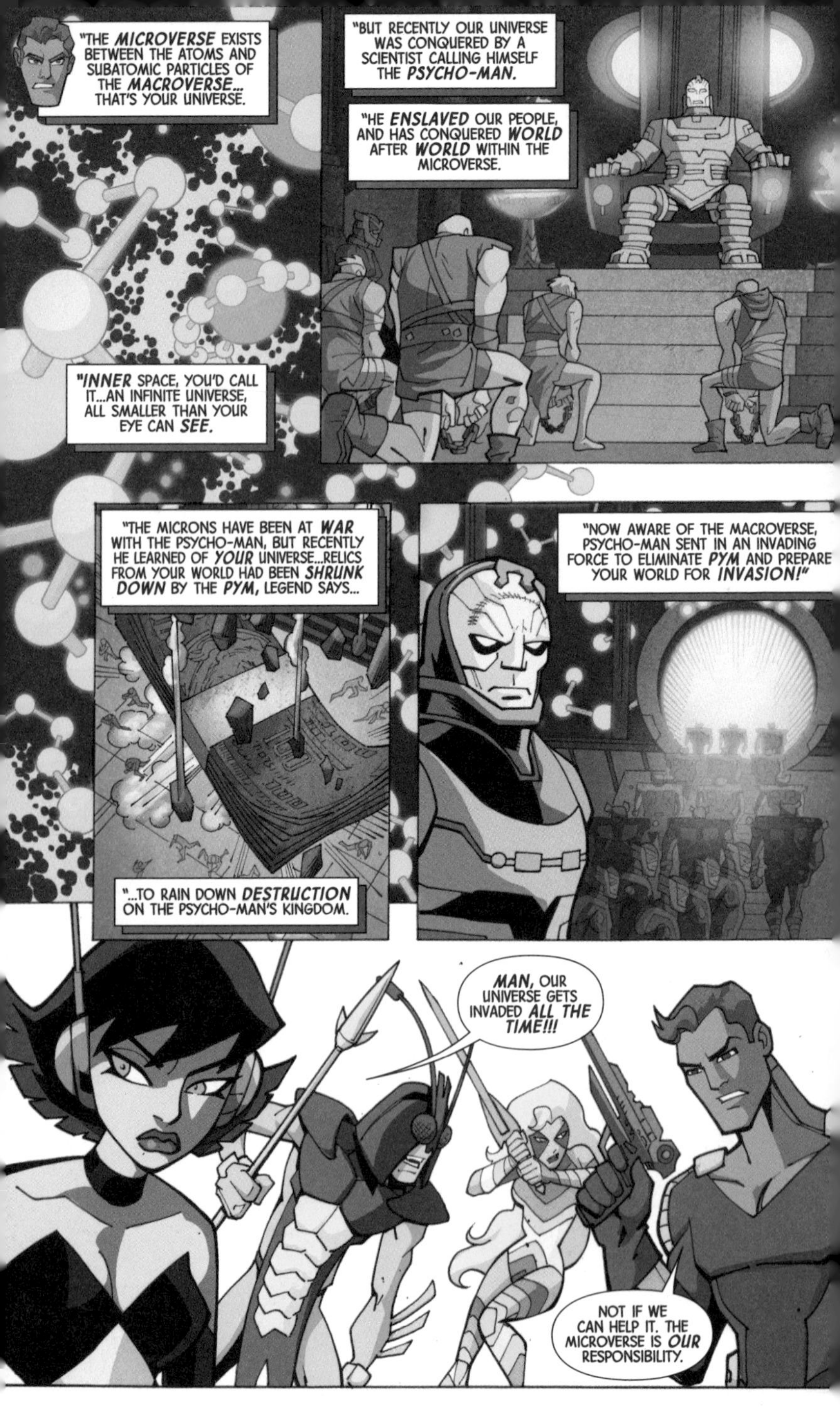
"THE MICROVERSE EXISTS BETWEEN THE ATOMS AND SUBATOMIC PARTICLES OF THE MACROVERSE... THAT'S YOUR UNIVERSE.
"INNER SPACE, YOU'D CALL IT...AN INFINITE UNIVERSE, ALL SMALLER THAN YOUR EYE CAN SEE.
"BUT RECENTLY OUR UNIVERSE WAS CONQUERED BY A SCIENTIST CALLING HIMSELF THE PSYCHO-MAN.
"HE ENSLAVED OUR PEOPLE, AND HAS CONQUERED WORLD AFTER WORLD WITHIN THE MICROVERSE.
"THE MICRONS HAVE BEEN AT WAR WITH THE PSYCHO-MAN, BUT RECENTLY HE LEARNED OF YOUR UNIVERSE...RELICS FROM YOUR WORLD HAD BEEN SHRUNK DOWN BY THE PYM, LEGEND SAYS...
"...TO RAIN DOWN DESTRUCTION ON THE PSYCHO-MAN'S KINGDOM.
"NOW AWARE OF THE MACROVERSE, PSYCHO-MAN SENT IN AN INVADING FORCE TO ELIMINATE PYM AND PREPARE YOUR WORLD FOR INVASION!"
MAN, OUR UNIVERSE GETS INVADED ALL THE TIME!!!
NOT IF WE CAN HELP IT. THE MICROVERSE IS OUR RESPONSIBILITY.

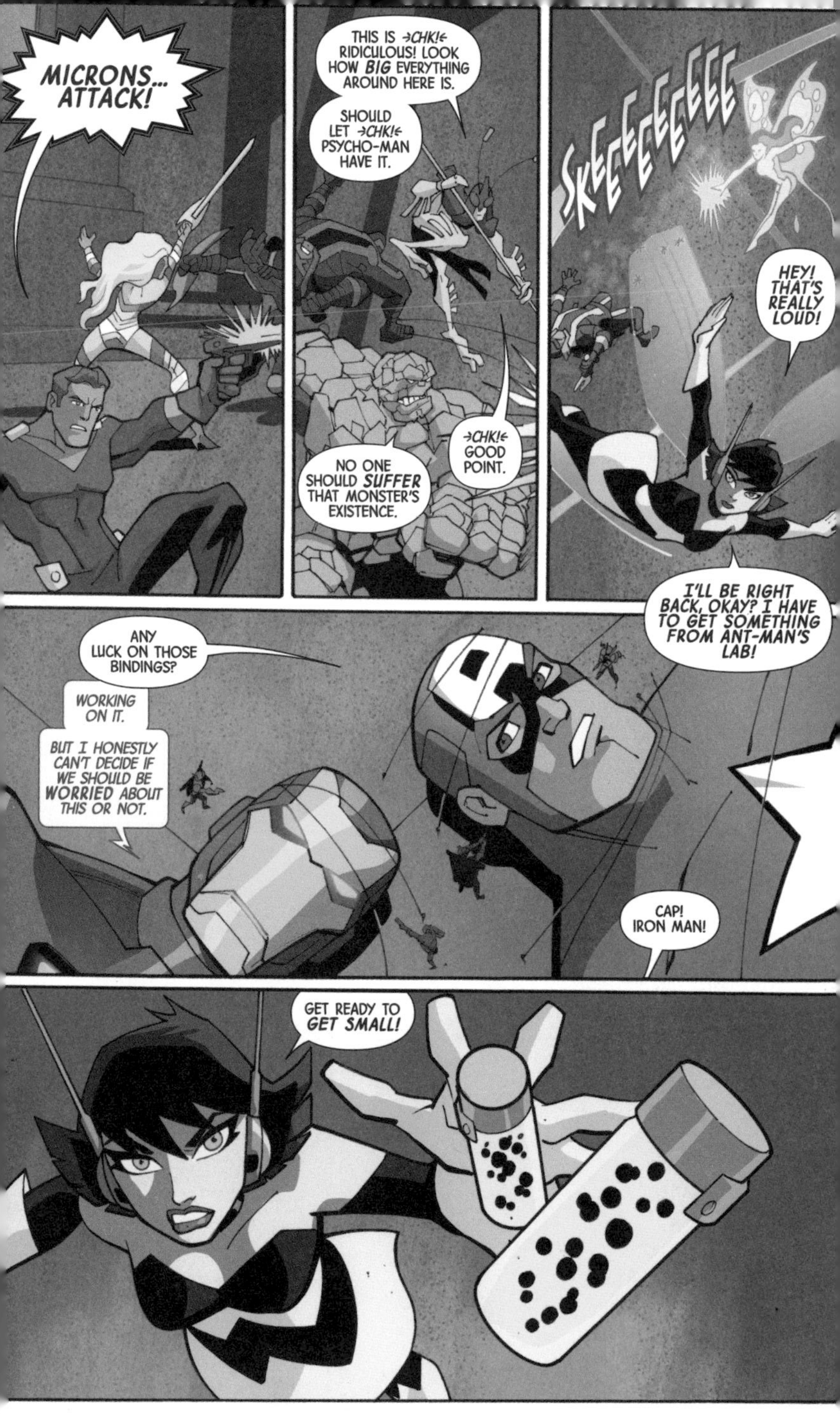
MICRONS... ATTACK!
THIS IS →CHK!← RIDICULOUS! LOOK HOW BIG EVERYTHING AROUND HERE IS.
SHOULD LET →CHK!← PSYCHO-MAN HAVE IT.
NO ONE SHOULD SUFFER THAT MONSTER'S EXISTENCE.
→CHK!← GOOD POINT.
SKEEEEEEEEE
HEY! THAT'S REALLY LOUD!
I'LL BE RIGHT BACK, OKAY? I HAVE TO GET SOMETHING FROM ANT-MAN'S LAB!
ANY LUCK ON THOSE BINDINGS?
WORKING ON IT.
BUT I HONESTLY CAN'T DECIDE IF WE SHOULD BE WORRIED ABOUT THIS OR NOT.
CAP! IRON MAN!
GET READY TO GET SMALL!

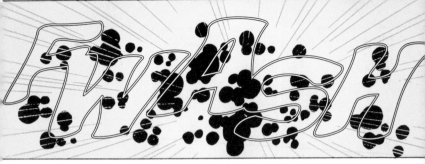

WASP... WHAT DID YOU *DO*?!

ANT-MAN HAS SOME EXTRA CAPSULES OF *PYM PARTICLES* IN HIS LAB, THE SAME STUFF *HE* USES! I SHRUNK YOU!

YOU'RE *FREE!* NOW YOU CAN FIGHT OUR *ITTY-BITTY* INVADERS!

WHY WOULD YOU DO THAT?

I...I FEEL SO SMALL...

TINY AVENGERS...

ASSEMBLE

UHN!

JARVIS! CAN YOU READ ME?

OOF!

NEGATIVE, SIR. I BELIEVE I AM COMMUNICATING WITH AN IRON MAN *ACTION FIGURE* AT THE MOMENT.

HA, HA. VERY FUNNY.

INDEE SIR.

BEWARE THE GIANT BLADES! BIGGER THAN TREES!

AAAHH!

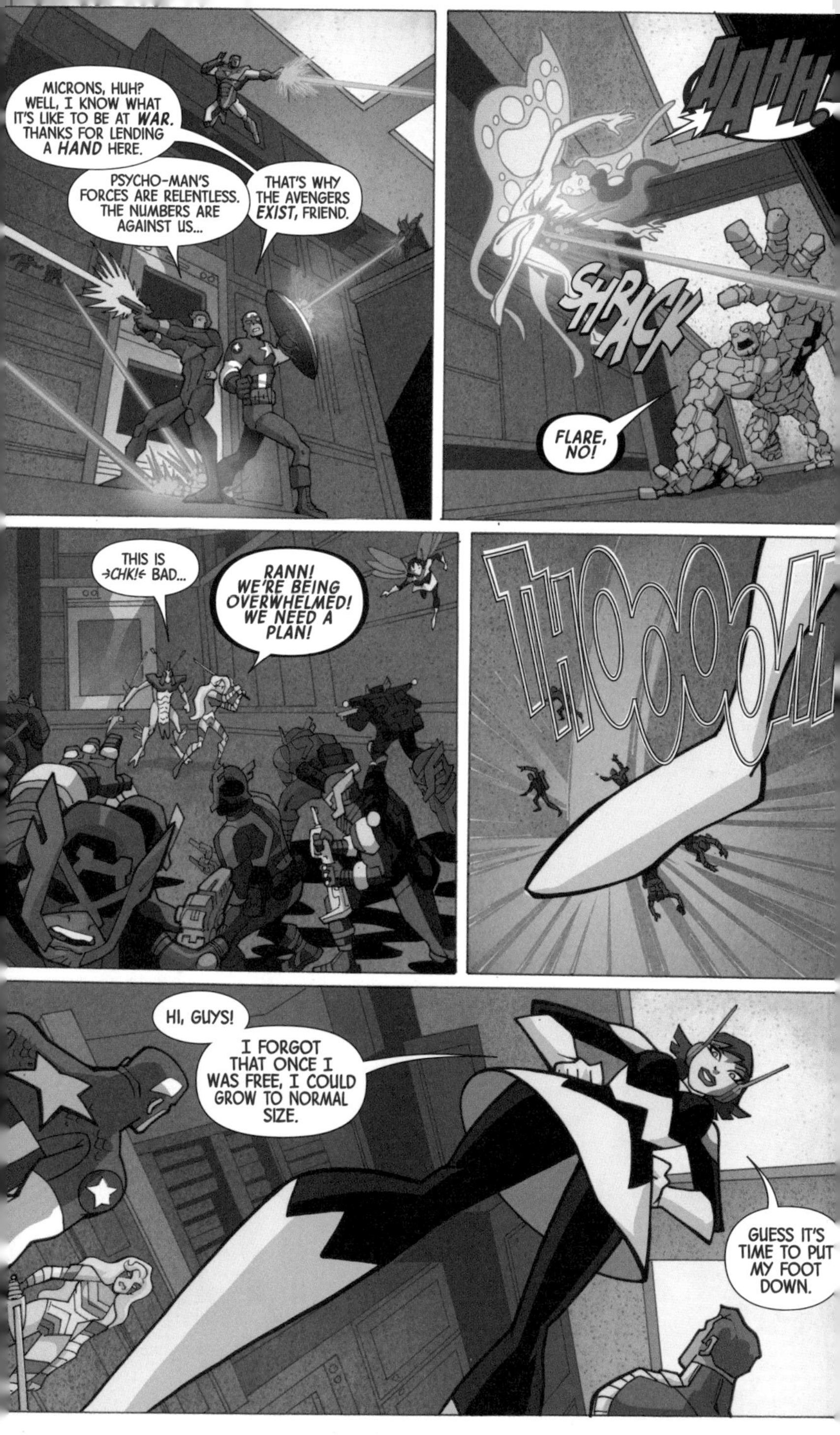
MICRONS, HUH? WELL, I KNOW WHAT IT'S LIKE TO BE AT WAR. THANKS FOR LENDING A HAND HERE.
PSYCHO-MAN'S FORCES ARE RELENTLESS. THE NUMBERS ARE AGAINST US...
THAT'S WHY THE AVENGERS EXIST, FRIEND.
AAHH!
SHRACK
FLARE, NO!
THIS IS →CHK!← BAD...
RANN! WE'RE BEING OVERWHELMED! WE NEED A PLAN!
THOOOOM
HI, GUYS!
I FORGOT THAT ONCE I WAS FREE, I COULD GROW TO NORMAL SIZE.
GUESS IT'S TIME TO PUT MY FOOT DOWN.

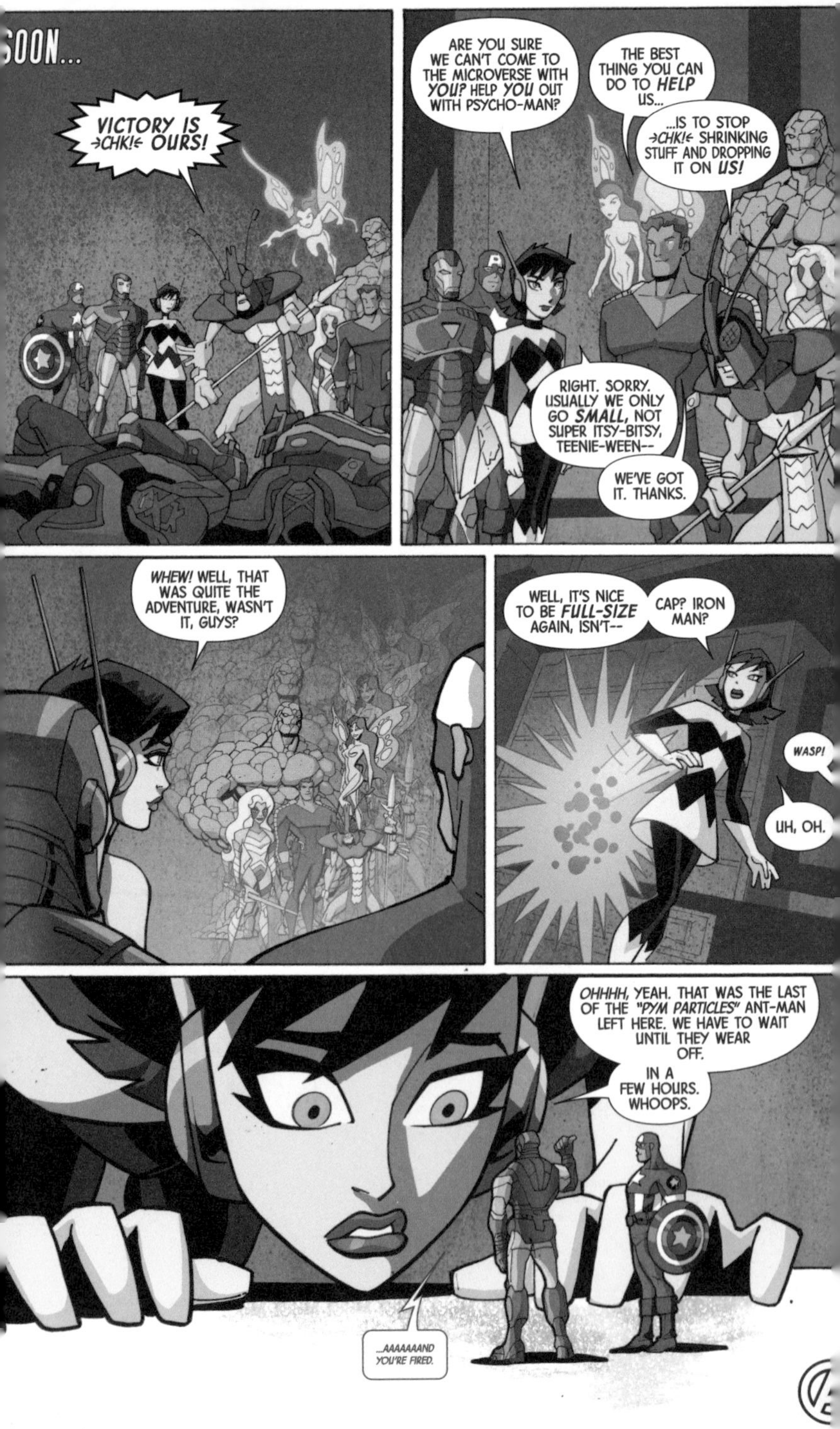

SOON...
VICTORY IS →CHK!← OURS!
ARE YOU SURE WE CAN'T COME TO THE MICROVERSE WITH YOU? HELP YOU OUT WITH PSYCHO-MAN?
THE BEST THING YOU CAN DO TO HELP US...
...IS TO STOP →CHK!← SHRINKING STUFF AND DROPPING IT ON US!
RIGHT. SORRY. USUALLY WE ONLY GO SMALL, NOT SUPER ITSY-BITSY, TEENIE-WEEN--
WE'VE GOT IT. THANKS.
WHEW! WELL, THAT WAS QUITE THE ADVENTURE, WASN'T IT, GUYS?
WELL, IT'S NICE TO BE FULL-SIZE AGAIN, ISN'T--
CAP? IRON MAN?
WASP!
UH, OH.
OHHHH, YEAH. THAT WAS THE LAST OF THE "PYM PARTICLES" ANT-MAN LEFT HERE. WE HAVE TO WAIT UNTIL THEY WEAR OFF.
IN A FEW HOURS. WHOOPS.
...AAAAAAAND YOU'RE FIRED.

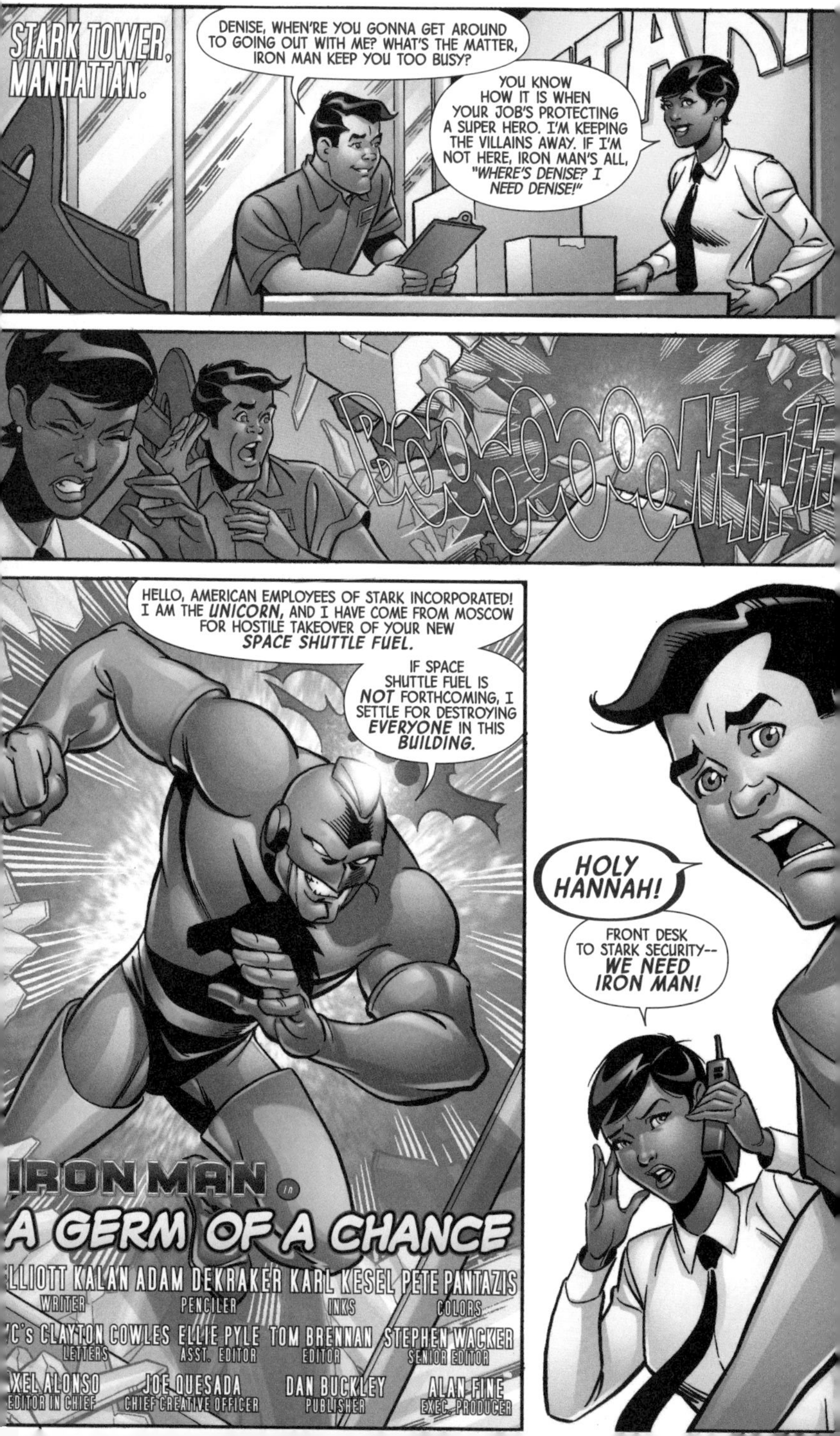
STARK TOWER, MANHATTAN.
DENISE, WHEN'RE YOU GONNA GET AROUND TO GOING OUT WITH ME? WHAT'S THE MATTER, IRON MAN KEEP YOU TOO BUSY?
YOU KNOW HOW IT IS WHEN YOUR JOB'S PROTECTING A SUPER HERO. I'M KEEPING THE VILLAINS AWAY. IF I'M NOT HERE, IRON MAN'S ALL, "WHERE'S DENISE? I NEED DENISE!"
BOOOOOOOOMMM!!!
HELLO, AMERICAN EMPLOYEES OF STARK INCORPORATED! I AM THE UNICORN, AND I HAVE COME FROM MOSCOW FOR HOSTILE TAKEOVER OF YOUR NEW SPACE SHUTTLE FUEL.
IF SPACE SHUTTLE FUEL IS NOT FORTHCOMING, I SETTLE FOR DESTROYING EVERYONE IN THIS BUILDING.
HOLY HANNAH!
FRONT DESK TO STARK SECURITY-- WE NEED IRON MAN!
IRON MAN in
A GERM OF A CHANCE
LLIOTT KALAN WRITER
ADAM DEKRAKER PENCILER
KARL KESEL INKS
PETE PANTAZIS COLORS
C's CLAYTON COWLES LETTERS
ELLIE PYLE ASST. EDITOR
TOM BRENNAN EDITOR
STEPHEN WACKER SENIOR EDITOR
XEL ALONSO EDITOR IN CHIEF
JOE QUESADA CHIEF CREATIVE OFFICER
DAN BUCKLEY PUBLISHER
ALAN FINE EXEC. PRODUCER

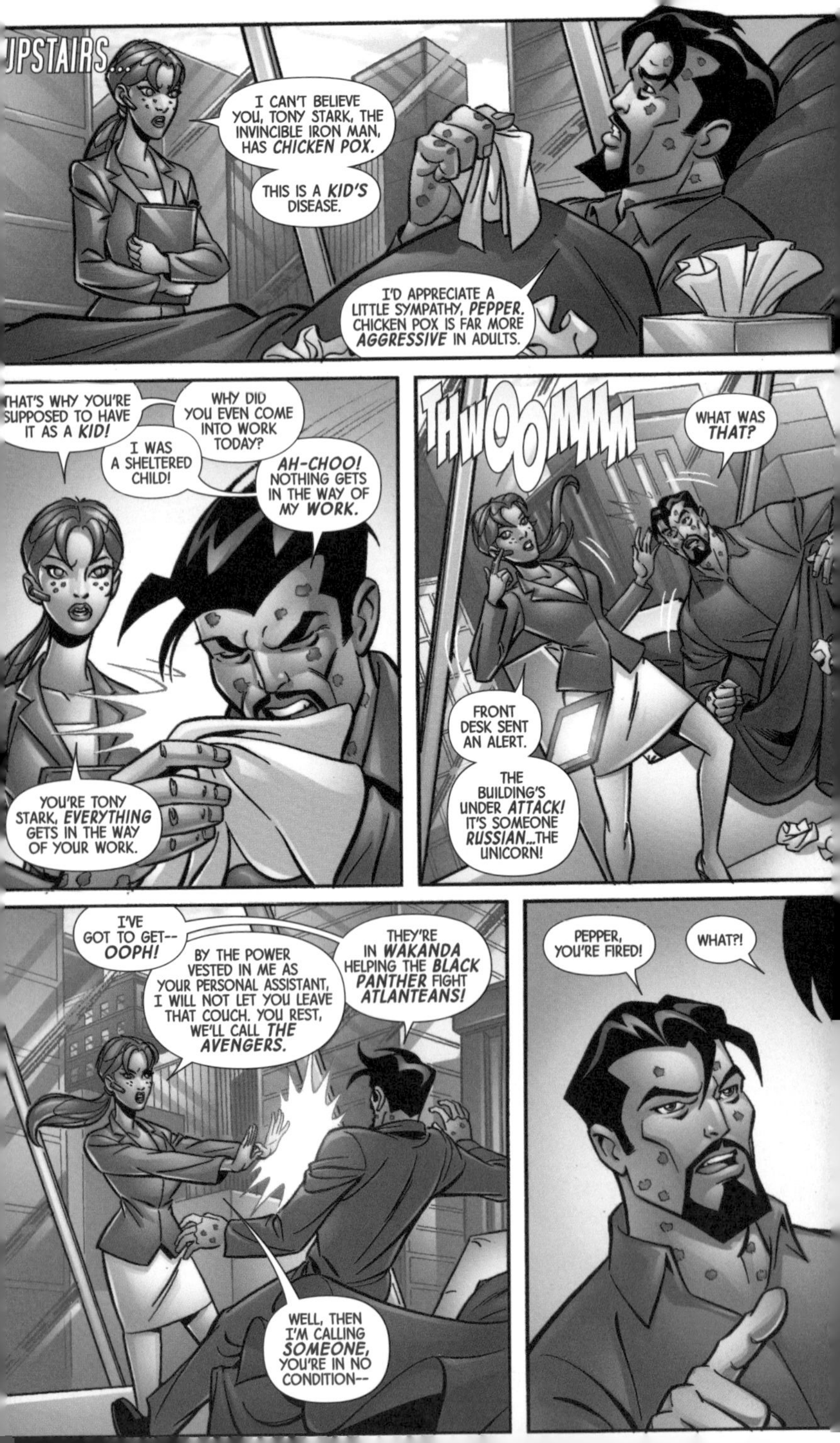
UPSTAIRS...
I CAN'T BELIEVE YOU, TONY STARK, THE INVINCIBLE IRON MAN, HAS CHICKEN POX.
THIS IS A KID'S DISEASE.
I'D APPRECIATE A LITTLE SYMPATHY, PEPPER. CHICKEN POX IS FAR MORE AGGRESSIVE IN ADULTS.
THAT'S WHY YOU'RE SUPPOSED TO HAVE IT AS A KID!
I WAS A SHELTERED CHILD!
WHY DID YOU EVEN COME INTO WORK TODAY?
AH-CHOO! NOTHING GETS IN THE WAY OF MY WORK.
YOU'RE TONY STARK, EVERYTHING GETS IN THE WAY OF YOUR WORK.
THWOOMMMM
WHAT WAS THAT?
FRONT DESK SENT AN ALERT.
THE BUILDING'S UNDER ATTACK! IT'S SOMEONE RUSSIAN...THE UNICORN!
I'VE GOT TO GET-- OOPH!
BY THE POWER VESTED IN ME AS YOUR PERSONAL ASSISTANT, I WILL NOT LET YOU LEAVE THAT COUCH. YOU REST, WE'LL CALL THE AVENGERS.
THEY'RE IN WAKANDA HELPING THE BLACK PANTHER FIGHT ATLANTEANS!
WELL, THEN I'M CALLING SOMEONE, YOU'RE IN NO CONDITION--
PEPPER, YOU'RE FIRED!
WHAT?!

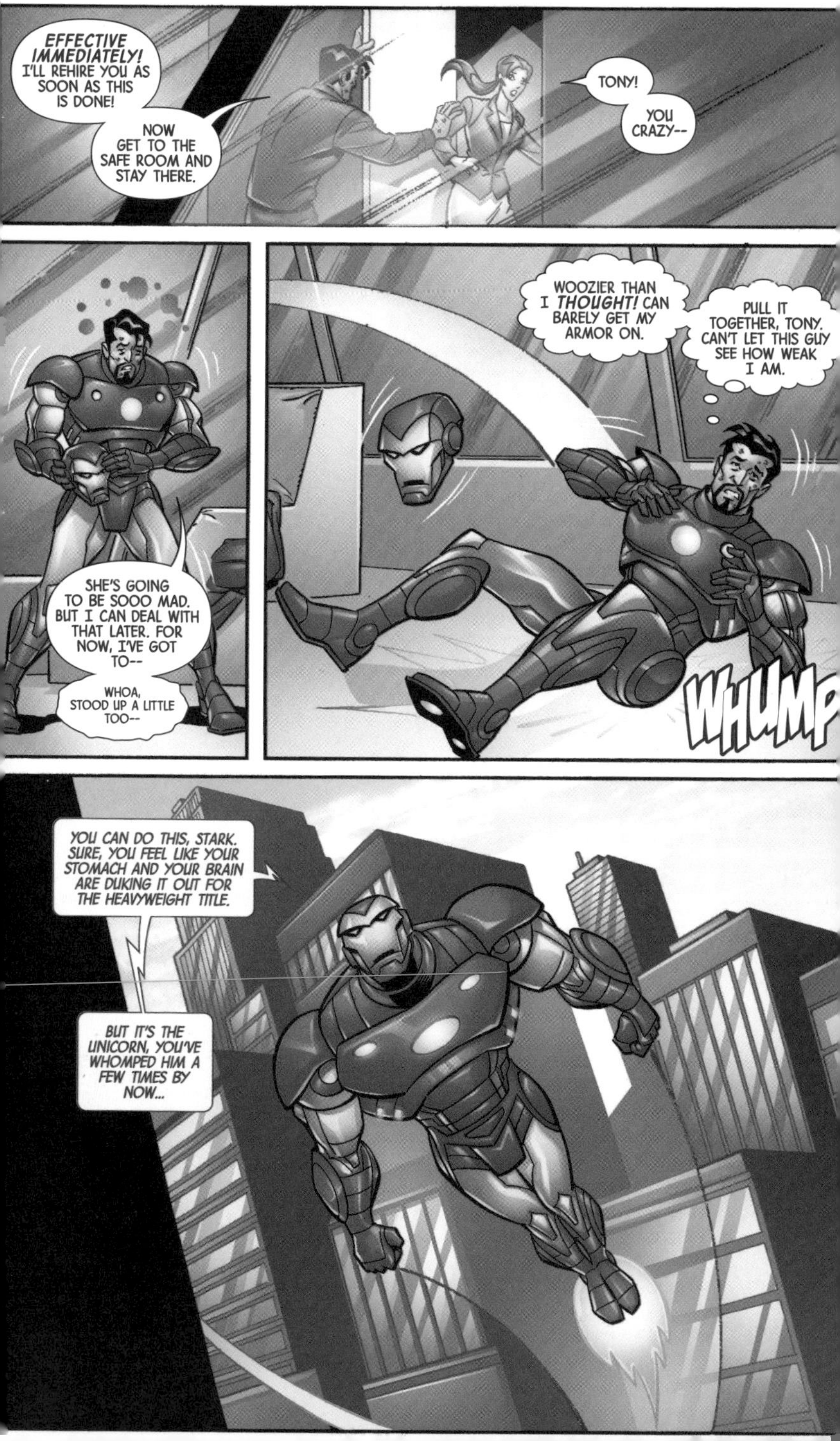
EFFECTIVE IMMEDIATELY! I'LL REHIRE YOU AS SOON AS THIS IS DONE!
NOW GET TO THE SAFE ROOM AND STAY THERE.
TONY!
YOU CRAZY--
SHE'S GOING TO BE SOOO MAD. BUT I CAN DEAL WITH THAT LATER. FOR NOW, I'VE GOT TO--
WHOA, STOOD UP A LITTLE TOO--
WOOZIER THAN I THOUGHT! CAN BARELY GET MY ARMOR ON.
PULL IT TOGETHER, TONY. CAN'T LET THIS GUY SEE HOW WEAK I AM.
WHUMP
YOU CAN DO THIS, STARK. SURE, YOU FEEL LIKE YOUR STOMACH AND YOUR BRAIN ARE DUKING IT OUT FOR THE HEAVYWEIGHT TITLE.
BUT IT'S THE UNICORN, YOU'VE WHOMPED HIM A FEW TIMES BY NOW...

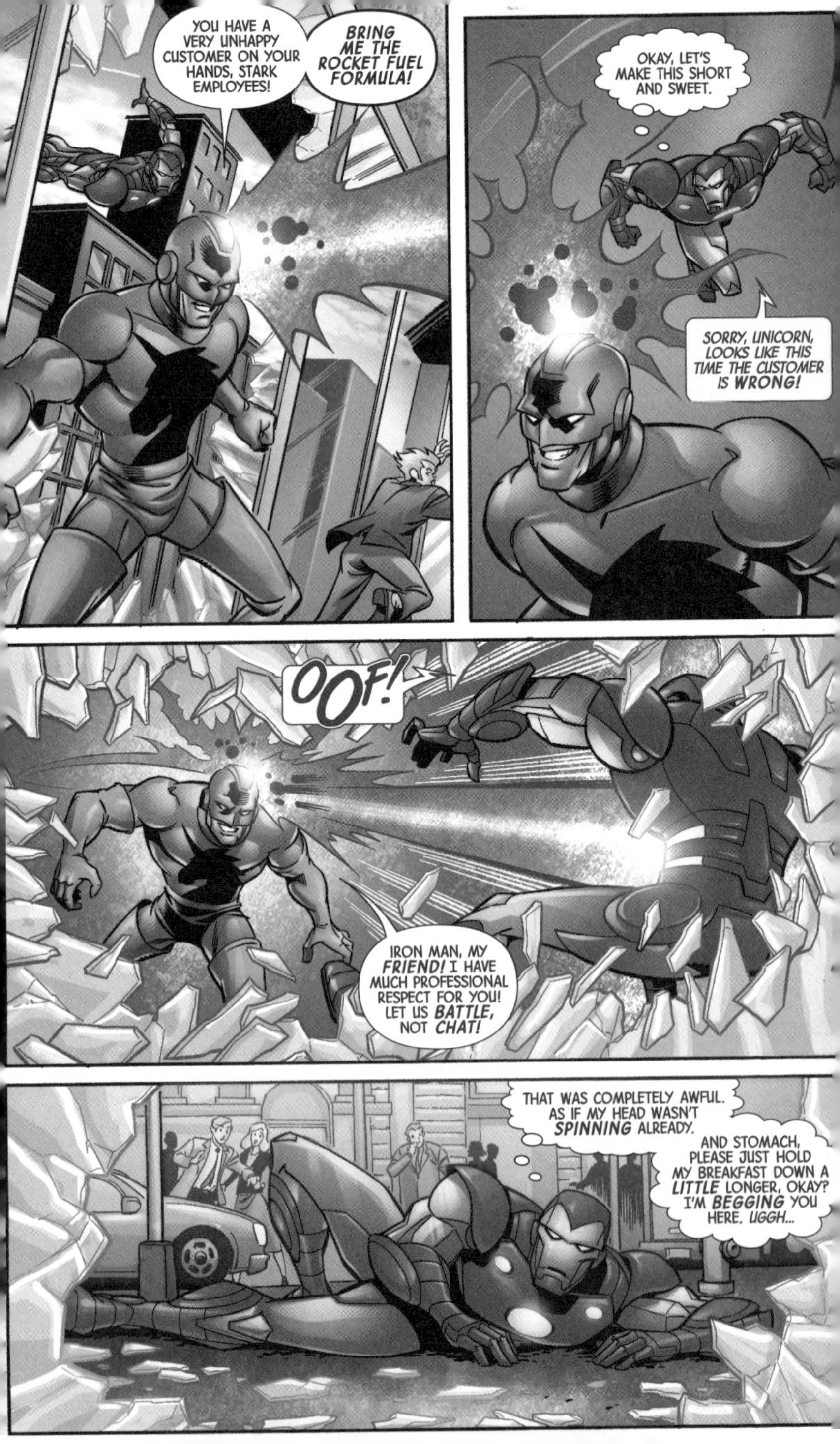
YOU HAVE A VERY UNHAPPY CUSTOMER ON YOUR HANDS, STARK EMPLOYEES!
BRING ME THE ROCKET FUEL FORMULA!
OKAY, LET'S MAKE THIS SHORT AND SWEET.
SORRY, UNICORN, LOOKS LIKE THIS TIME THE CUSTOMER IS WRONG!
OOF!
IRON MAN, MY FRIEND! I HAVE MUCH PROFESSIONAL RESPECT FOR YOU! LET US BATTLE, NOT CHAT!
THAT WAS COMPLETELY AWFUL. AS IF MY HEAD WASN'T SPINNING ALREADY.
AND STOMACH, PLEASE JUST HOLD MY BREAKFAST DOWN A LITTLE LONGER, OKAY? I'M BEGGING YOU HERE. UGGH...

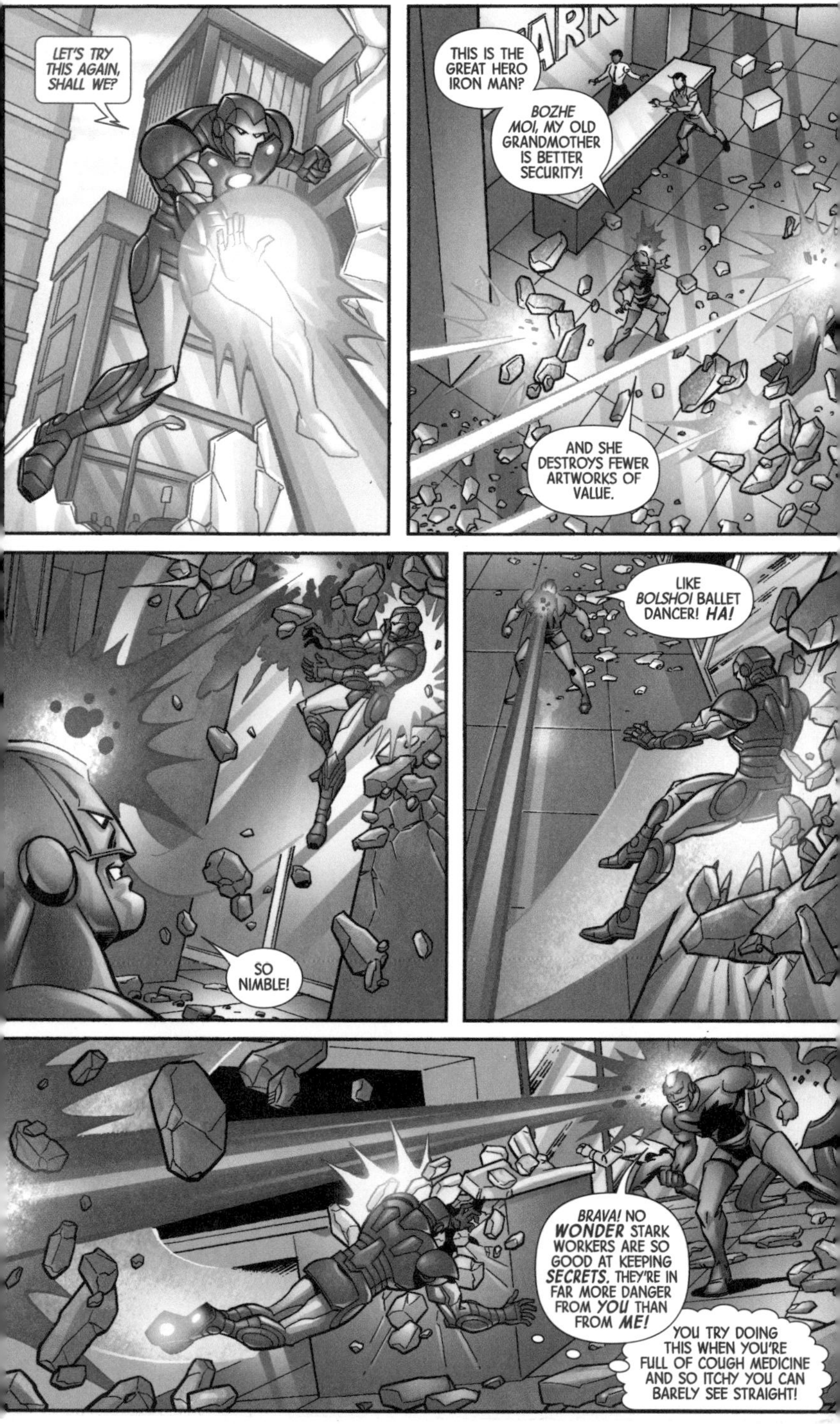
LET'S TRY THIS AGAIN, SHALL WE?
THIS IS THE GREAT HERO IRON MAN?
BOZHE MOI, MY OLD GRANDMOTHER IS BETTER SECURITY!
AND SHE DESTROYS FEWER ARTWORKS OF VALUE.
SO NIMBLE!
LIKE BOLSHOI BALLET DANCER! HA!
BRAVA! NO WONDER STARK WORKERS ARE SO GOOD AT KEEPING SECRETS. THEY'RE IN FAR MORE DANGER FROM YOU THAN FROM ME!
YOU TRY DOING THIS WHEN YOU'RE FULL OF COUGH MEDICINE AND SO ITCHY YOU CAN BARELY SEE STRAIGHT!

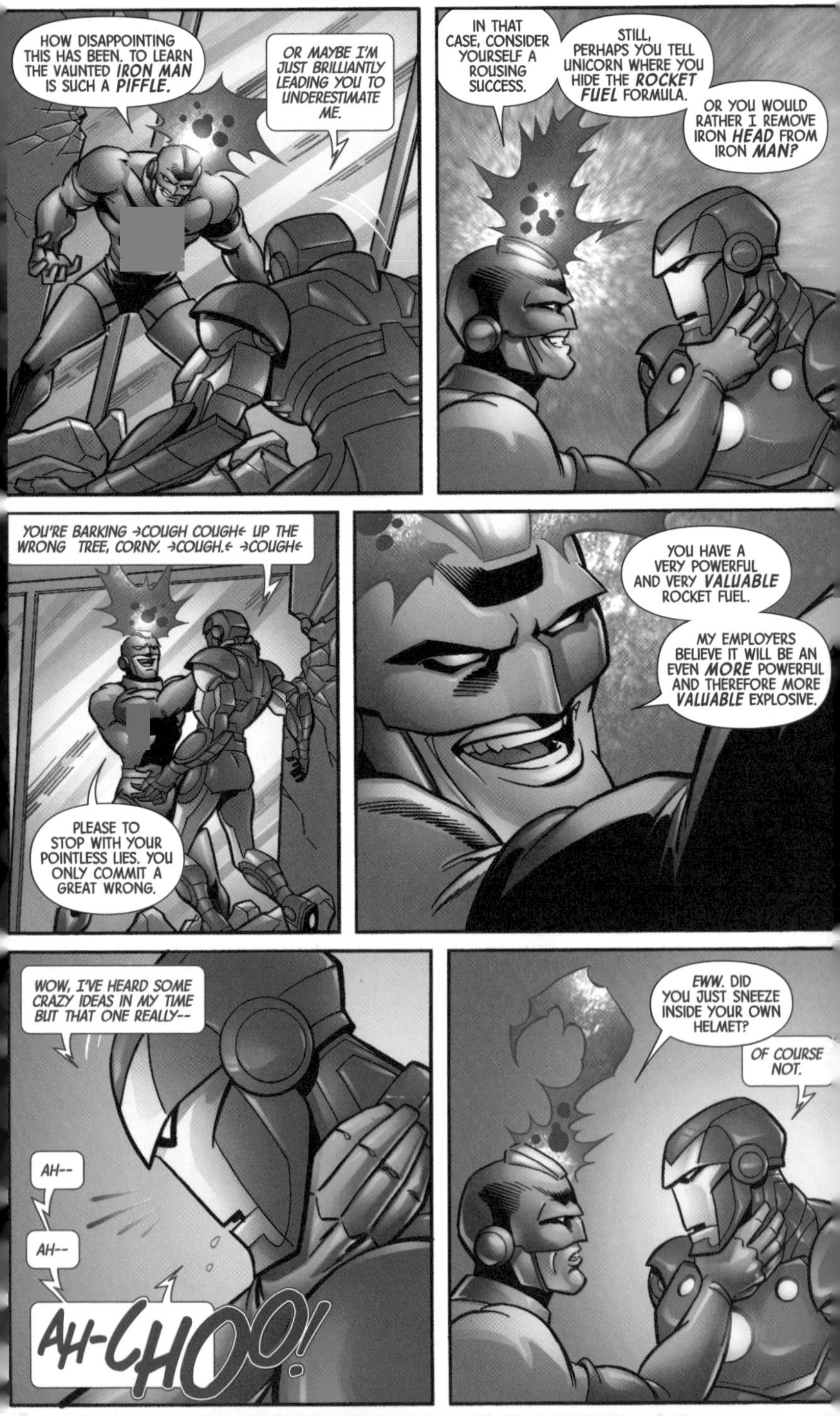
HOW DISAPPOINTING THIS HAS BEEN. TO LEARN THE VAUNTED IRON MAN IS SUCH A PIFFLE.
OR MAYBE I'M JUST BRILLIANTLY LEADING YOU TO UNDERESTIMATE ME.
IN THAT CASE, CONSIDER YOURSELF A ROUSING SUCCESS.
STILL, PERHAPS YOU TELL UNICORN WHERE YOU HIDE THE ROCKET FUEL FORMULA.
OR YOU WOULD RATHER I REMOVE IRON HEAD FROM IRON MAN?
YOU'RE BARKING →COUGH COUGH← UP THE WRONG TREE, CORNY. →COUGH.← →COUGH←
PLEASE TO STOP WITH YOUR POINTLESS LIES. YOU ONLY COMMIT A GREAT WRONG.
YOU HAVE A VERY POWERFUL AND VERY VALUABLE ROCKET FUEL.
MY EMPLOYERS BELIEVE IT WILL BE AN EVEN MORE POWERFUL AND THEREFORE MORE VALUABLE EXPLOSIVE.
WOW, I'VE HEARD SOME CRAZY IDEAS IN MY TIME BUT THAT ONE REALLY--
AH--
AH--
AH-CHOO!
EWW. DID YOU JUST SNEEZE INSIDE YOUR OWN HELMET?
OF COURSE NOT.

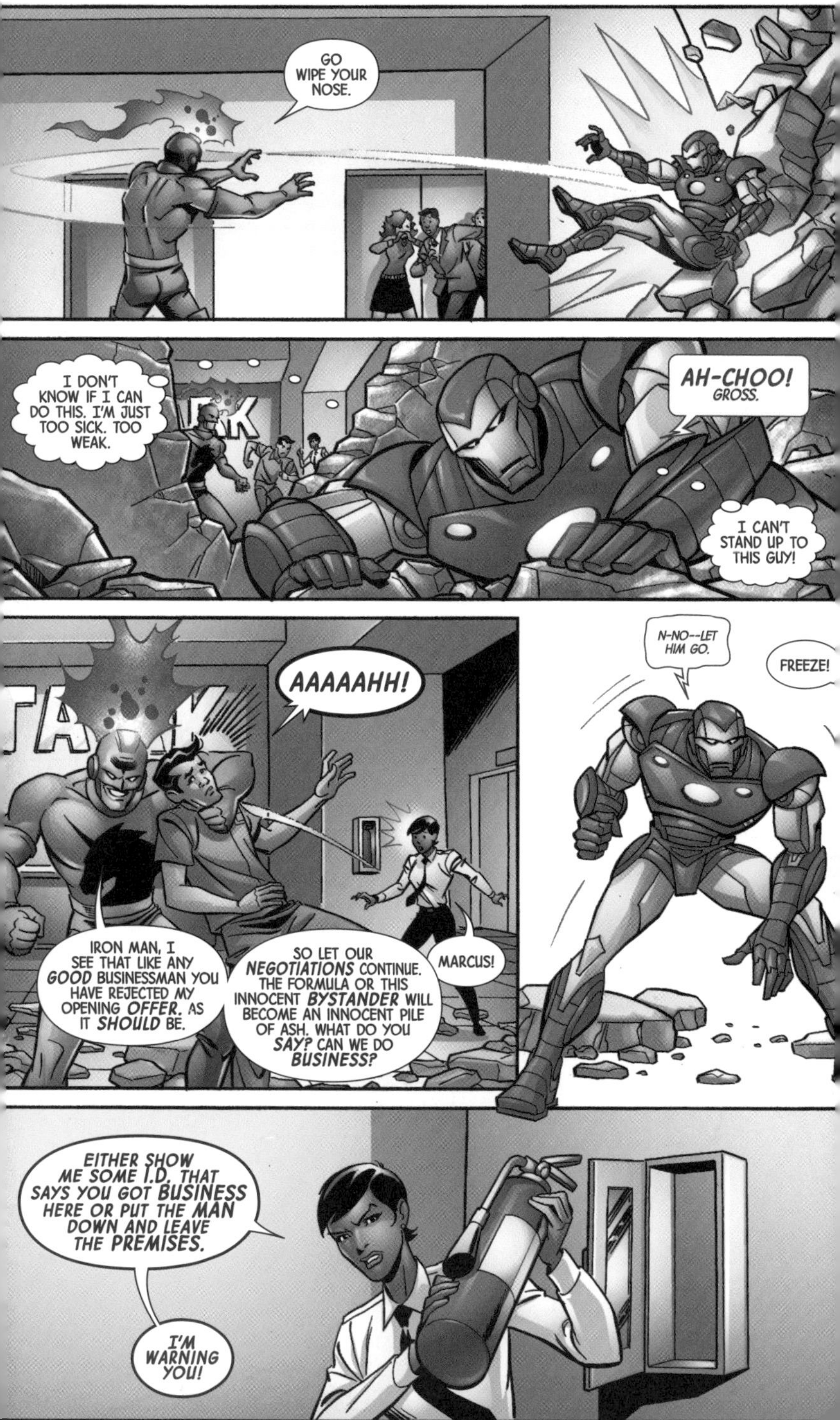

GO WIPE YOUR NOSE.
I DON'T KNOW IF I CAN DO THIS. I'M JUST TOO SICK. TOO WEAK.
AH-CHOO! GROSS.
I CAN'T STAND UP TO THIS GUY!
AAAAAHH!
IRON MAN, I SEE THAT LIKE ANY GOOD BUSINESSMAN YOU HAVE REJECTED MY OPENING OFFER. AS IT SHOULD BE.
SO LET OUR NEGOTIATIONS CONTINUE. THE FORMULA OR THIS INNOCENT BYSTANDER WILL BECOME AN INNOCENT PILE OF ASH. WHAT DO YOU SAY? CAN WE DO BUSINESS?
MARCUS!
N-NO--LET HIM GO.
FREEZE!
EITHER SHOW ME SOME I.D. THAT SAYS YOU GOT BUSINESS HERE OR PUT THE MAN DOWN AND LEAVE THE PREMISES.
I'M WARNING YOU!

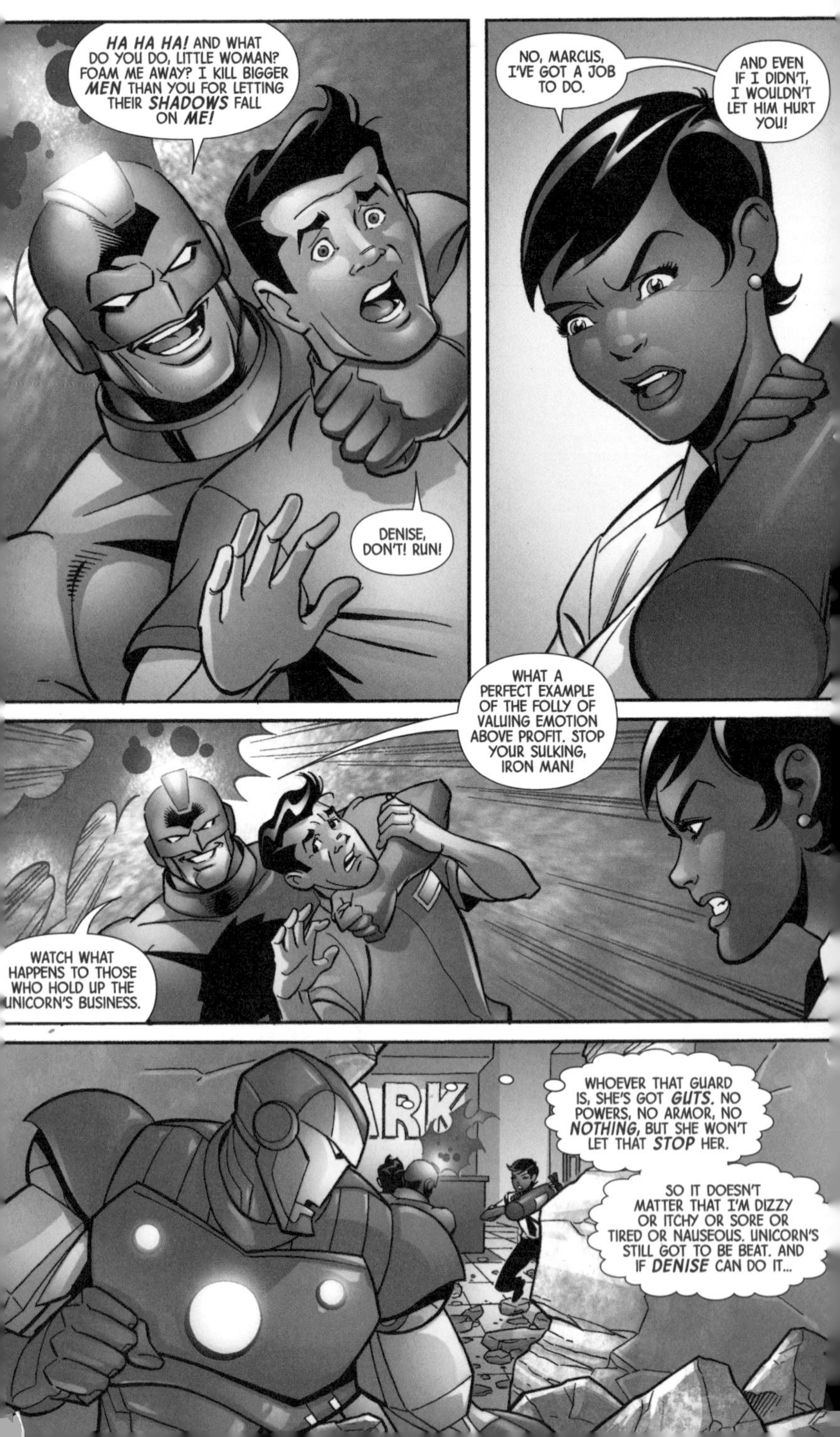
HA HA HA! AND WHAT DO YOU DO, LITTLE WOMAN? FOAM ME AWAY? I KILL BIGGER MEN THAN YOU FOR LETTING THEIR SHADOWS FALL ON ME!
DENISE, DON'T! RUN!
NO, MARCUS, I'VE GOT A JOB TO DO.
AND EVEN IF I DIDN'T, I WOULDN'T LET HIM HURT YOU!
WHAT A PERFECT EXAMPLE OF THE FOLLY OF VALUING EMOTION ABOVE PROFIT. STOP YOUR SULKING, IRON MAN!
WATCH WHAT HAPPENS TO THOSE WHO HOLD UP THE UNICORN'S BUSINESS.
WHOEVER THAT GUARD IS, SHE'S GOT GUTS. NO POWERS, NO ARMOR, NO NOTHING, BUT SHE WON'T LET THAT STOP HER.
SO IT DOESN'T MATTER THAT I'M DIZZY OR ITCHY OR SORE OR TIRED OR NAUSEOUS. UNICORN'S STILL GOT TO BE BEAT. AND IF DENISE CAN DO IT...

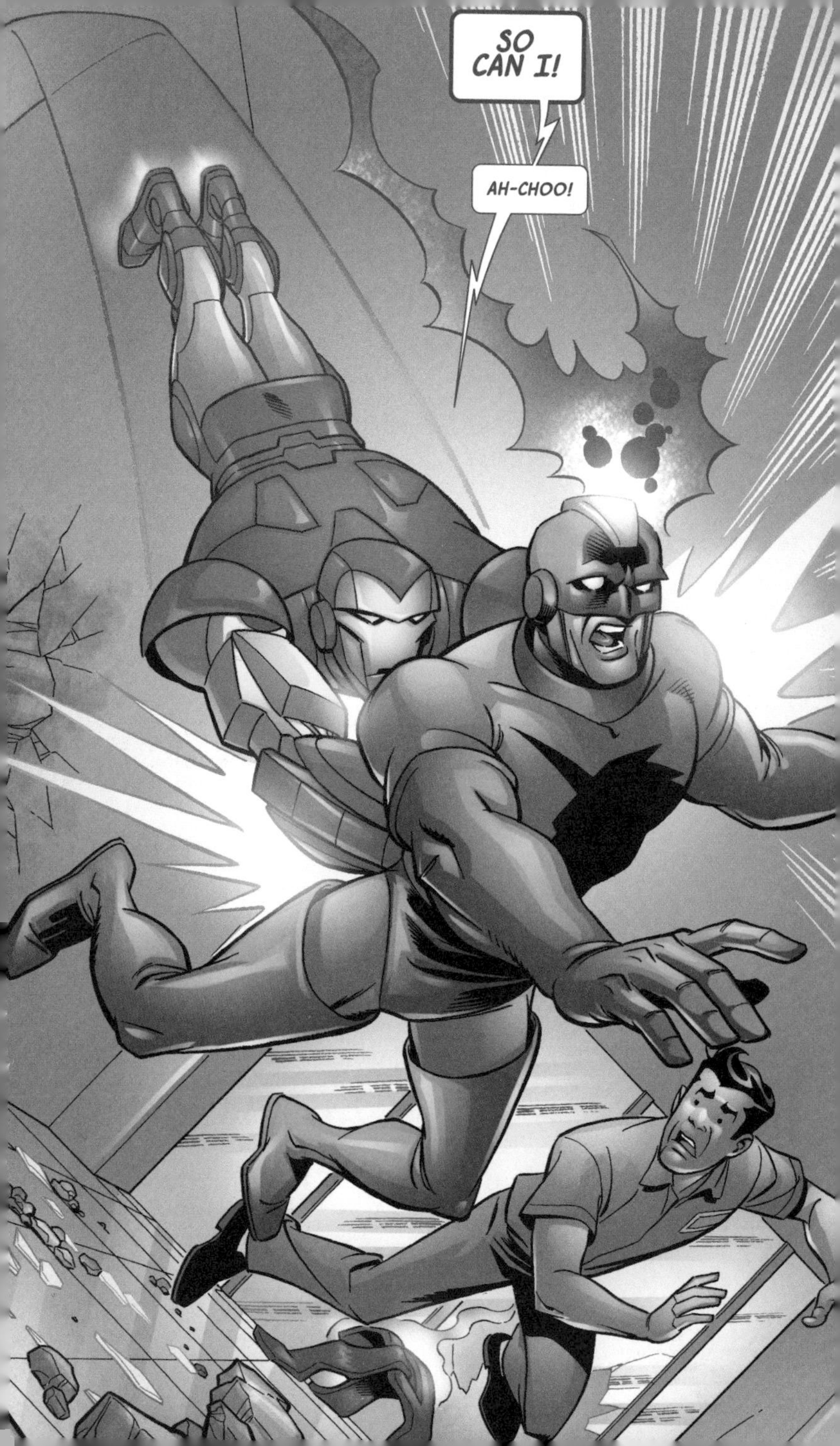

SO CAN I!
AH-CHOO!

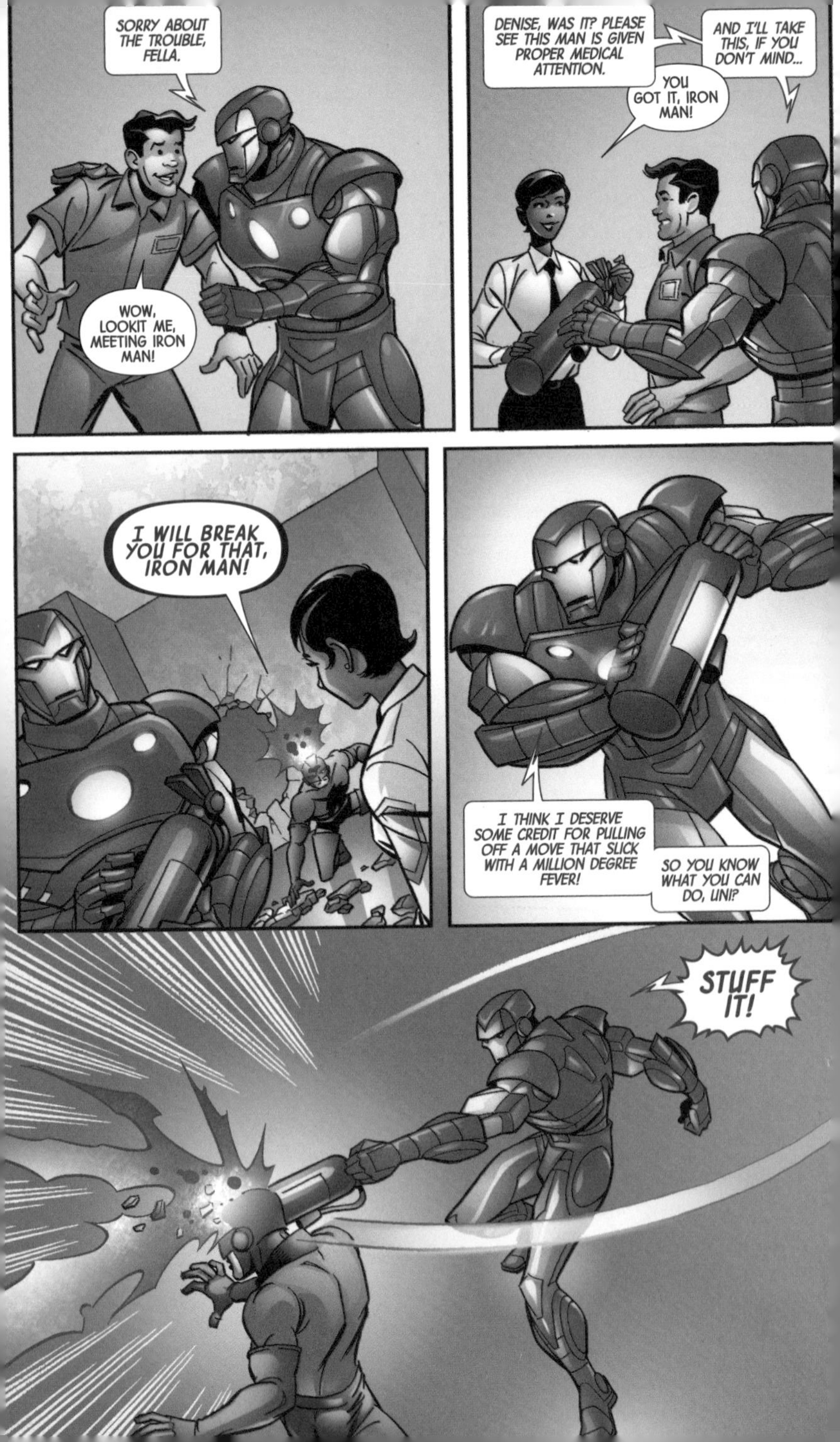
SORRY ABOUT THE TROUBLE, FELLA.
WOW, LOOKIT ME, MEETING IRON MAN!
DENISE, WAS IT? PLEASE SEE THIS MAN IS GIVEN PROPER MEDICAL ATTENTION.
YOU GOT IT, IRON MAN!
AND I'LL TAKE THIS, IF YOU DON'T MIND...
I WILL BREAK YOU FOR THAT, IRON MAN!
I THINK I DESERVE SOME CREDIT FOR PULLING OFF A MOVE THAT SLICK WITH A MILLION DEGREE FEVER!
SO YOU KNOW WHAT YOU CAN DO, UNI?
STUFF IT!

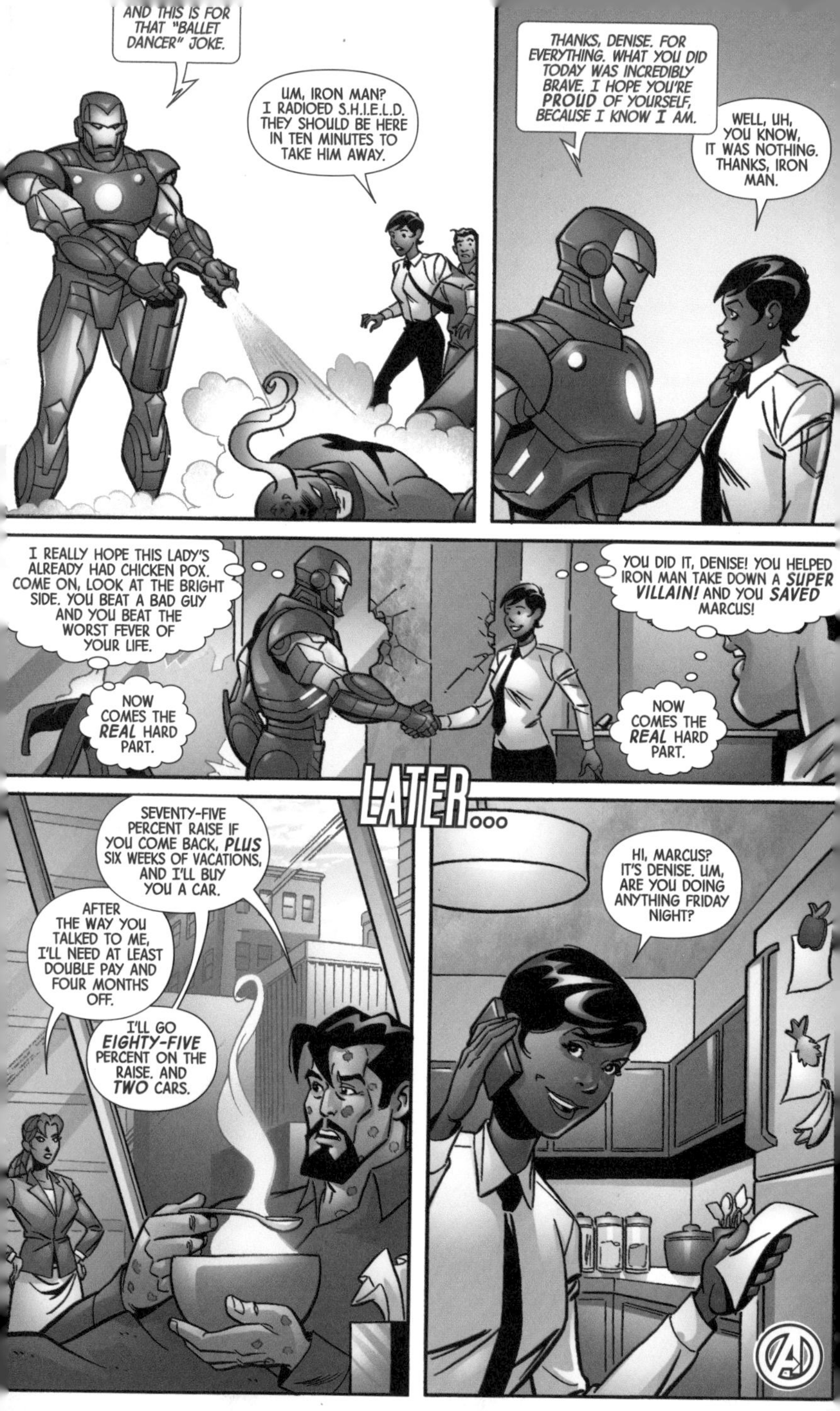
AND THIS IS FOR THAT "BALLET DANCER" JOKE.
UM, IRON MAN? I RADIOED S.H.I.E.L.D. THEY SHOULD BE HERE IN TEN MINUTES TO TAKE HIM AWAY.
THANKS, DENISE. FOR EVERYTHING. WHAT YOU DID TODAY WAS INCREDIBLY BRAVE. I HOPE YOU'RE PROUD OF YOURSELF, BECAUSE I KNOW I AM.
WELL, UH, YOU KNOW, IT WAS NOTHING. THANKS, IRON MAN.
I REALLY HOPE THIS LADY'S ALREADY HAD CHICKEN POX. COME ON, LOOK AT THE BRIGHT SIDE. YOU BEAT A BAD GUY AND YOU BEAT THE WORST FEVER OF YOUR LIFE.
NOW COMES THE REAL HARD PART.
YOU DID IT, DENISE! YOU HELPED IRON MAN TAKE DOWN A SUPER VILLAIN! AND YOU SAVED MARCUS!
NOW COMES THE REAL HARD PART.
LATER...
SEVENTY-FIVE PERCENT RAISE IF YOU COME BACK, PLUS SIX WEEKS OF VACATIONS, AND I'LL BUY YOU A CAR.
AFTER THE WAY YOU TALKED TO ME, I'LL NEED AT LEAST DOUBLE PAY AND FOUR MONTHS OFF.
I'LL GO EIGHTY-FIVE PERCENT ON THE RAISE. AND TWO CARS.
HI, MARCUS? IT'S DENISE. UM, ARE YOU DOING ANYTHING FRIDAY NIGHT?

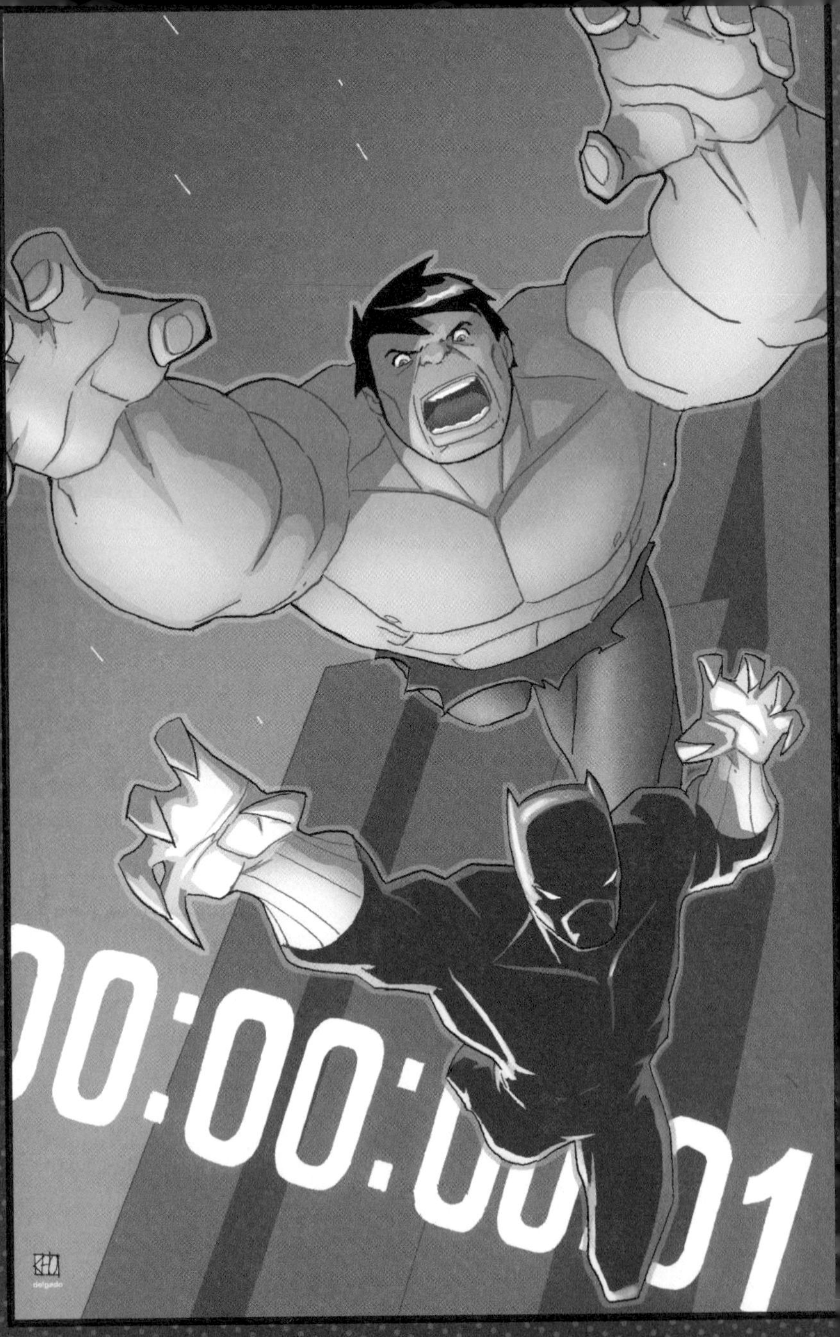
00:00:00
01

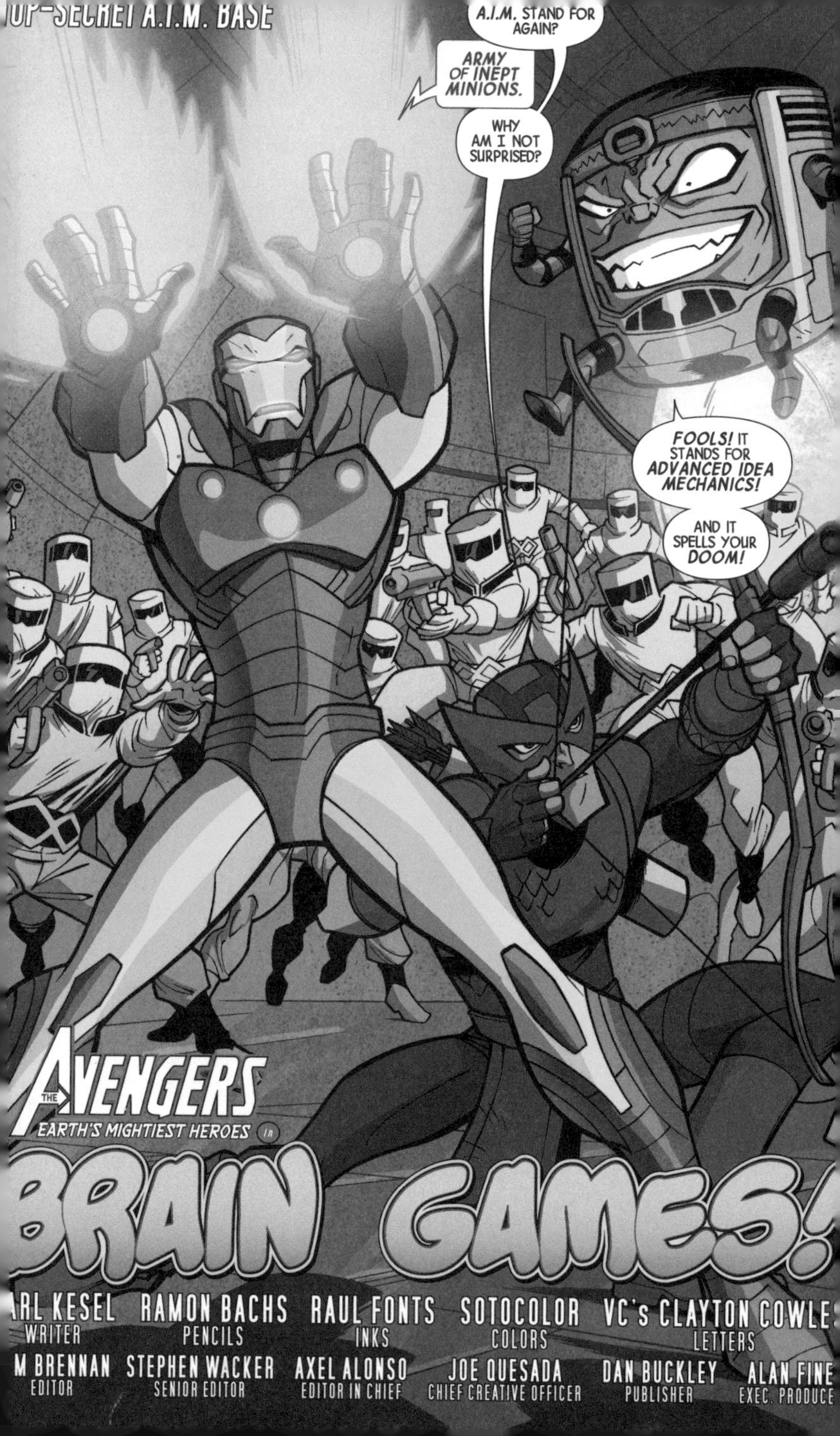
OP-SECRET A.I.M. BASE
A.I.M. STAND FOR AGAIN?
ARMY OF INEPT MINIONS.
WHY AM I NOT SURPRISED?
FOOLS! IT STANDS FOR ADVANCED IDEA MECHANICS!
AND IT SPELLS YOUR DOOM!
THE AVENGERS EARTH'S MIGHTIEST HEROES in
BRAIN GAMES!
ARL KESEL WRITER
RAMON BACHS PENCILS
RAUL FONTS INKS
SOTOCOLOR COLORS
VC's CLAYTON COWLES LETTERS
M BRENNAN EDITOR
STEPHEN WACKER SENIOR EDITOR
AXEL ALONSO EDITOR IN CHIEF
JOE QUESADA CHIEF CREATIVE OFFICER
DAN BUCKLEY PUBLISHER
ALAN FINE EXEC. PRODUCE

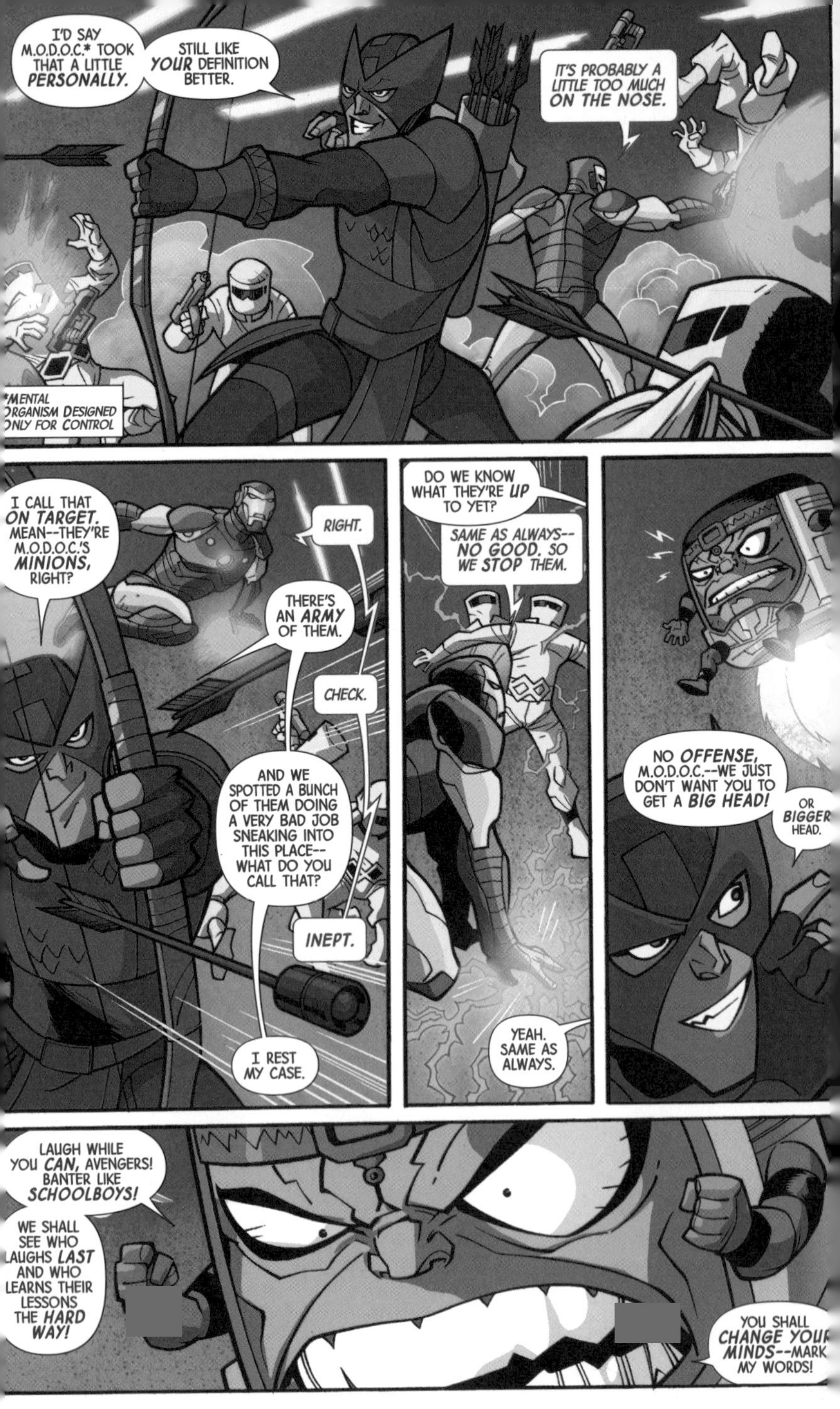
I'D SAY M.O.D.O.C.* TOOK THAT A LITTLE PERSONALLY.
STILL LIKE YOUR DEFINITION BETTER.
IT'S PROBABLY A LITTLE TOO MUCH ON THE NOSE.
*MENTAL ORGANISM DESIGNED ONLY FOR CONTROL
I CALL THAT ON TARGET. MEAN--THEY'RE M.O.D.O.C.'S MINIONS, RIGHT?
RIGHT.
THERE'S AN ARMY OF THEM.
CHECK.
AND WE SPOTTED A BUNCH OF THEM DOING A VERY BAD JOB SNEAKING INTO THIS PLACE--WHAT DO YOU CALL THAT?
INEPT.
I REST MY CASE.
DO WE KNOW WHAT THEY'RE UP TO YET?
SAME AS ALWAYS--NO GOOD. SO WE STOP THEM.
YEAH. SAME AS ALWAYS.
NO OFFENSE, M.O.D.O.C.--WE JUST DON'T WANT YOU TO GET A BIG HEAD!
OR BIGGER HEAD.
LAUGH WHILE YOU CAN, AVENGERS! BANTER LIKE SCHOOLBOYS!
WE SHALL SEE WHO LAUGHS LAST AND WHO LEARNS THEIR LESSONS THE HARD WAY!
YOU SHALL CHANGE YOUR MINDS--MARK MY WORDS!

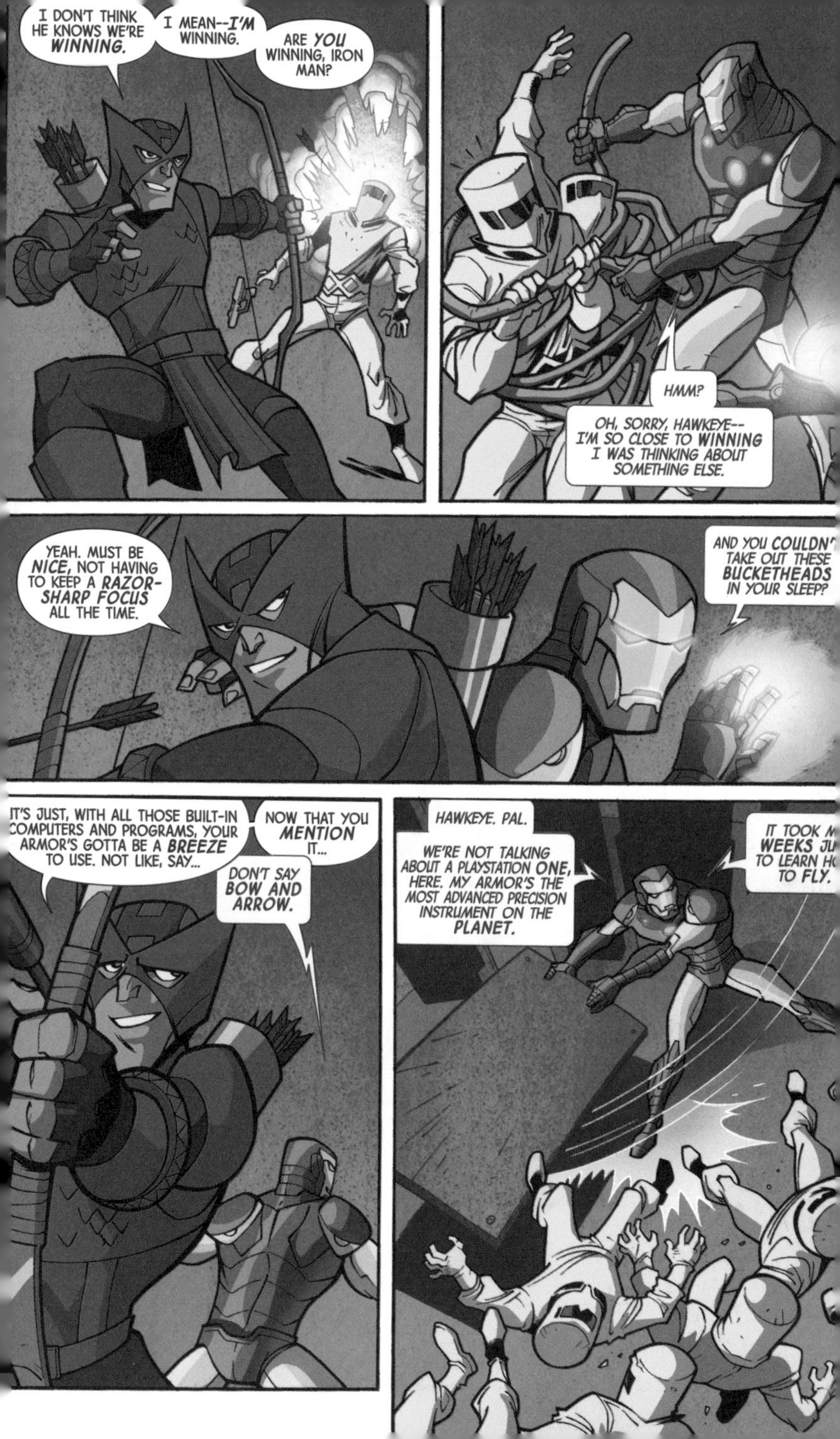
I DON'T THINK HE KNOWS WE'RE WINNING.
I MEAN--I'M WINNING.
ARE YOU WINNING, IRON MAN?
HMM?
OH, SORRY, HAWKEYE-- I'M SO CLOSE TO WINNING I WAS THINKING ABOUT SOMETHING ELSE.
YEAH. MUST BE NICE, NOT HAVING TO KEEP A RAZOR-SHARP FOCUS ALL THE TIME.
AND YOU COULDN' TAKE OUT THESE BUCKETHEADS IN YOUR SLEEP?
IT'S JUST, WITH ALL THOSE BUILT-IN COMPUTERS AND PROGRAMS, YOUR ARMOR'S GOTTA BE A BREEZE TO USE. NOT LIKE, SAY...
NOW THAT YOU MENTION IT...
DON'T SAY BOW AND ARROW.
HAWKEYE. PAL.
WE'RE NOT TALKING ABOUT A PLAYSTATION ONE, HERE. MY ARMOR'S THE MOST ADVANCED PRECISION INSTRUMENT ON THE PLANET.
IT TOOK M WEEKS JU TO LEARN H TO FLY.

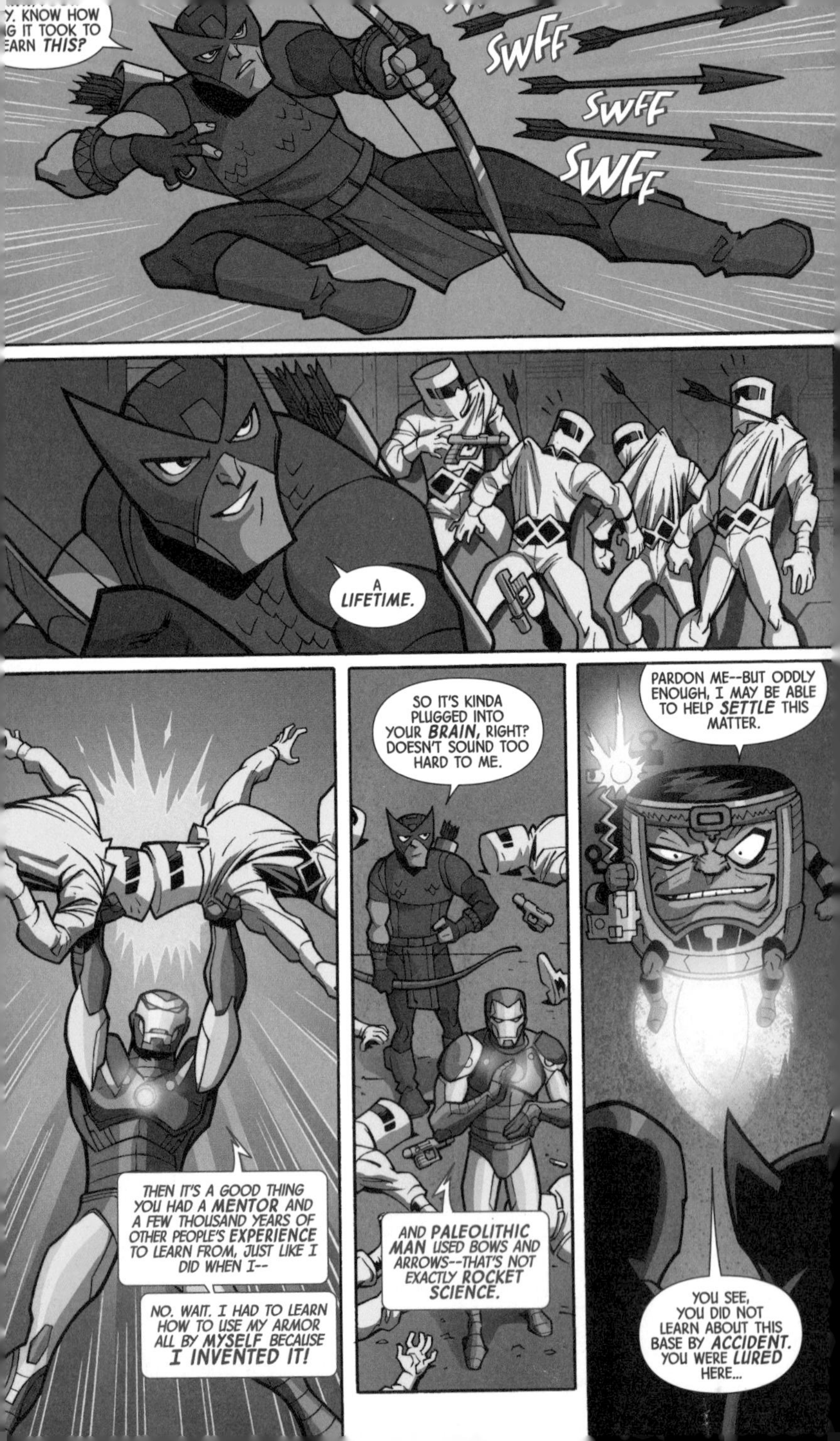
Y. KNOW HOW
G IT TOOK TO
EARN THIS?
SWFF
SWFF
SWFF
A LIFETIME.
THEN IT'S A GOOD THING YOU HAD A MENTOR AND A FEW THOUSAND YEARS OF OTHER PEOPLE'S EXPERIENCE TO LEARN FROM, JUST LIKE I DID WHEN I--
NO. WAIT. I HAD TO LEARN HOW TO USE MY ARMOR ALL BY MYSELF BECAUSE I INVENTED IT!
SO IT'S KINDA PLUGGED INTO YOUR BRAIN, RIGHT? DOESN'T SOUND TOO HARD TO ME.
AND PALEOLITHIC MAN USED BOWS AND ARROWS--THAT'S NOT EXACTLY ROCKET SCIENCE.
PARDON ME--BUT ODDLY ENOUGH, I MAY BE ABLE TO HELP SETTLE THIS MATTER.
YOU SEE, YOU DID NOT LEARN ABOUT THIS BASE BY ACCIDENT. YOU WERE LURED HERE...

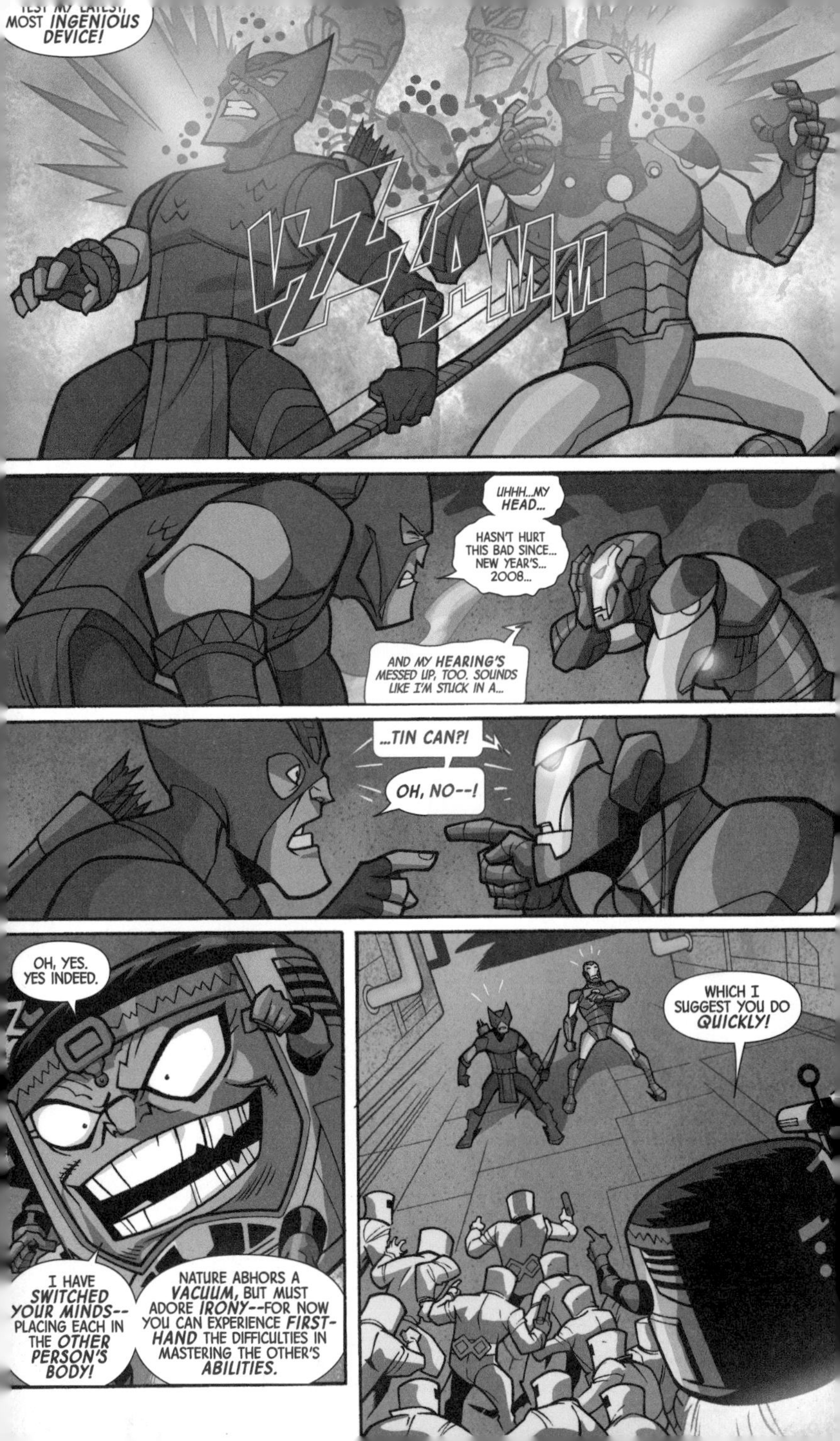
MOST INGENIOUS DEVICE!
VZZZAMM
UHHH...MY HEAD...
HASN'T HURT THIS BAD SINCE... NEW YEAR'S... 2008...
AND MY HEARING'S MESSED UP, TOO. SOUNDS LIKE I'M STUCK IN A...
...TIN CAN?!
OH, NO--!
OH, YES. YES INDEED.
I HAVE SWITCHED YOUR MINDS--PLACING EACH IN THE OTHER PERSON'S BODY!
NATURE ABHORS A VACUUM, BUT MUST ADORE IRONY--FOR NOW YOU CAN EXPERIENCE FIRST-HAND THE DIFFICULTIES IN MASTERING THE OTHER'S ABILITIES.
WHICH I SUGGEST YOU DO QUICKLY!

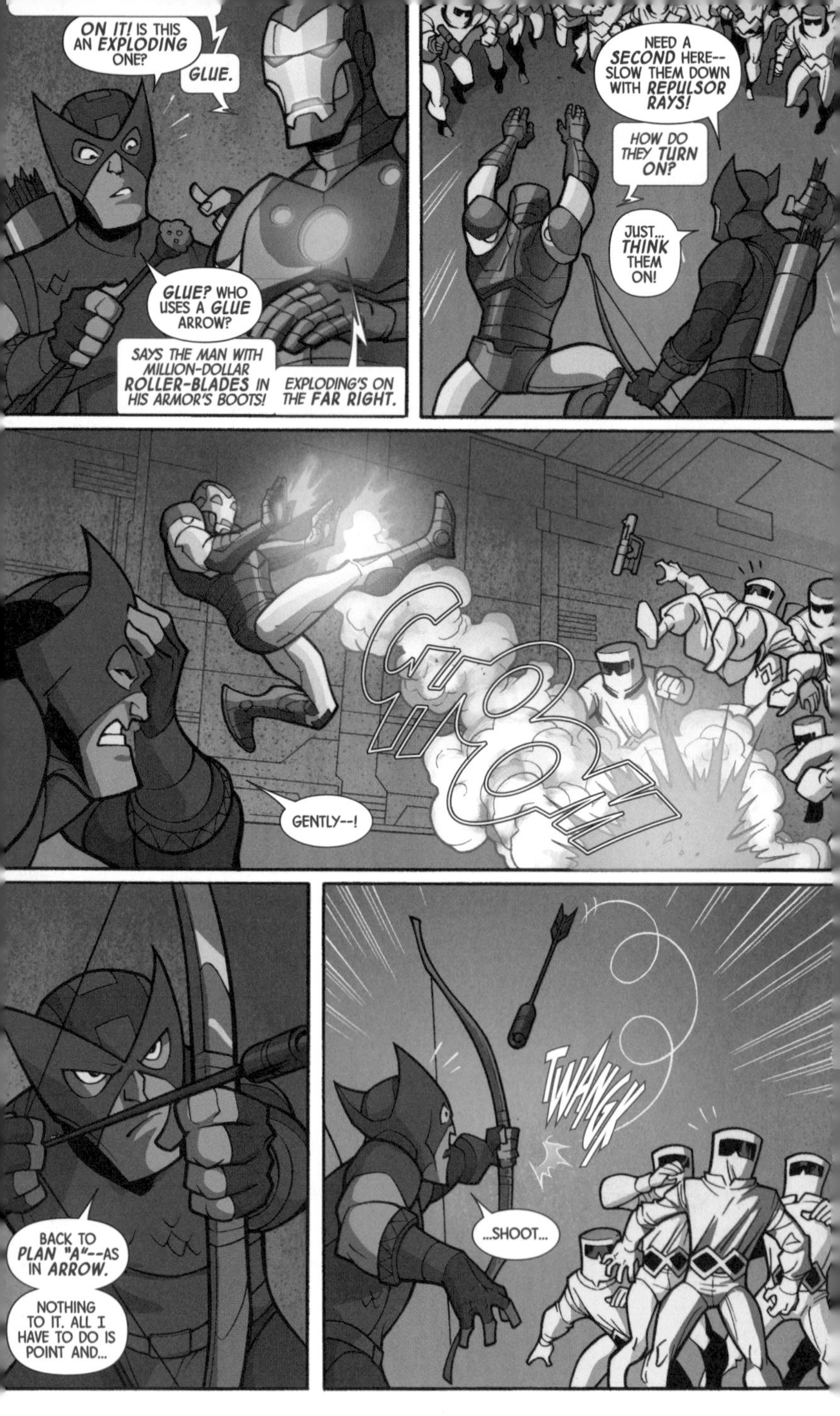
ON IT! IS THIS AN EXPLODING ONE?
GLUE.
GLUE? WHO USES A GLUE ARROW?
SAYS THE MAN WITH MILLION-DOLLAR ROLLER-BLADES IN HIS ARMOR'S BOOTS!
EXPLODING'S ON THE FAR RIGHT.
NEED A SECOND HERE--SLOW THEM DOWN WITH REPULSOR RAYS!
HOW DO THEY TURN ON?
JUST... THINK THEM ON!
GENTLY--!
BACK TO PLAN "A"--AS IN ARROW.
NOTHING TO IT. ALL I HAVE TO DO IS POINT AND...
TWANG
...SHOOT...

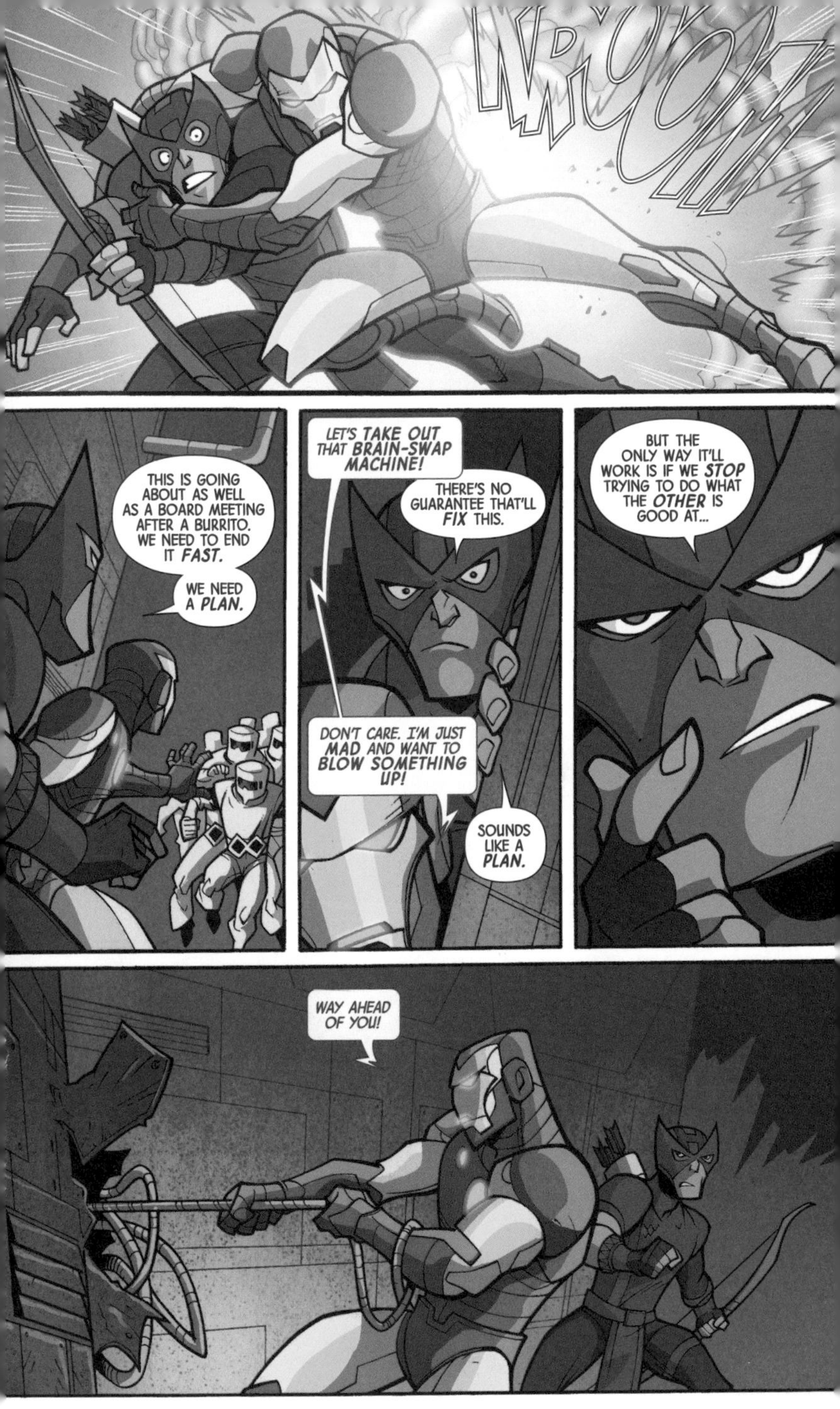
WRROOOM
THIS IS GOING ABOUT AS WELL AS A BOARD MEETING AFTER A BURRITO. WE NEED TO END IT FAST.
WE NEED A PLAN.
LET'S TAKE OUT THAT BRAIN-SWAP MACHINE!
THERE'S NO GUARANTEE THAT'LL FIX THIS.
DON'T CARE. I'M JUST MAD AND WANT TO BLOW SOMETHING UP!
SOUNDS LIKE A PLAN.
BUT THE ONLY WAY IT'LL WORK IS IF WE STOP TRYING TO DO WHAT THE OTHER IS GOOD AT...
WAY AHEAD OF YOU!

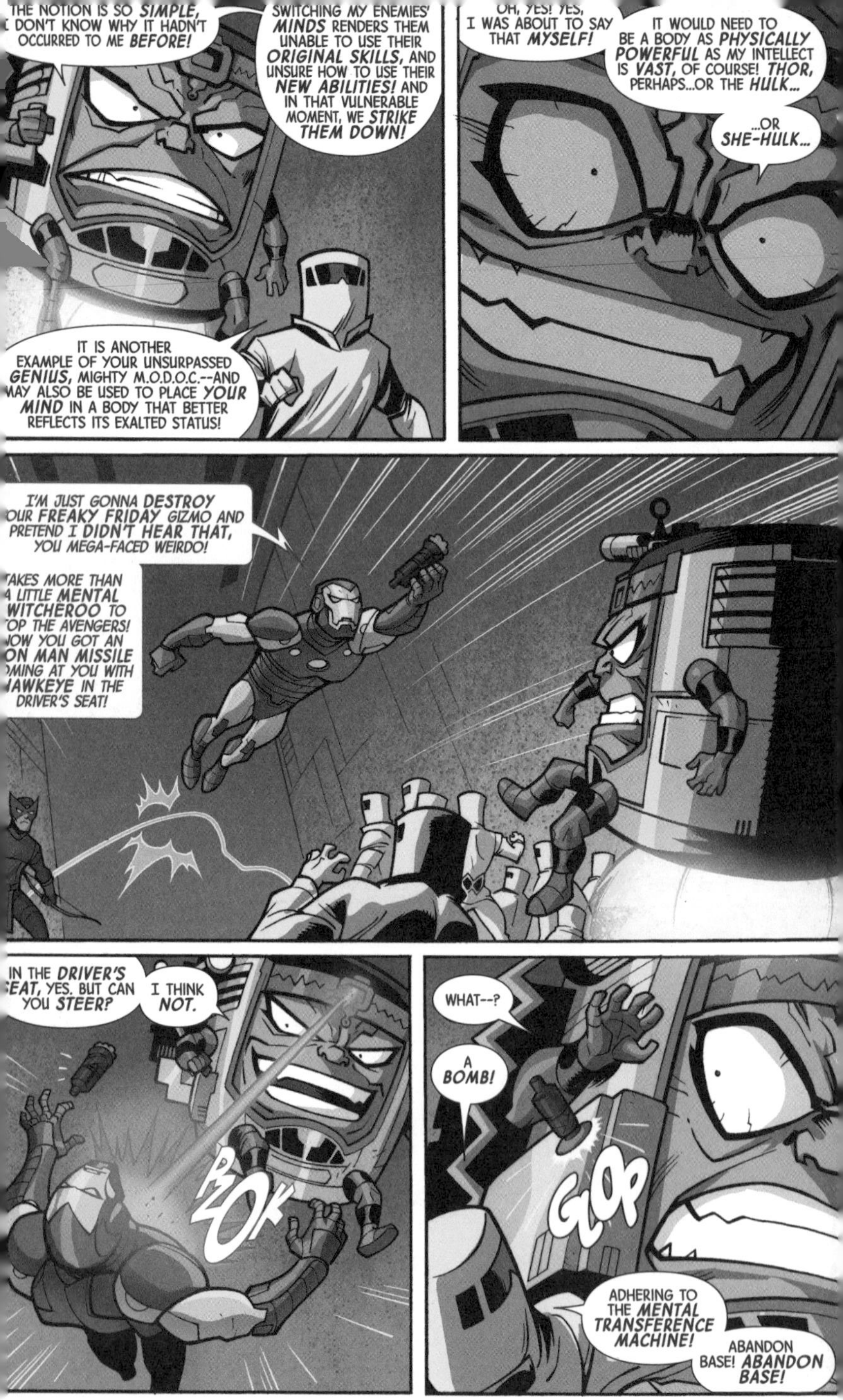
THE NOTION IS SO SIMPLE, DON'T KNOW WHY IT HADN'T OCCURRED TO ME BEFORE!
SWITCHING MY ENEMIES' MINDS RENDERS THEM UNABLE TO USE THEIR ORIGINAL SKILLS, AND UNSURE HOW TO USE THEIR NEW ABILITIES! AND IN THAT VULNERABLE MOMENT, WE STRIKE THEM DOWN!
IT IS ANOTHER EXAMPLE OF YOUR UNSURPASSED GENIUS, MIGHTY M.O.D.O.C.--AND MAY ALSO BE USED TO PLACE YOUR MIND IN A BODY THAT BETTER REFLECTS ITS EXALTED STATUS!
OH, YES! YES, I WAS ABOUT TO SAY THAT MYSELF!
IT WOULD NEED TO BE A BODY AS PHYSICALLY POWERFUL AS MY INTELLECT IS VAST, OF COURSE! THOR, PERHAPS...OR THE HULK...
...OR SHE-HULK...
I'M JUST GONNA DESTROY OUR FREAKY FRIDAY GIZMO AND PRETEND I DIDN'T HEAR THAT, YOU MEGA-FACED WEIRDO!
AKES MORE THAN A LITTLE MENTAL WITCHEROO TO OP THE AVENGERS! OW YOU GOT AN ON MAN MISSILE OMING AT YOU WITH AWKEYE IN THE DRIVER'S SEAT!
IN THE DRIVER'S EAT, YES. BUT CAN YOU STEER?
I THINK NOT.
BZOK
WHAT--?
A BOMB!
GLOP
ADHERING TO THE MENTAL TRANSFERENCE MACHINE!
ABANDON BASE! ABANDON BASE!

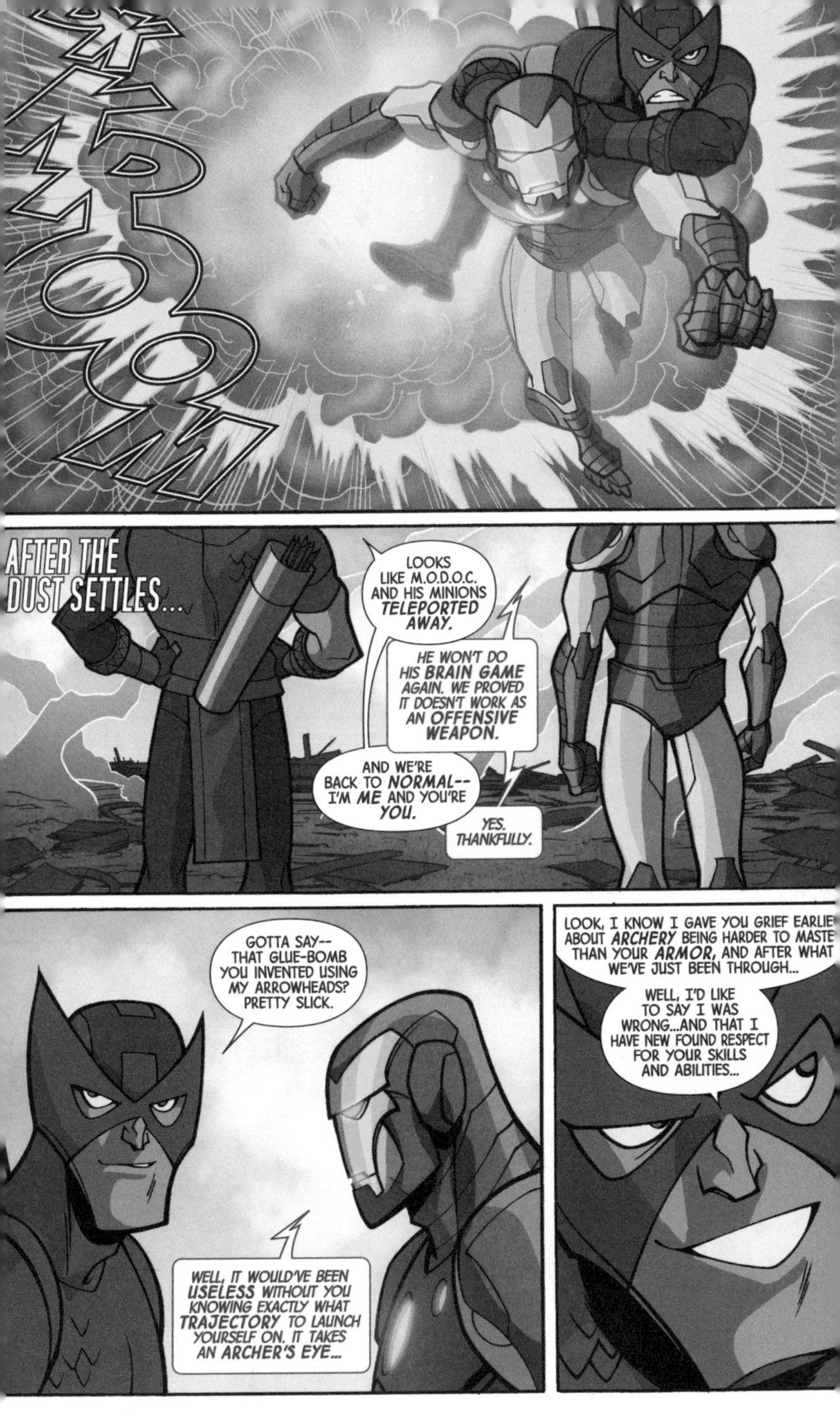

KA-THOOOOM
AFTER THE DUST SETTLES...
LOOKS LIKE M.O.D.O.C. AND HIS MINIONS TELEPORTED AWAY.
HE WON'T DO HIS BRAIN GAME AGAIN. WE PROVED IT DOESN'T WORK AS AN OFFENSIVE WEAPON.
AND WE'RE BACK TO NORMAL-- I'M ME AND YOU'RE YOU.
YES. THANKFULLY.
GOTTA SAY-- THAT GLUE-BOMB YOU INVENTED USING MY ARROWHEADS? PRETTY SLICK.
WELL, IT WOULD'VE BEEN USELESS WITHOUT YOU KNOWING EXACTLY WHAT TRAJECTORY TO LAUNCH YOURSELF ON. IT TAKES AN ARCHER'S EYE...
LOOK, I KNOW I GAVE YOU GRIEF EARLIE ABOUT ARCHERY BEING HARDER TO MASTE THAN YOUR ARMOR, AND AFTER WHAT WE'VE JUST BEEN THROUGH...
WELL, I'D LIKE TO SAY I WAS WRONG...AND THAT I HAVE NEW FOUND RESPECT FOR YOUR SKILLS AND ABILITIES...

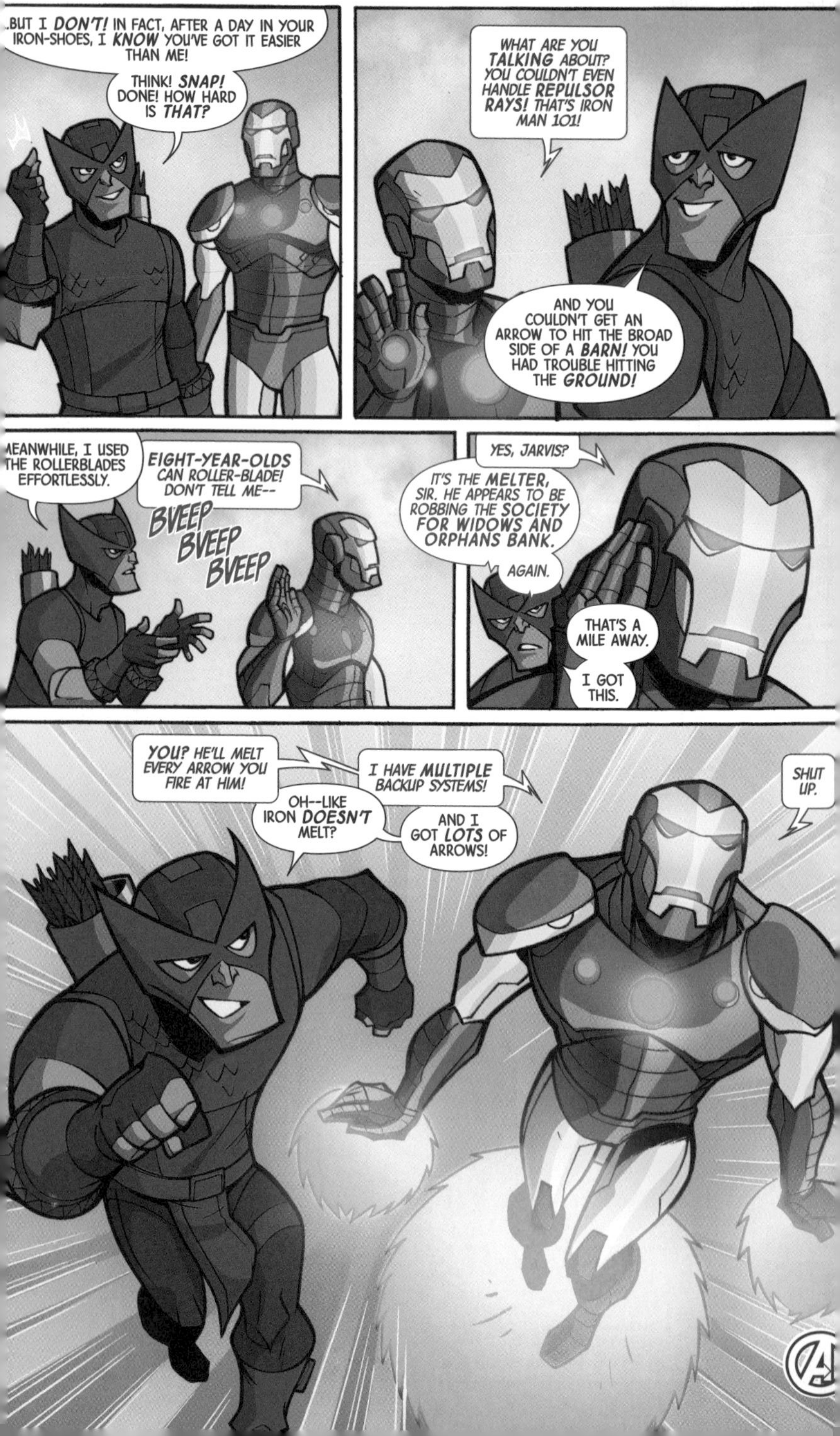
..BUT I DON'T! IN FACT, AFTER A DAY IN YOUR IRON-SHOES, I KNOW YOU'VE GOT IT EASIER THAN ME!
THINK! SNAP! DONE! HOW HARD IS THAT?
WHAT ARE YOU TALKING ABOUT? YOU COULDN'T EVEN HANDLE REPULSOR RAYS! THAT'S IRON MAN 101!
AND YOU COULDN'T GET AN ARROW TO HIT THE BROAD SIDE OF A BARN! YOU HAD TROUBLE HITTING THE GROUND!
MEANWHILE, I USED THE ROLLERBLADES EFFORTLESSLY.
EIGHT-YEAR-OLDS CAN ROLLER-BLADE! DON'T TELL ME--
BVEEP BVEEP BVEEP
YES, JARVIS?
IT'S THE MELTER, SIR. HE APPEARS TO BE ROBBING THE SOCIETY FOR WIDOWS AND ORPHANS BANK.
AGAIN.
THAT'S A MILE AWAY.
I GOT THIS.
YOU? HE'LL MELT EVERY ARROW YOU FIRE AT HIM!
I HAVE MULTIPLE BACKUP SYSTEMS!
OH--LIKE IRON DOESN'T MELT?
AND I GOT LOTS OF ARROWS!
SHUT UP.

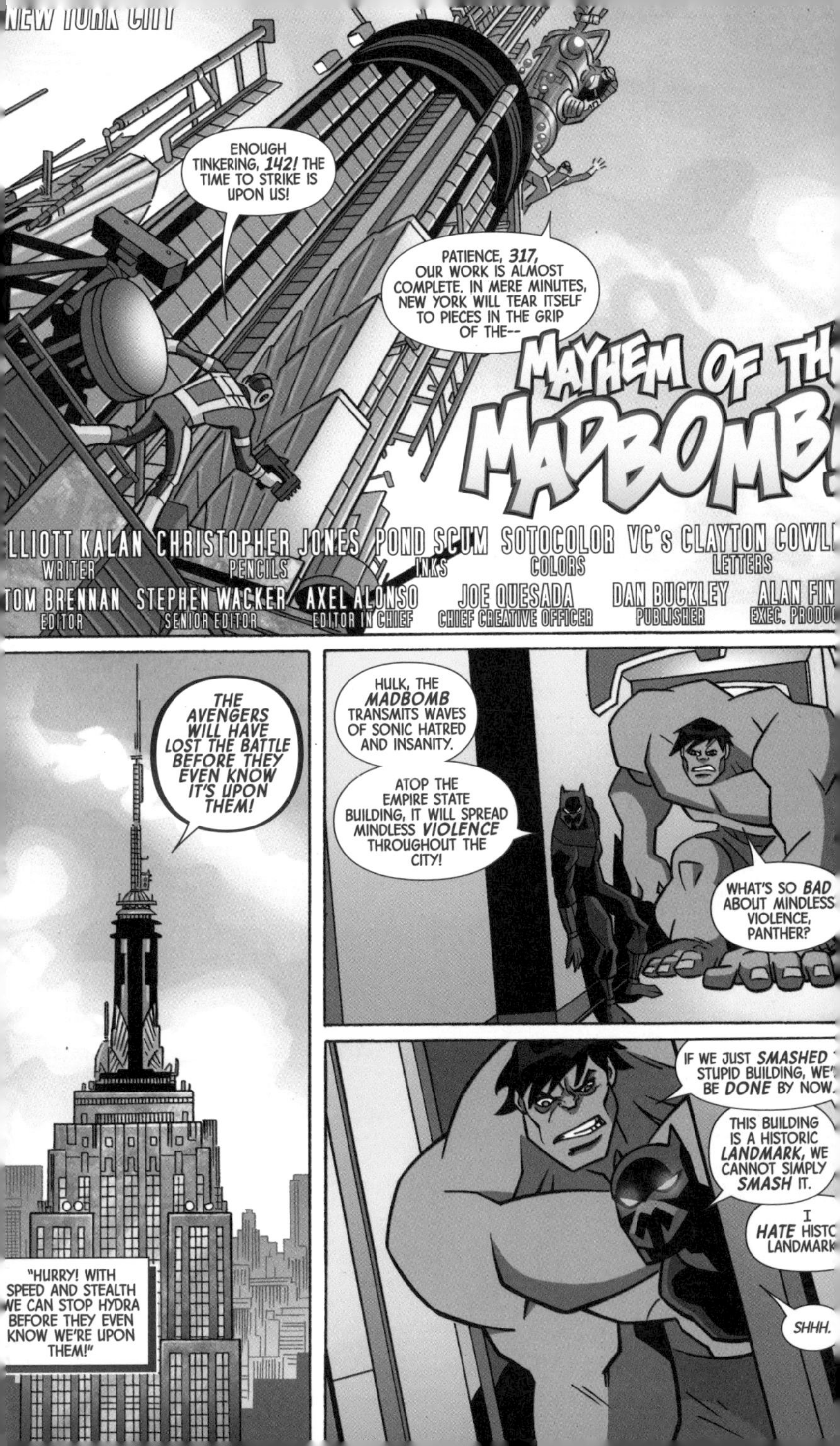
NEW YORK CITY
ENOUGH TINKERING, 142! THE TIME TO STRIKE IS UPON US!
PATIENCE, 317, OUR WORK IS ALMOST COMPLETE. IN MERE MINUTES, NEW YORK WILL TEAR ITSELF TO PIECES IN THE GRIP OF THE--
MAYHEM OF TH
MADBOMB
LLIOTT KALAN WRITER
CHRISTOPHER JONES PENCILS
POND SCUM INKS
SOTOCOLOR COLORS
VC's CLAYTON COWL LETTERS
TOM BRENNAN EDITOR
STEPHEN WACKER SENIOR EDITOR
AXEL ALONSO EDITOR IN CHIEF
JOE QUESADA CHIEF CREATIVE OFFICER
DAN BUCKLEY PUBLISHER
ALAN FIN EXEC. PRODUC
THE AVENGERS WILL HAVE LOST THE BATTLE BEFORE THEY EVEN KNOW IT'S UPON THEM!
"HURRY! WITH SPEED AND STEALTH WE CAN STOP HYDRA BEFORE THEY EVEN KNOW WE'RE UPON THEM!"
HULK, THE MADBOMB TRANSMITS WAVES OF SONIC HATRED AND INSANITY.
ATOP THE EMPIRE STATE BUILDING, IT WILL SPREAD MINDLESS VIOLENCE THROUGHOUT THE CITY!
WHAT'S SO BAD ABOUT MINDLESS VIOLENCE, PANTHER?
IF WE JUST SMASHED STUPID BUILDING, WE' BE DONE BY NOW.
THIS BUILDING IS A HISTORIC LANDMARK, WE CANNOT SIMPLY SMASH IT.
I HATE HISTO LANDMARK
SHHH.

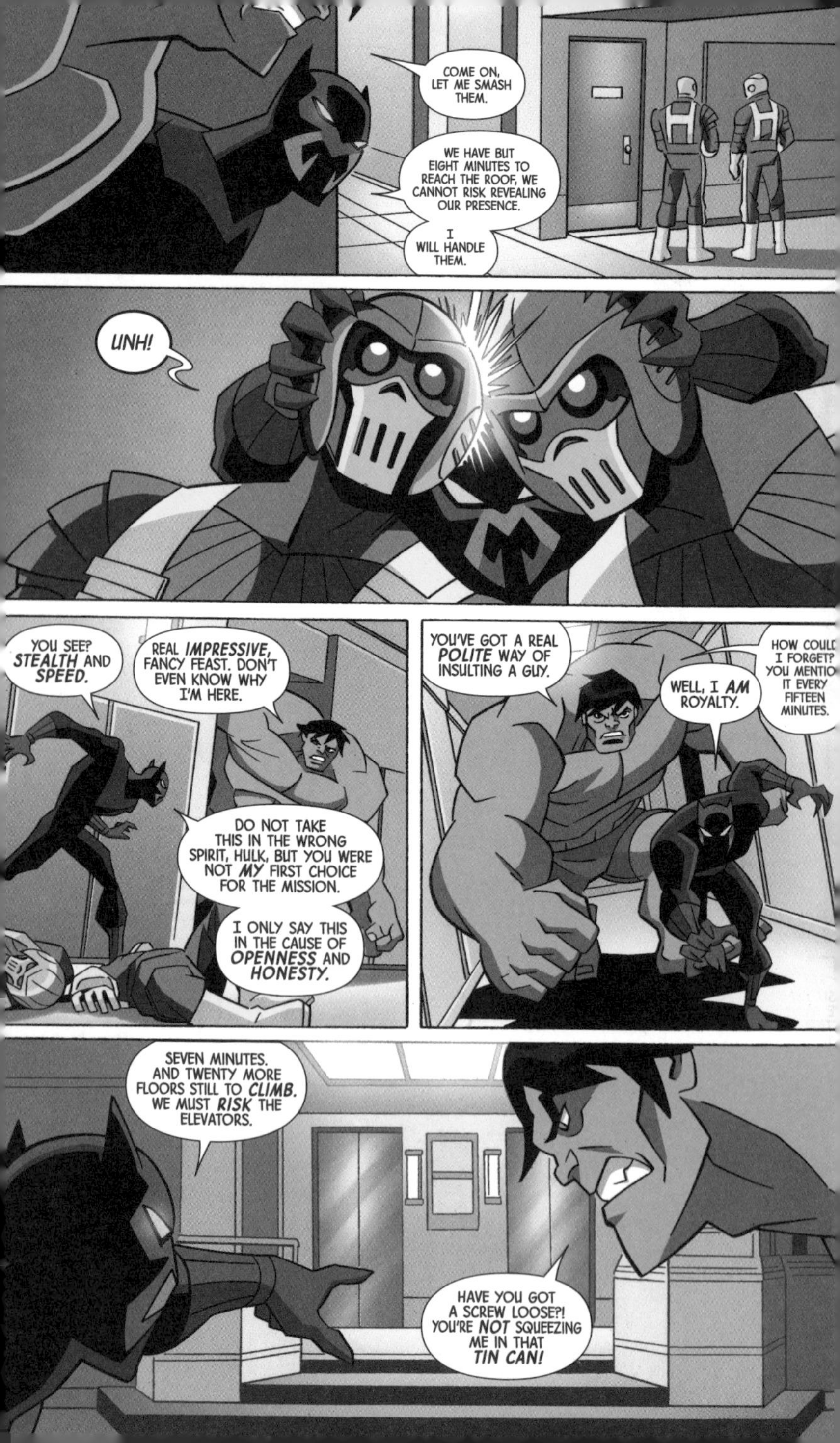
COME ON, LET ME SMASH THEM.
WE HAVE BUT EIGHT MINUTES TO REACH THE ROOF, WE CANNOT RISK REVEALING OUR PRESENCE.
I WILL HANDLE THEM.
UNH!
YOU SEE? STEALTH AND SPEED.
REAL IMPRESSIVE, FANCY FEAST. DON'T EVEN KNOW WHY I'M HERE.
DO NOT TAKE THIS IN THE WRONG SPIRIT, HULK, BUT YOU WERE NOT MY FIRST CHOICE FOR THE MISSION.
I ONLY SAY THIS IN THE CAUSE OF OPENNESS AND HONESTY.
YOU'VE GOT A REAL POLITE WAY OF INSULTING A GUY.
WELL, I AM ROYALTY.
SEVEN MINUTES. AND TWENTY MORE FLOORS STILL TO CLIMB. WE MUST RISK THE ELEVATORS.
HAVE YOU GOT A SCREW LOOSE?! YOU'RE NOT SQUEEZING ME IN THAT TIN CAN!

HAWKEYE APPRECIATES *STEALTH*, BUT HE'S UNDERCOVER IN THE RINGMASTER'S *CIRCUS OF CRIME*.

BLACK WIDOW IS AN INFILTRATION EXPERT, BUT SHE'S SHUTTING DOWN THE TASKMASTER'S SUPER VILLAIN ACADEMY.

IT'S LIKE YOU *WANT* ME TO SMASH YOU.

DING

ANT-MAN AND WASP ARE IDEAL FOR *QUIET* RAIDS, BUT THEY'RE DISARMING COUNT NEFARIA AND MADAME MASQUE.

WHOA!

PLEASE LET ME TAKE THESE GUYS OUT.

NO NEED!

OOF!

NUMBER 407, WHO WAS IN THE ELEVATOR?

FALSE ALARM. AN AUTOMATIC PROGRAM, *NOTHING* MORE.

SIX MINUTES. WE MUST MOVE FASTER. PLEASE TRY TO KEEP UP.

OKAY, THAT'S IT, PUSS N' BOOTS. I DON'T CARE ABOUT ANY MADBOMB.

I'M MAD ENOUGH RIGHT NOW!

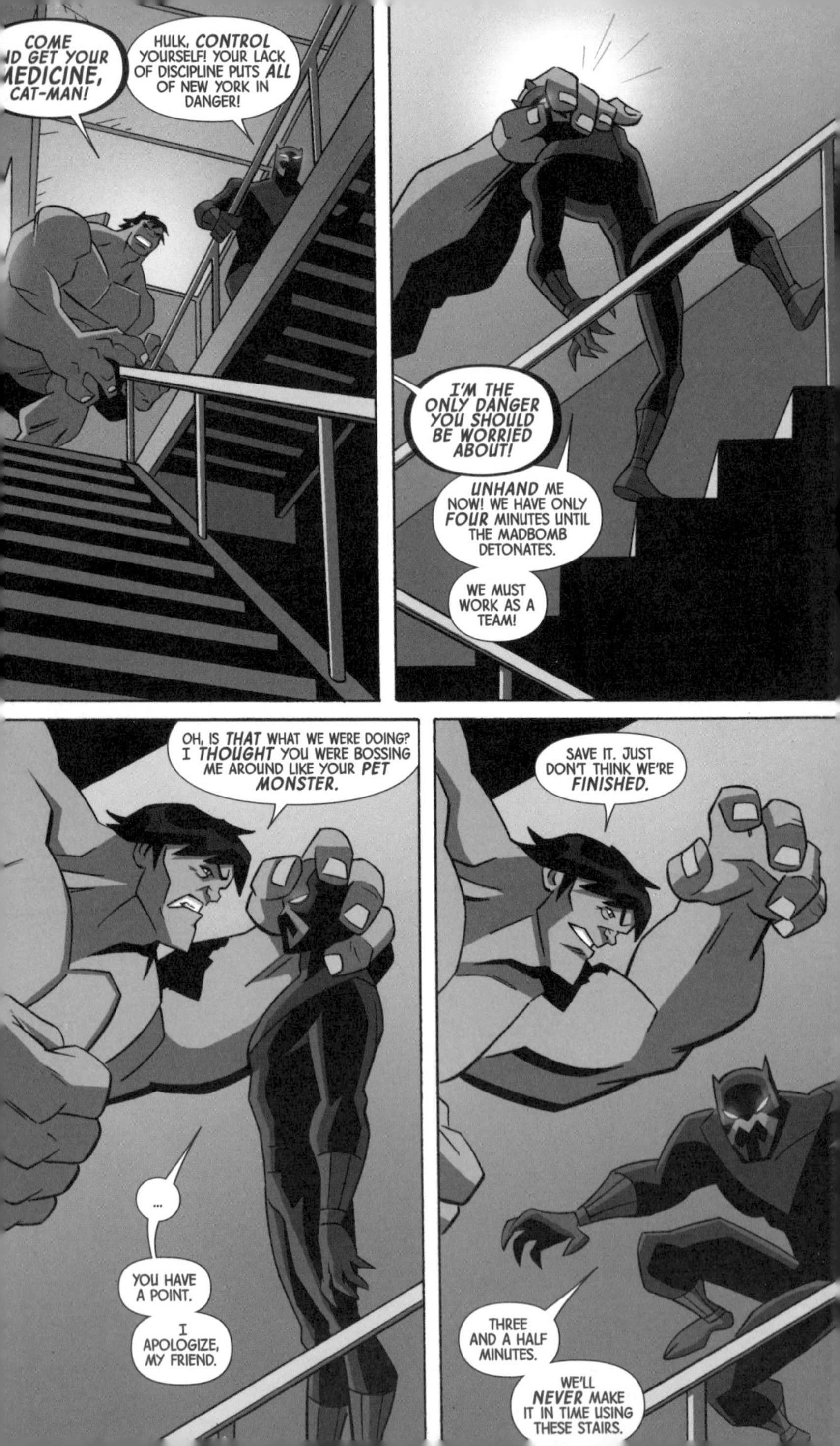

COME
ID GET YOUR
MEDICINE,
CAT-MAN!
HULK, CONTROL YOURSELF! YOUR LACK OF DISCIPLINE PUTS ALL OF NEW YORK IN DANGER!
I'M THE ONLY DANGER YOU SHOULD BE WORRIED ABOUT!
UNHAND ME NOW! WE HAVE ONLY FOUR MINUTES UNTIL THE MADBOMB DETONATES.
WE MUST WORK AS A TEAM!
OH, IS THAT WHAT WE WERE DOING? I THOUGHT YOU WERE BOSSING ME AROUND LIKE YOUR PET MONSTER.
...
YOU HAVE A POINT.
I APOLOGIZE, MY FRIEND.
SAVE IT. JUST DON'T THINK WE'RE FINISHED.
THREE AND A HALF MINUTES.
WE'LL NEVER MAKE IT IN TIME USING THESE STAIRS.

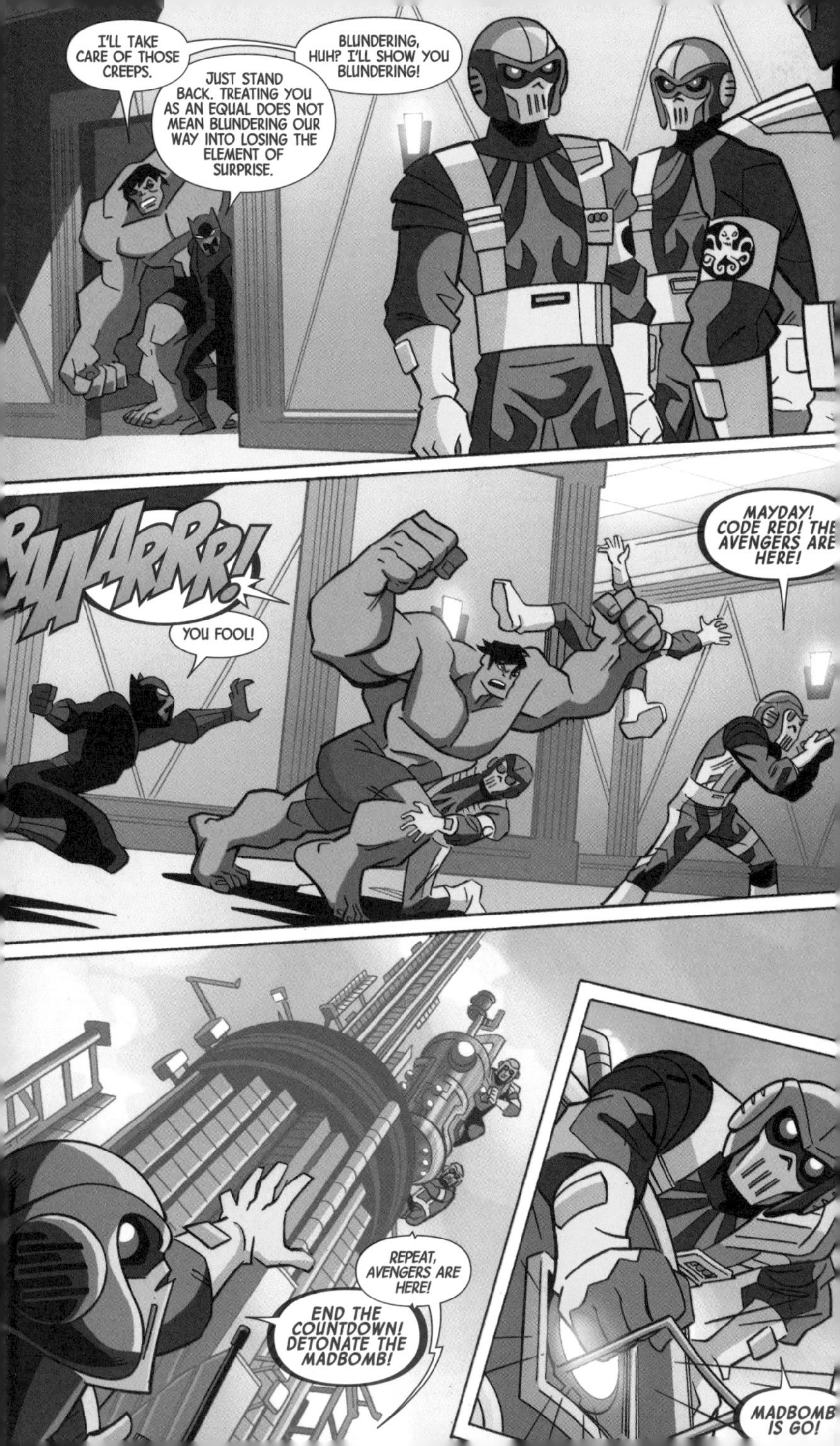

I'LL TAKE CARE OF THOSE CREEPS.
JUST STAND BACK. TREATING YOU AS AN EQUAL DOES NOT MEAN BLUNDERING OUR WAY INTO LOSING THE ELEMENT OF SURPRISE.
BLUNDERING, HUH? I'LL SHOW YOU BLUNDERING!
BWAARRR!
YOU FOOL!
MAYDAY! CODE RED! THE AVENGERS ARE HERE!
REPEAT, AVENGERS ARE HERE!
END THE COUNTDOWN! DETONATE THE MADBOMB!
MADBOMB IS GO!

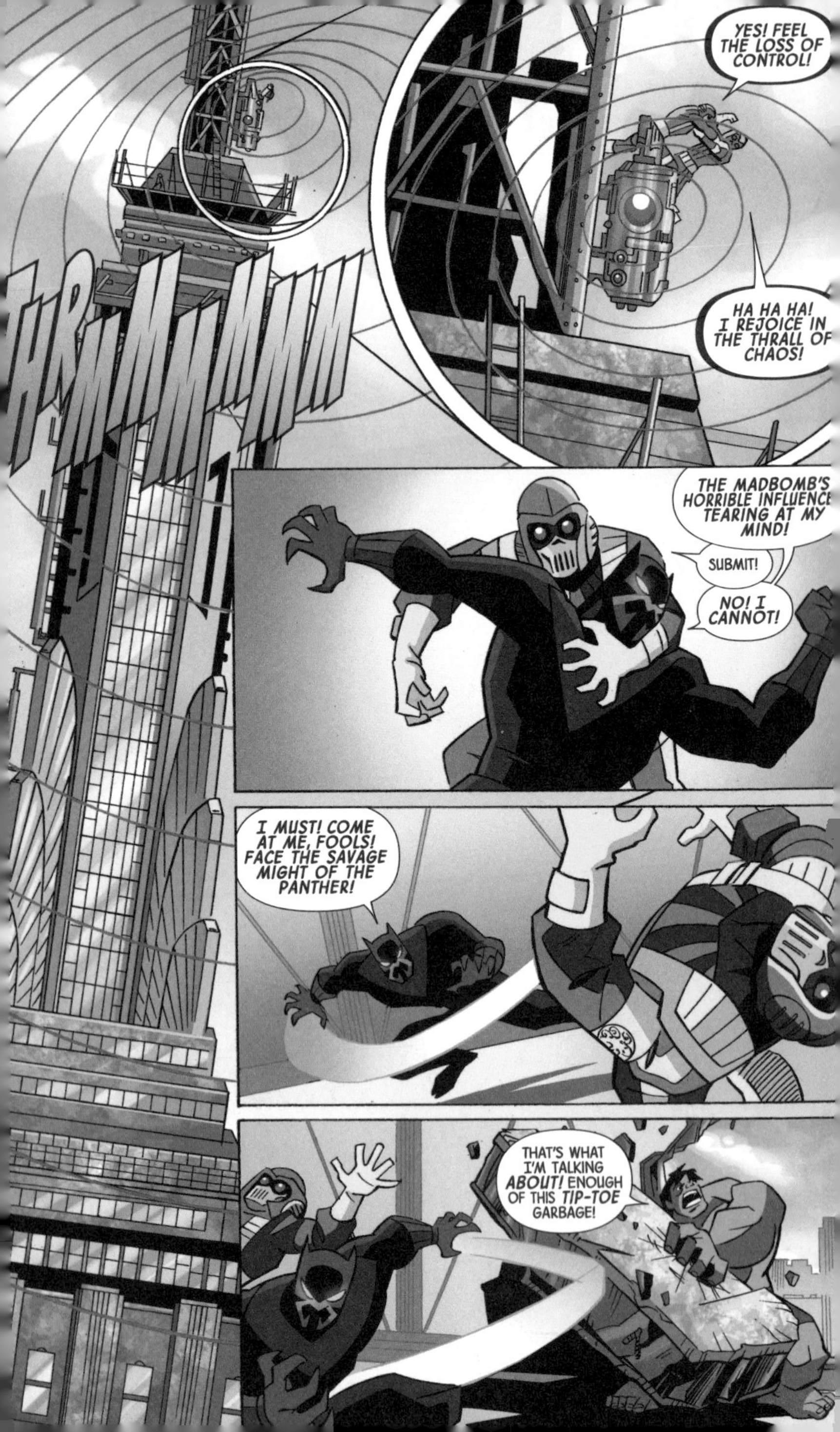
THRMMMMMMMMM
YES! FEEL THE LOSS OF CONTROL!
HA HA HA! I REJOICE IN THE THRALL OF CHAOS!
THE MADBOMB'S HORRIBLE INFLUENCE TEARING AT MY MIND!
SUBMIT!
NO! I CANNOT!
I MUST! COME AT ME, FOOLS! FACE THE SAVAGE MIGHT OF THE PANTHER!
THAT'S WHAT I'M TALKING ABOUT! ENOUGH OF THIS TIP-TOE GARBAGE!

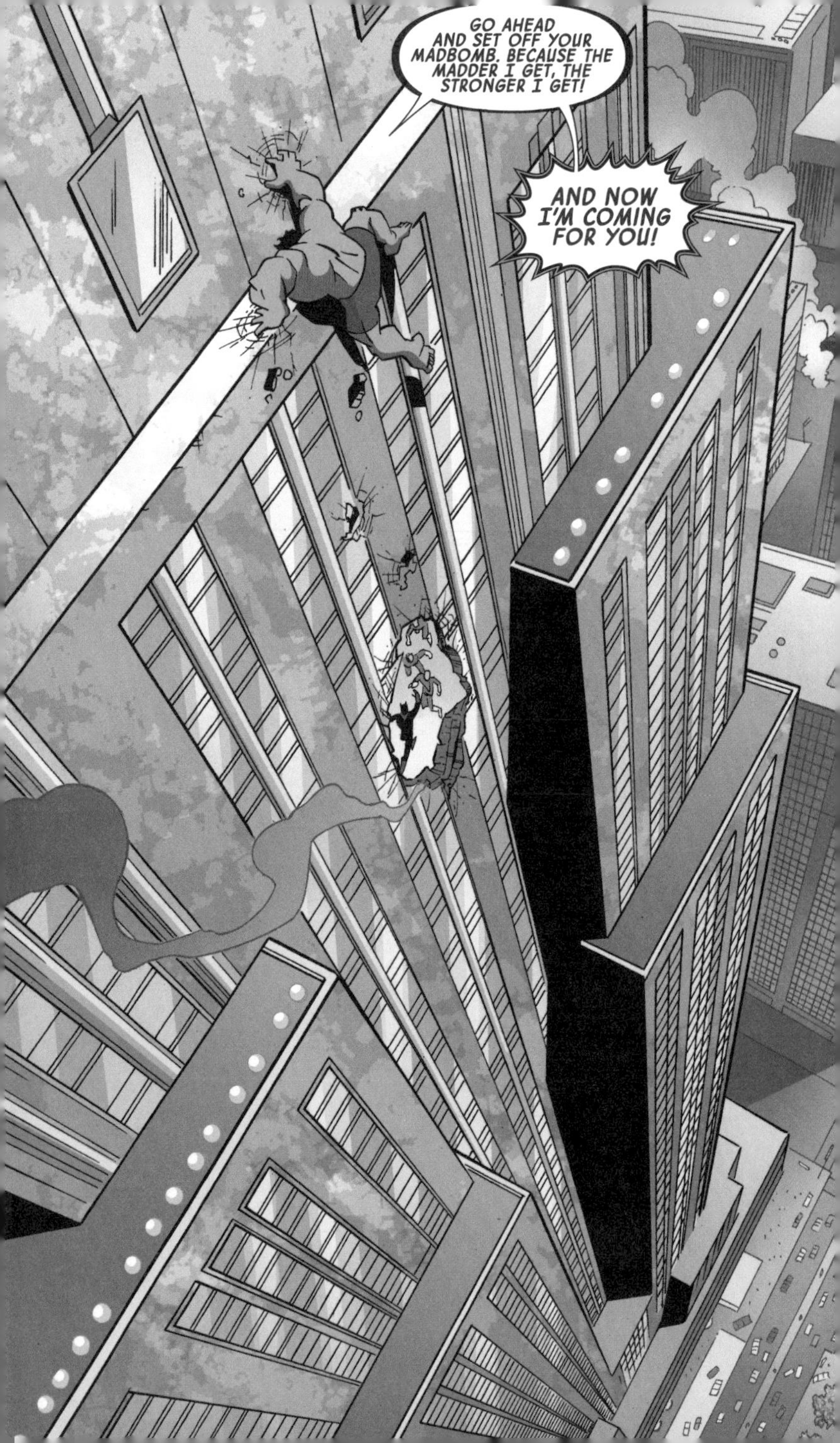
GO AHEAD AND SET OFF YOUR MADBOMB. BECAUSE THE MADDER I GET, THE STRONGER I GET!
AND NOW I'M COMING FOR YOU!

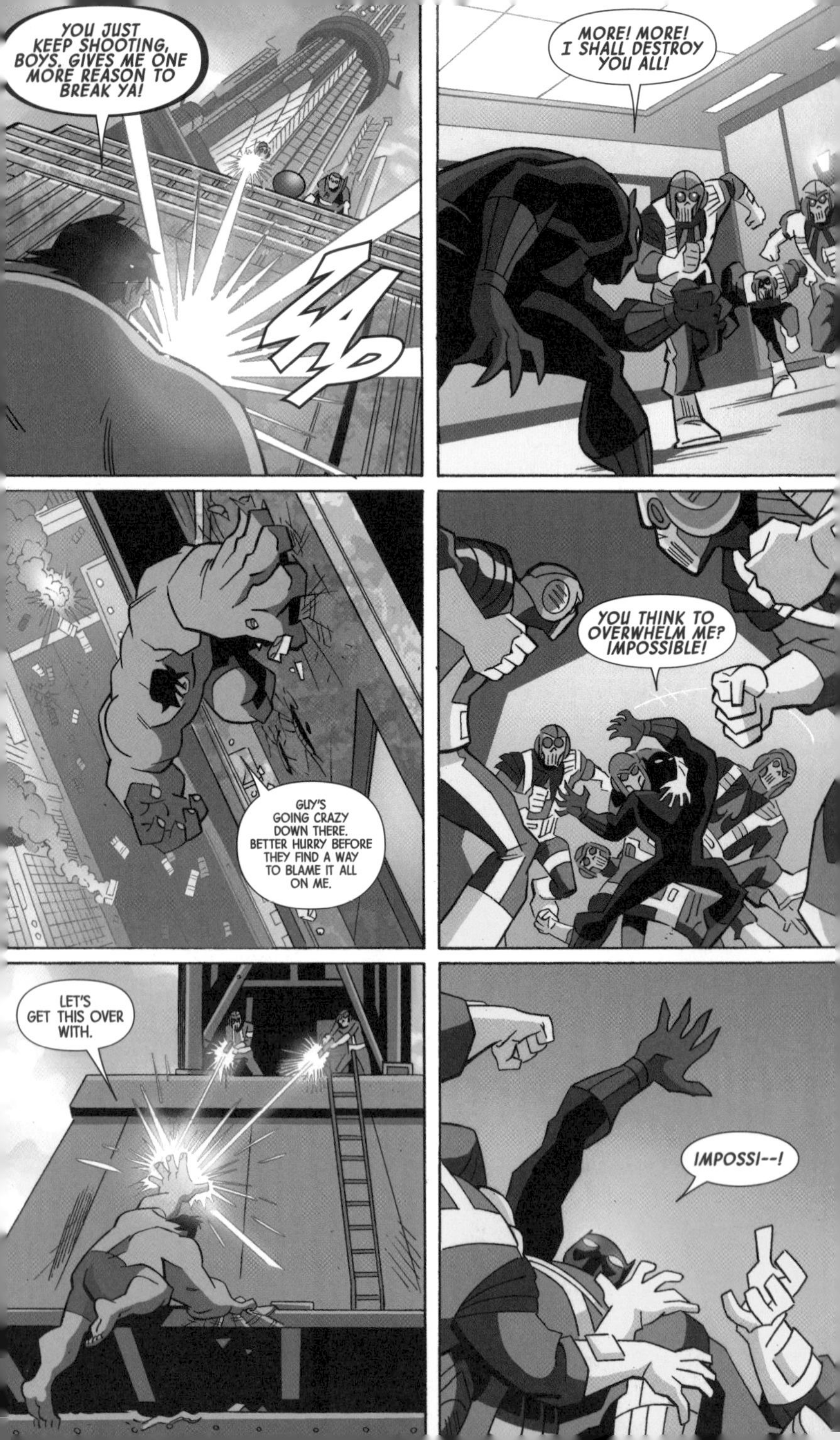
YOU JUST KEEP SHOOTING, BOYS. GIVES ME ONE MORE REASON TO BREAK YA!
ZAP
MORE! MORE! I SHALL DESTROY YOU ALL!
GUY'S GOING CRAZY DOWN THERE. BETTER HURRY BEFORE THEY FIND A WAY TO BLAME IT ALL ON ME.
YOU THINK TO OVERWHELM ME? IMPOSSIBLE!
LET'S GET THIS OVER WITH.
IMPOSSI--!

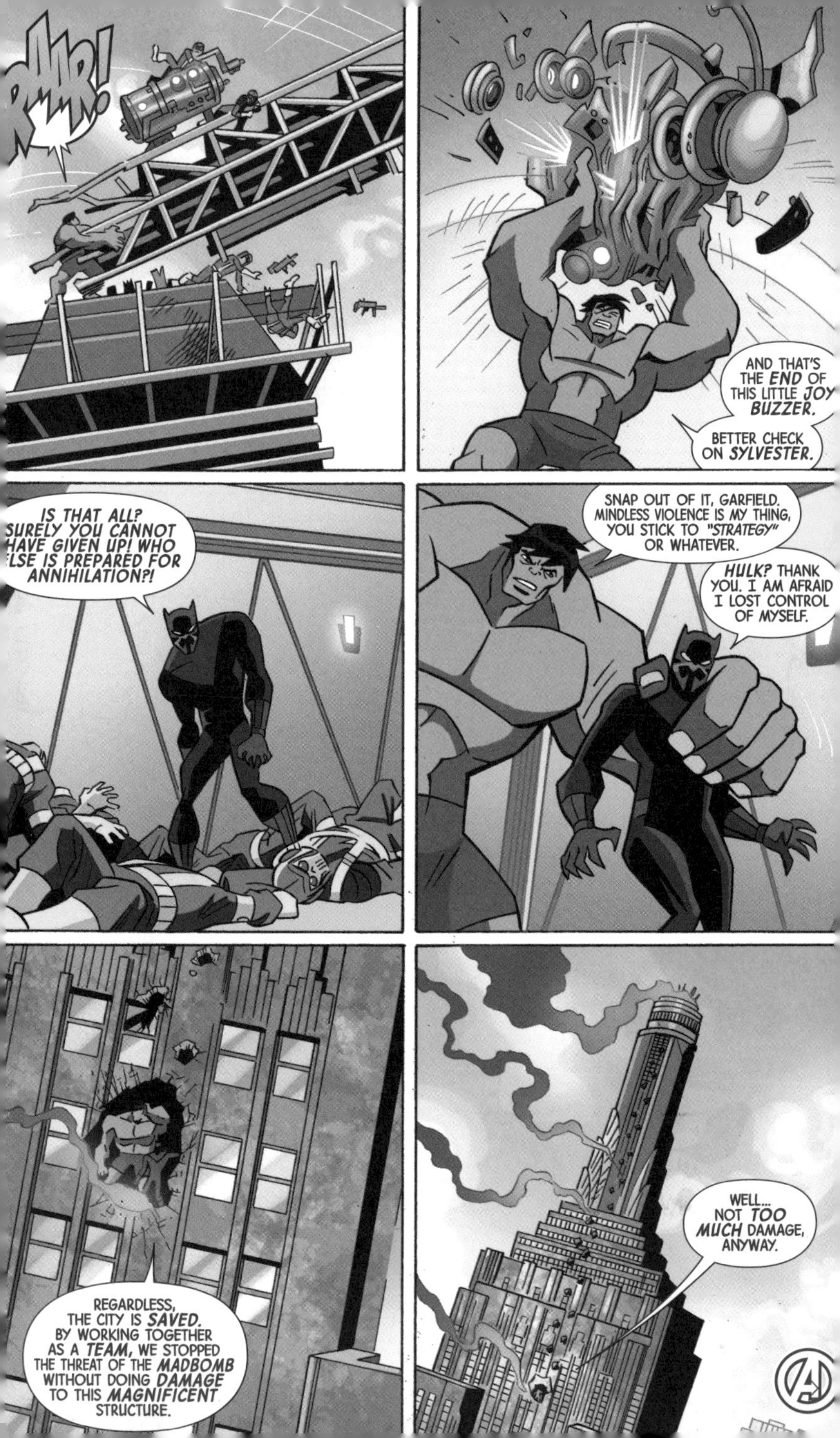
RAAR!
AND THAT'S THE END OF THIS LITTLE JOY BUZZER.
BETTER CHECK ON SYLVESTER.
IS THAT ALL? SURELY YOU CANNOT HAVE GIVEN UP! WHO ELSE IS PREPARED FOR ANNIHILATION?!
SNAP OUT OF IT, GARFIELD. MINDLESS VIOLENCE IS MY THING, YOU STICK TO "STRATEGY" OR WHATEVER.
HULK? THANK YOU. I AM AFRAID I LOST CONTROL OF MYSELF.
REGARDLESS, THE CITY IS SAVED. BY WORKING TOGETHER AS A TEAM, WE STOPPED THE THREAT OF THE MADBOMB WITHOUT DOING DAMAGE TO THIS MAGNIFICENT STRUCTURE.
WELL... NOT TOO MUCH DAMAGE, ANYWAY.

MARVEL UNIVERSE PRESENTS: # MINI-HULKS IN HULK SWIM TEAM

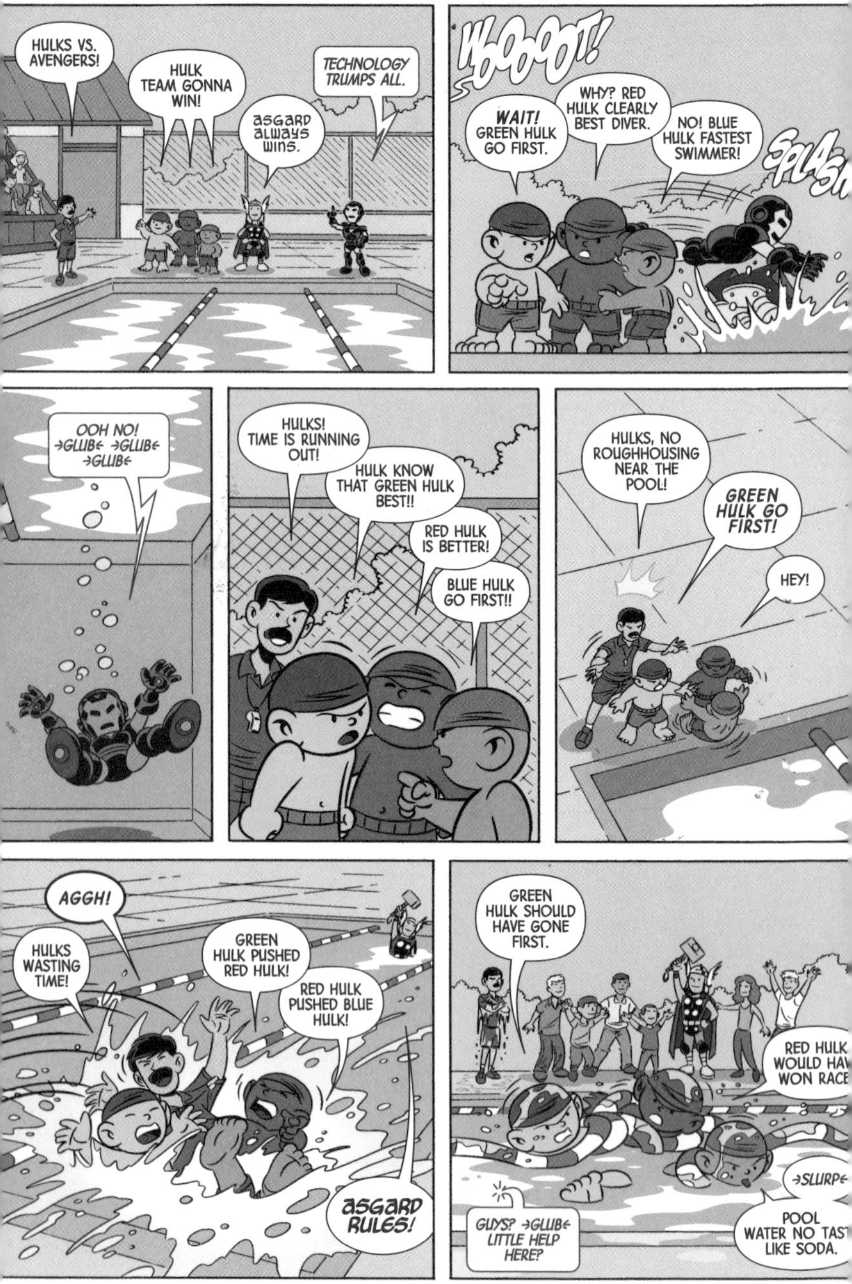

HULKS VS. AVENGERS!
HULK TEAM GONNA WIN!
asgard always wins.
TECHNOLOGY TRUMPS ALL.
WOOOOT!
WAIT! GREEN HULK GO FIRST.
WHY? RED HULK CLEARLY BEST DIVER.
NO! BLUE HULK FASTEST SWIMMER!
SPLAS
OOH NO! →GLUB← →GLUB← →GLUB←
HULKS! TIME IS RUNNING OUT!
HULK KNOW THAT GREEN HULK BEST!!
RED HULK IS BETTER!
BLUE HULK GO FIRST!!
HULKS, NO ROUGHHOUSING NEAR THE POOL!
GREEN HULK GO FIRST!
HEY!
AGGH!
HULKS WASTING TIME!
GREEN HULK PUSHED RED HULK!
RED HULK PUSHED BLUE HULK!
asgard RULES!
GREEN HULK SHOULD HAVE GONE FIRST.
RED HULK WOULD HAV WON RACE
GUYS? →GLUB← LITTLE HELP HERE?
→SLURP←
POOL WATER NO TAST LIKE SODA.

AUDREY LOEB, WRITER DARIO BRIZUELA, ARTIST VC'S CLAYTON COWLES, LETTER
TOM BRENNAN, LIFEGUARD